The Long European Reformation

European History in Perspective

General Editor: Jeremy Black

Benjamin Arnold *Medieval Germany*
Ronald Asch *The Thirty Years' War*
Nigel Aston *The French Revolution, 1789–1804*
Nicholas Atkin *The Fifth French Republic*
Christopher Bartlett *Peace, War and the European Powers, 1814–1914*
Robert Bireley *The Refashioning of Catholicism, 1450–1700*
Donna Bohanan *Crown and Nobility in Early Modern France*
Arden Bucholz *Moltke and the German Wars, 1864–1871*
Patricia Clavin *The Great Depression, 1929–1939*
Paula Sutter Fichtner *The Habsburg Monarchy, 1490–1848*
Mark R. Forster *Catholic Germany from the Reformation to the Enlightenment*
Mark Galeotti *Gorbachev and his Revolution*
David Gates *Warfare in the Nineteenth Century*
Alexander Grab *Napoleon and the Transformation of Europe*
Martin P. Johnson *The Dreyfus Affair*
Tim Kirk *Nazi Germany*
Ronald Kowalski *European Communism*
Paul Douglas Lockhart *Sweden in the Seventeenth Century*
Kevin McDermott *Stalin*
Graeme Murdock *Beyond Calvin*
Peter Musgrave *The Early Modern European Economy*
J. L. Price *The Dutch Republic in the Seventeenth Century*
A. W. Purdue *The Second World War*
Christopher Read *The Making and Breaking of the Soviet System*
Francisco J. Romero-Salvado *Twentieth-Century Spain*
Matthew S. Seligmann and Roderick R. McLean
Germany from Reich to Republic, 1871–1918
David A. Shafer *The Paris Commune*
David Sturdy *Louis XIV*
David J. Sturdy *Richelieu and Mazarin*
Hunt Tooley *The Western Front*
Peter Waldron *The End of Imperial Russia, 1855–1917*
Peter Waldron *Governing Tsarist Russia*
Peter G. Wallace *The Long European Reformation*
James D. White *Lenin*
Patrick Williams *Philip II*
Peter H. Wilson *From Reich to Revolution*

European History in Perspective
Series Standing Order
ISBN 0–333–71694–9 hardcover
ISBN 0–333–69336–1 paperback
(outside North America only)

You can receive future titles in this series as they are published by placing a standing order. Please contact your bookseller or, in the case of difficulty, write to us at the address below with your name and address, the title of the series and the ISBN quoted above.

Customer Services Department, Palgrave Ltd
Houndmills, Basingstoke, Hampshire RG21 6XS, England

THE LONG EUROPEAN REFORMATION

RELIGION, POLITICAL CONFLICT, AND THE SEARCH FOR CONFORMITY, 1350–1750

Peter G. Wallace

First published 2004 by
PALGRAVE MACMILLAN
Houndmills, Basingstoke, Hampshire RG21 6XS and
175 Fifth Avenue, New York, N.Y. 10010
Companies and representatives throughout the world

PALGRAVE MACMILLAN is the global academic imprint of the Palgrave
Macmillan division of St. Martin's Press, LLC and of Palgrave Macmillan Ltd.
Macmillan® is a registered trademark in the United States, United Kingdom
and other countries. Palgrave is a registered trademark in the European
Union and other countries.

ISBN 978–0–333–64450–8 hardback
ISBN 978–0 333–64451–5 paperback

This book is printed on paper suitable for recycling and made
from fully managed and sustained forest sources. Logging, pulping
and manufacturing processes are expected to conform to the
environmental regulations of the country of origin.

A catalogue record for this book is available from the British Library.

Library of Congress Cataloging in Publication Data
Wallace, Peter George, 1952–
    The long European Reformation : religion, political conflict, and the search
for conformity, 1350–1750 / Peter G. Wallace.
       p.   cm. — (European history in perspective)
    Includes bibliographical references (p.) and index.
    ISBN 0–333–64450–6 — ISBN 0–333–64451–4 (pbk.)
    1. Reformation.   2. Europe—Politics and government.   3. Christianity—
    Europe.   I. Title.   II. European history in perspective (Palgrave (Firm))

    BR305.3.W35 2003
    274—dc21

                                                                    2003042969

10   9   8   7
13   12   11   10   09

Printed and bound in Great Britain by
CPI Antony Rowe, Chippenham, Wiltshire

To Shelley, Erik, and Evan

CONTENTS

LIST OF MAPS

ABBREVIATIONS

AAEB	Archives de l'Ancien Evêché de Bâle, Porrentruy (Switzerland).
AHR	*The American Historical Review.*
ARG	*Archiv für Reformationsgeschichte / Archive for Reformation History.*
EME	*Early Modern Europe: An Oxford History*, ed. Euan Cameron (Oxford: Oxford University Press, 1999).
ERE	Pettegree, Andrew (ed.), *The Early Reformation in Europe* (Cambridge: Cambridge University Press, 1992).
HEH	Brady, Thomas A., Jr, Heiko A. Oberman, and James D. Tracy (eds), *The Handbook of European History, 1400–1600* (Leiden: E. J. Brill, 1994–5), 2 vols.
JMH	*Journal of Modern History.*
OER	*The Oxford Encyclopedia of the Reformation*, edited by Hans Hillerbrand (New York: Oxford University Press, 1996), 4 vols.
P&P	*Past and Present.*
RNC	Scribner, Bob, Roy Porter, and Mikuláš Teich (eds), *The Reformation in National Context* (Cambridge: Cambridge University Press, 1994).

Convention on dates

When appearing with a set of dates (e.g. *1547–1560), the asterisk signifies the years of a monarch or pope's reign. Sets of dates without an asterisk mark the individual's life span.

ACKNOWLEDGEMENTS

Any book project involves many, many people. It is impossible to fully recognize all who have helped shape this work. I would like to thank Jeremy Black for inviting me to participate in this series and for his continued guidance and encouragement. I also wish to recognize the late Heiko Oberman for his critical reading of the initial proposal, and for the suggestions that dramatically altered its form. Tom and Kathy Brady, as life-long mentors, have provided critical advice throughout the long process of bringing this work to fruition. I owe intellectual debts to many other colleagues whose writings have informed my argument, for the search for historical understanding is a collective endeavour and the fruit of an ongoing intellectual conversation. I would, however, like to offer special recognition to Marc Forster, Merry Wiesner-Hanks, Jim Farr, and Kaspar von Greyerz, who in conversations and their written work have left a deep impression on my own thinking. I would like to thank Felicity Noble and Sonya Barker at Palgrave for their guidance through various stages in the process of bringing this book to print and, especially, to thank Terka Acton for her patience, encouragement, and critical reading of the manuscript. She along with the readers at Palgrave offered insights and suggested revisions that have made this a better text. My work on this manuscript received financial support through a Trustees Research Grant from Hartwick College and through release time provided by an appointment as Winifred Wandersee Scholar in Residence. I would like to thank my colleagues at Hartwick College, especially the Dean of the Faculty, Susan Gotsch, and my dear friends in the History Department, for their support of my research and writing agenda. I would also like to acknowledge the input of my students whose curiosity about aspects of the Reformation have helped frame this text, and especially Megan

Raphoon and Courtney DeMayo, who have served as my ideal audience for this work. Finally and most importantly, I dedicate this work to my wife Shelley, for her faith in me and for the innumerable sacrifices she has made to help this book become a reality, and to our sons Erik and Evan, who shared that burden.

INTRODUCTION

In the spring of 1776, the Catholic pastor for the small town of Munster in Upper Alsace, Antoine Maurer, petitioned his religious superior, the bishop of Basel, to order Maurer's patron, the Benedictine abbot in Munster, for an increase in wages. Maurer served Munster and a half-dozen hamlets peppering the surrounding ridges. The petition listed the religious services which the priest performed to meet the spiritual needs of his flock. One duty was to bring the consecrated host (the *viaticum*) to sick and dying parishioners day or night in all weather. Maurer would ride a donkey while the churchwarden preceded him with an illuminated lantern and a handbell. When they encountered someone on the road, the churchwarden rang the bell to let the mountain folk know that they should kneel to honour the real presence of Christ as it passed. Maurer commented that, because it was a new practice, Lutherans needed to be told what it was about, and that he had "not yet met a single one who has refused to [kneel] after having been instructed".[1]

Except for the presence of Lutherans, Maurer's frustrations with his ecclesiastical superiors and his experiences with the mountain folk could easily have occurred in 1376, four hundred years earlier. For centuries pastors and patrons had bickered over fees and obligations, while rural Christians relied on town-dwelling priests to provide for their spiritual needs. Martin Luther and other sixteenth-century reformers had sought to shift the religious leadership's focus away from fees and payments as part of a renewal of the medieval Church. More importantly, the reformers hoped to restore and clarify the core tenets of the faith, which they would then make accessible to all Christians. Maurer's experience, 260 years after Luther posted his theses, suggests that this realization of a reformed Christianity had been gradual and incomplete. Great distances

1

still separated the image of coherent pastoral blocks of indoctrinated Roman Catholic or Lutheran subjects harboured by spiritual and secular officials, and the reality of local conditions.

Most students, when asked to describe some aspect of the European Reformation, recall dramatic events such as Luther's obstinate self-defence at the Imperial Diet of Worms, Calvin's triumphant return to Geneva in 1541 after three years in exile, Henry VIII's quest for a divorce and a male heir, or the bloody repression in 1535 of the Anabaptists at Münster in Westphalia. Their stories begin with Luther's nailing of ninety-five theses to the church door at Wittenberg, and end sometime in the 1550s with the religious peace of Augsburg or the Elizabethan Settlement. This has been the narrative framework for many textbook histories of the Reformation.[2] This traditional model normally assumes that the late medieval Catholic Church was institutionally corrupt, spiritually bankrupt, and theologically muddled, until courageous reformers such as Luther and Calvin offered morally grounded and theologically coherent visions of reformed religious practice, which promised to restore their followers to the pristine state of primitive Christianity. In this older view, Protestants swept away the Church's decadent "popish" structure and replaced it with a more disciplined ecclesiastical order, while in preaching God's word, the reformers would root out the barely Christianized and superstitious practices of folk religions and lay the foundation for modern, rational faith.

Much of Reformation history has been written from the Protestant reformers' perspective and has embraced this historical model, yet even sympathetic studies of the sixteenth-century Catholic Reformation have emphasized its distance from medieval faith and its role in instituting modern Catholicism.[3] Thus whatever their own religious background, historians have taken the reformers at their word and viewed fifteenth-century Christianity as in need of reform, and from that perspective have emphasized the differences between post-Reformation religiosity and the practices of unreformed medieval Christians. In this dramatic vision of Christian history, the Reformation ushers in modern Christianity.[4]

Thinking Historically

People use the word "history" to define two distinct phenomena: past events and the accounts of past events.[5] In the historical past, wars, famines, and revolutions happened as people confronted difficult and often poorly understood choices and acted on them, with results that, more often than not, did not meet their expectations. We also apply the term "history" to accounts of past events and their impact on the historical present, but ironically in historical accounts the present also filters our understanding of the past.[6] The ancient Greeks coined the word "history", by which they meant learning by inquiry, and until the Enlightenment, historical research and writing maintained this open intellectual agenda. In the last 200 years, history has become a professional discipline practised by rigorously trained research scholars, who, through the systematic exploration of documents contemporary to the events under analysis, combined with the "objective", non-partisan, and scientific demeanour required of a professional, construct "as accurately as possible" accounts of past historical events.[7] Recently, however, this commitment to historical objectivity and scientific methods has come under fire from a cluster of theories loosely gathered into a perspective labelled post-modernist.

In light of post-modernist critiques, Keith Jenkins's brief essay *Re-thinking History* provides a helpful introduction to historiography; that is, the study of writing histories.[8] Jenkins argues that from the perspective of post-modernism, the past must be understood as a complex, chaotic, and unknowable landscape. Historical accounts construct window frames through which we may view this landscape. Both the way we build our frames and the way we look through them are habits learned as we are taught to think historically. What we see, when we read any historical account of the Reformation, is framed both by the text's author and by our own learned preconceptions. My window frame could highlight theologians, or peasants, or princes. You as a reader will view the landscape, which I have framed, through your own unique perspective. It is in your effort to resolve the tension between your frame and mine that learning occurs. What follows, then, is an account of the European Reformation based on my reading of the landscape of historical events through the "sediment of previous interpretations" or, more precisely, what I have learned in resolving the tension between my preconceptions and the accounts or frames of other authors, who themselves have wrestled with the same learning process.

As a teacher of Reformation history, I have learned that recognizing the personal values and baggage we all bring to this subject is important in how we understand its historical legacies. Those of you who read this book bring to it extremely diverse religious and personal backgrounds. Many of you have had no formal contact with Christianity, and even those of you who have been raised as Christians or have come to faith later in your lives confront Christian history differently. Some of you seek to understand the world through the prism of faith, while others do not. As your guide, you should know that I was raised in the Catholic faith and as a young man briefly studied for the priesthood. I have since parted ways with the Roman Catholic Church. As a trained historian, my goal is to approach the material carefully from a critical and self-critical perspective, but my understanding of the subject remains entangled in my life experiences, as will yours.

Historical Accounts of the Reformation

The historical participants in the sixteenth-century reform movements defended and justified their actions as part of an over-arching historical drama written by God. At the core of the conflict between the reformers and the Church lay the account of this drama, the Bible, which human authors had composed through divine inspiration. The last chapter of the Word of God had been written less than a century after Jesus's death. Medieval spiritual leaders envisioned their Church as the living Body of Christ guided through history by the Holy Spirit, and thus whatever new traditions they established served merely as continuing expressions of the *kerygma*, the original model of Christian life in the Bible. Nevertheless, at issue were conflicting interpretations of that model, and any cry for reform (*reformatio*) of the Church or renewal (*renovatio*) of Christian life hinged on the relationship between the textual word of God and its "inspired" re-articulation throughout history by the Church. For all parties, the earliest Christian community of Jesus's apostles and disciples, the original Church (*ekklesia*), served as the spiritual template for the "true" Church.

We normally see faith as a personal commitment and experience, but pre-modern reformers understood faith as a communal expression and practised their faith in public collective rituals. Shared commitment and correct ritual were essential for salvation. Moreover, then as now, the Christian community's identity derived from imagined bonds to the historical past of the apostolic Church and the historical future of Christ's second coming, when unbelievers would be cast into lakes of fire and the saved, both living and dead, would gather under God as a "communion of saints" in a millennial kingdom of Christ. For sixteenth-century men and women, imbued with Christian faith, this historical model not only helped make sense of their experiences, it also endowed their lives with meaning. Nearly all of them also believed that Christ's second coming was at hand, and their conviction gave them courage to act.

In this charged atmosphere, Martin Luther's opposition to the Church openly challenged its claim to both the apostolic past and the apocalyptic future and triggered wide-scale political, religious, and social unrest. In the violent struggles which followed, chroniclers in all camps defended their actions and interpreted their successes and setbacks in light of a spiritual struggle between God and the Devil waged in temporal history. Most of these earliest accounts of the Reformation were written by active participants, in the heat of controversy, whose texts smeared their opponents and glorified their own party.[9] Over the ensuing generations, the bloodshed among Protestants and Catholics only deepened religious divisions, and partisan historians shaped their accounts of the reform movements as propaganda, calumny, or apologetics. The thirst for the security of divine sanction for one's actions made it extremely difficult to see anything of value in an opposing view.

By the end of the sixteenth century, the reform groups had gelled into separate religious camps, which historians have come to call "confessions", from the Latin word *confessio* (acknowledgement). Reform leaders, both Catholic and Protestant, hammered out tenets of faith that their followers had to acknowledge to affirm their membership in the true Christian community. Meanwhile decades of civil and inter-dynastic war had added massacres, martyrdoms, and persecutions to be commemorated in historical accounts, but the skein of violence had also exhausted the participants without determining God's chosen Church. By 1695, when Veit Ludwig von Seckendorff first defined the Reformation as an era in Church history rather than a movement, confessionally minded historians had to accept that the Reformation's historical legacy had been to divide Christianity rather than cleanse and restore it.[10] By the beginning of the eighteenth century, all four major confessions, Catholic, Lutheran, Calvinist, and Anglican, had spawned minority factions or non-conformist movements whose members read the historical roots of these churches differently. Henceforth, there could be no consensus account, no single window frame, to illuminate the Reformation landscape.

By 1750 European politics, society, and culture had begun to undergo a set of tectonic shifts which ushered in the modern era. The Enlightenment movement, philosophical idealism, and liberalism promoted new, secular visions of history. Confessional historical scholarship continued to operate, but the Reformation's historical significance came into question. The emerging professional approach to history relegated the study of the Reformation to its role in nurturing the modern state, modern society, and modern individualism.[11] In this framework, Protestantism, which predominated in the industrial powers of England, Germany, and the United States, emerged as a modernizing force. Leopold von Ranke, Max Weber, and Ernst Troeltsch composed critical assessments of the relationship between the Reformation and modernity, but Reformation studies never spawned a paradigmatic account, a widely accepted view, of the era's place in the origins of modern history.[12] Meanwhile in an increasingly professionalized environment, Reformation historiography became almost exclusively the provenance of Church historians, most of whom were churchmen themselves.

The historical profession and the volume of Reformation scholarship have mushroomed in the past fifty years. Much of the new research, loosely described as social history, has turned away from accounts of the political, social, and intellectual elites to explore the historical landscape of the common folk, of women rich and poor, of children, and of marginalized groups. Down to the mid-1970s the dialogue between social and Church historians remained limited, but recently Reformation studies have opened themselves to numerous new influences. The diversity and depth of the scholarship prohibit any short overview, but this text will attempt to highlight these new insights and perspectives where they apply.[13]

Framing this Text

Most recent reinterpretations of the European Reformation have challenged the decadent image of late medieval Christianity, the ability of the reformers to distance themselves from earlier patterns of belief, and the success of the reformers in indoctrinating their religious values into the hearts and minds of their followers. In light of these challenges, the following account of the European Reformation movements will broaden its scope in terms of both time and perspectives of inquiry. First, it will begin with the fourteenth-century demographic and social crisis and its effects on the Christian Church, which was so deeply embedded in late medieval society. Secondly, it will connect the fifteenth-century efforts at ecclesiastical renewal and reform with the Protestant evangelical movements of the first half of the sixteenth century, which sought to redefine social and moral order on the basis of the gospels. We will see how the political, social, and religious forces unleashed by Luther and other reformers drove their movements in unanticipated directions that ultimately divided Christians into separate religious communities. Thirdly, the text will trace the efforts in the late sixteenth century to rebuild social and religious order on a local and regional basis through the establishment of official churches, closely aligned with political authorities in towns, principalities, and kingdoms. Unfortunately, within a generation the blending of political ambition with religious righteousness would produce a bloody round of civil and inter-dynastic wars which embroiled the entire continent. Finally, this text will highlight the late seventeenth- and early eighteenth-century efforts of reformed elites to inculcate "established" doctrines and practices among congregations and parish communities, who would resist and refine these confessionalizing agendas to meet communal and personal needs.

Throughout this study, the various confessional communities will be treated as analogous movements. Though one might argue that there were multiple reformations, this essay frames its subject in the singular. This comparative perspective will focus on the common issues faced by all reformers, but it is not intended to obscure their different resolutions. Lutherans, Calvinists, Anglicans, Anabaptists, and Catholics fashioned dissimilar church structures, worshipped in self-consciously distinct ways, and defined the proper social behaviour of a Christian man or woman differently. As religious acculturation progressed, misconceptions regarding other Christians who observed their faith differently produced animosity, alienation, and sometimes violence. In time, however, the quest for order within emerging states and the growing emphasis on newer forms of social cohesion and animosity, defined in ethnic or national terms, produced grudging religious toleration among most Christians.[14] In all, by exploring the gradual integration of reformed values into the belief systems of common Christians, this text offers its readers a bridge between the dramatic course of structural change and the more mundane progress of new beliefs and practices in the churches, homes, and death-beds of early modern Europe.

All religions are imbedded in the societies and cultures to which they bring meaning. Religious history cannot be separated from the study of political, social, or economic change. Thus Reformation history cannot confine itself to Church history or to a study of the evolution of theology. Nor can students of the Reformation effectively make sense of the historical experience from a single secular perspective such as class struggle or state building.[15] Religious beliefs were deeply woven into the fabric of early modern European culture from the princely courts to the village green. Ecclesiastical institutions supported social elites economically, justified their superiority, and defended the political culture they dominated. To study the Reformation any text must consider historical changes in society and politics.

The scope of analysis which I have proposed would require a large volume, if not a multi-volume study, bringing together a team of interdisciplinary specialists from diverse national and confessional backgrounds.[16] This is impractical for a short introductory text. Thus the following essay can only offer a framework for a comprehensive analysis of a cluster of historical experiences extending over four centuries. To introduce the reader to the long European Reformation, the text will mix narrative and analytical sections grounded on current scholarship in the field. In a sense it will serve as a web-site. I have divided the text into two parts. The first chronicles key events from 1350 to 1650 in order to plot institutional, ideological, and political changes over time and to provide a background for the analytical chapters. The second part explores the Reformation's legacies and limits in the century after the Peace of Westphalia. In weaving the fabric of this book, the warp will be the narrative account and the weft the analytical threads of argument. Finally the notes and selected bibliography will identify important recent works, primarily those available in English, so that the reader will be able to conduct further research on the topics addressed in the book.

Ancient Christianities: The Templates for the True Church

To begin to build a common frame for our account of the Reformation, we need to consider the religious, political, and social legacies medieval Christianity presented its reformers. What follows is a brief and schematic account of Christian church history up until 1350 with a particular focus on aspects that will re-emerge later in the book. This synopsis will emphasize the impact of changing social and political contexts on Christian faith, which, you must remember, was not how the reformers approached this story. They perceived ancient Christian writings and the primitive Church as an unchanging and divinely constructed whole. For the reformers, the medieval Church had deviated from its true original form, which they strove to realize once again. Even those Roman Catholics who defended the historical innovations of the medieval papacy did so with the assumption that these new traditions derived from the inspiration of the Holy Spirit as part of a divine historical plan.

The original followers of Jesus of Nazareth were Jews. During his life-time, neither he nor they wrote down his message or their experiences. What we know of Jesus derives from diverse and sometimes conflicting texts written thirty to seventy years after his death by followers who interwove personal memories and oral traditions with their developing sense of his mission.[17] Sometime in the late 20s CE Jesus of Nazareth preached and attracted a band of followers in Galilee, a region in north-ern Palestine within the Roman Empire. Roman officials normally toler-ated local religions, but unlike most subjects the Jews adhered to a single faith and felt that they were the chosen people of their God, Yahweh. Centuries earlier the Jews had forged a significant regional kingdom, which had fallen, they believed, because of their failure to honour Yahweh. Through the words of prophets, who literally served as God's mouthpieces, Yahweh had promised to restore this kingdom. Under Roman rule many poorer Jews had come to anticipate a political revival through a *messiah*, one anointed by God. Before, during, and after Jesus's lifetime, a number of messiahs had risen on waves of social anger directed against both the Romans and collaborating Jewish elites in Jerusalem. Jesus was one of them. He claimed intimate knowledge of God, preached the coming of God's kingdom, taught through parables drawn from the experiences of the common folk, and practised a social and gender egalitarianism which troubled Jewish elites. When Jesus confronted Jewish officials with the threat of disorder in Jerusalem, the local Roman officials had him arrested and put to death. Many messianic Jews believed that Yahweh would raise the dead to help restore the king-dom. Following his execution by crucifixion, Jesus's disciples claimed that he had risen from the dead, ascended into heaven, and would soon come again to establish God's kingdom on earth. Scholars refer to this collective expectation of a "second coming" as "apocalyptic".

These first Jewish Christians were Aramaic-speakers, who formed an apocalyptic church in Palestine, pooled their economic resources, and lived in common, waiting for signs of Jesus's return. Most Jews, however, lived outside of Palestine in the urban centres of the ancient Mediterra-nean basin and western Asia. These Jews of the diaspora (dispersal) spoke Greek, which was the common language for discourse in this ethnic and cultural melting pot.[18] Early on, the Jewish Christians of Palestine spread the gospel or "good news" to the diaspora communities. Paul of Tarsus, a Greek-speaking Jew of the diaspora, a Roman citizen, and an early Christian convert, carried his conviction in Jesus's messianic mission throughout the countries of the eastern Mediterranean. His epistles (letters) are among the oldest Christian texts we have. Paul, who had never met Jesus, translated Christian faith beyond its initial Jewish context. He defined Christian ethics, how individuals come to the faith and how communities of faith should live in this world. He broadcast the gospel to the Gentiles (non-Jews), and insisted that they did not need to embrace the complexity of Mosaic law – literally to become Jews – in order to embrace Jesus. He thus opened Church membership to the world. Finally he concentrated on the events surrounding Jesus's death, the Last Supper, the Crucifixion, and the Resurrection, as the purpose of Jesus's life. Paul saw Jesus as the anointed one, the Messiah (or *Christos*, in Greek), whose redeeming death granted salvation for every individual soul and whose resurrection confirmed the resurrection of all true believers when Jesus would come again. According to Paul, all that God required was faith in these truths.

Paul's historical vision for Christianity would have a profound effect on the future Church; however, Paul's personal mission troubled Jewish Christians, many of whom found it too difficult to embrace Gentile Christians as brethren. He also angered non-Christian Jews, who became increasingly enraged over the blasphemous spiritual power which his followers assigned to Christ, and who regularly persecuted Jewish Christians. Meanwhile other messiahs spurred popular resistance to Roman rule; this escalated into a major uprising between 66 and 70 CE. In retaliation the Romans destroyed the Temple at Jerusalem and brutally repressed the Palestinian Jews, Christian and non-Christian alike.[19] Though Paul had not lived to see it, his vision of the Christian community separated from its Jewish roots had emerged victorious by default.

In the wake of the great rebellion, many of the first Christian writings appeared. These gospels offered accounts of Jesus's life, mission, and message, for audiences who had never met him. Soon Christian communities began to develop ceremonies that expressed their faith and defined membership. They gathered regularly to celebrate the Eucharist, a ritual meal which recalled the events surrounding Jesus's death and resurrection, and over time the feast condensed into a liturgy of communion during which bread and wine were blessed and shared. To join in Christian communion, a prospective adult convert, or *catechumen*, endured a lengthy initiation process culminating in baptism, a ceremonial washing away of the old self with water. Sometimes individuals broke faith or disrupted the communion among believers. Christians would forgive these "sins" but only after public acts of confession and penance by the sinner, normally carried out before the entire community.

In some cases unforgiven transgressors were shunned or excommunicated – denied access to the liturgy of communion.[20]

The Roman government officially tolerated nearly all religions and often encouraged integration or syncretism of beliefs to help bind its culturally diverse empire.[21] Nevertheless, officials expected all citizens and subjects to honour sanctioned imperial cults. The Jews and Christians refused to comply, which for the Roman authorities demonstrated disloyalty and fostered disorder. Furthermore, Christian cohesiveness and their mysterious rituals, which were closed to non-members, aroused suspicion among neighbours and local authorities. In this atmosphere, attacks on Christians had official approval and popular support, though persecution was normally sporadic and local.[22]

By the second century, Christian communities existed in towns all over the Roman Empire but were concentrated primarily in the Greek-speaking East. No Christian possessed a living memory of Jesus, and without an established leadership the fledgling Church faced a crisis of authority. In response a group of Christians, calling themselves "Catholic" (universal) Christians, fashioned an administrative hierarchy that distinguished between the laity (the people) and clergy (leaders).[23] Initially the laity probably elected their clergy, but under the emerging Catholic system the clergy co-opted new leaders. Each Catholic Christian community was headed by a bishop (from the Greek word *episkopos*, which means an "overseer"). Presbyters (elders) and deacons (servants) assisted him. Though women played key roles among Jesus's immediate followers and in the primitive Church, the emerging Catholic leadership was increasingly limited to males. Catholic Christians argued that the original bishops had received their authority directly from the apostles, who had "laid their hands" on their chosen successors, and this "apostolic succession", re-enacted in the consecration of each new bishop, justified episcopal authority in fashioning the norms of faith.[24]

In their drive to delineate a normative Christianity, Catholic bishops assembled in synods to discuss divergent interpretations of God's nature. They resolved these theological (*from theos* = God + *logos* = "discourse") debates with a trinitarian model of three "persons" (perhaps most easily understood as distinct "personalities") in one God: the Father, Son (Christ), and Spirit. Accepting Jesus's divinity within the Trinity, the bishops also wrestled with the Christological tension between Jesus as God and Jesus as man and determined that Jesus possessed both natures. Finally in their ecclesiology, they defined the Church as clergy-centred with leadership firmly in episcopal hands.[25] The synods drew up brief statements of beliefs, called "creeds", which all Catholic Christians seeking communion publicly acknowledged. Those who accepted these creeds embraced "orthodoxy" (from the Greek, meaning "upright doctrine"). Choosing to oppose orthodoxy labelled an individual as a "heretic" (from the Greek word *hairesis* meaning "choice"). Thus these synods designed a vocabulary of faith and the machinery for religious conformity. Ultimately, Catholic Christian bishops consolidated orthodox beliefs into the "Apostles' Creed", separating true believers from dozens of divergent "heretical" Christian communities.[26] By the year 200 CE, the Catholic Christians had designated the true, divinely inspired gospels and epistles as the New Testament, the sanctioned account of Jesus's life and mission.

In the third century the Roman Empire weathered an internal crisis exacerbated by foreign invasions, including the first major incursions by Germanic tribes. In response, Emperor Diocletian (*284–305 CE) sought to shore up public order by reinvigorating imperial cults. The unwillingness of Jews and Christians to participate triggered severe persecutions climaxing in 304–5 CE. Many of the smaller, "heretical", non-Catholic Christian communities disappeared, while martyrdom and abjuration severely weakened Catholic Christianity. After Diocletian retired in 305, his successors fought among themselves, and the winner, Constantine (*306–37), attributing his success to the intercession of the Christian God, legalized Christian worship in 313, offering tax exemptions and gifts of public properties to Catholic Christians. Finally, in 380, Emperor Theodosius (*379–95) declared Catholic Christianity the official religion of the Empire.

Ironically, imperial support and legalization shattered Christian communion.[27] Those who had held their faith during the great persecution and survived, bitterly refused to re-admit abjured backsliders and were suspicious of new "fair weather" converts. The crisis stimulated a debate, with two ecclesiological models advocated: a small, closed spiritual church of true believers; and a broader open church that would welcome all. When Catholic Christianity became the official imperial religion, the open-church model prevailed. Many, who insisted on a pure church, were labelled as "Donatist" heretics, after Donatus, one of their outspoken leaders; while others, advocates of a tiny spiritual church, fled to the desert to pursue a purer, saintly life as monks (solitaries). As isolated hermetic monks began to attract communities of disciples, episcopal authorities drew up rules to integrate monasticism into Catholic Christianity.[28]

In an effort to resolve the tensions in the rapidly growing legalized church, Constantine assembled a general or "ecumenical" council of Church leaders at Nicaea in 325. The council drew up the Nicene Creed, which refined the tenets of Catholic Christianity and cemented a new relationship between the Church and Imperial administration. None the less, despite the rallying power of an official church, the Empire's political decline continued, as its governmental structure soon split into eastern and western halves, each moving along a separate trajectory. The official Catholic Christian Church also divided between the poorer, rural, Latin-speaking West and the wealthier, urban, Greek-speaking East. Shared faith begins with shared language, and differences between Greek and Latin soon sparked a growing dissonance between the two communities' views on theology and church structure. Germanic migrations into the western provinces in the fifth century further alienated East and West. In the East the bishops continued to function under the guidance of the Emperor at Constantinople. In the West the imperial system collapsed, and bishops assumed the mantle of political leadership over Imperial administrative districts, known since Diocletian's rule as dioceses. The bishops of Rome, asserting apostolic succession from Peter and controlling the capital of the old Empire, eventually claimed symbolic authority as father, *papa*, over other Latin-speaking bishops. Though few initially honoured this title, no other Latin churchman could approach the spiritual prestige of Rome's bishop.[29]

As classical civilization began to disintegrate around them, the intellectual elite sought to preserve key pieces of the old culture and to influence the development of the new. Jerome of Aquileia (*c*.342–420) translated the Greek Bible into a Latin Vulgate edition which would be the standard throughout the Middle Ages. Meanwhile the African Augustine of Hippo (354–430) produced a mass of polemical religious writings that would be as prominent as the works of Paul of Tarsus in Latin Christian thought. In his youth Augustine had embraced the Manichaean faith, a dualist Persian religion. Manichaeans believed in two Gods: a holy God, Father of All, who ruled the realm of the spirit; and an evil God, Satan or Lucifer, who created and ruled the world. Under Manichaean Christology, Jesus Christ was the Son of the holy God, who "appeared" to take on human form to suppress Satan's power. Manichaean dualism extended to human beings, who also possessed two natures: the body (evil) and soul (good). Special knowledge, *Gnosis*, gained through a rigorous ascetic self-discipline, allowed the soul to control bodily appetites and so find union with the Father of All.

When Augustine converted, he brought with him much of his Gnostic Manichaean world view.[30]

Augustine believed that the carnal (bodily) union of our parents stained our souls with original sin, a legacy extending back to the first sexual union of Adam and Eve. Baptism washed away the sin, but did not change our sinful bodily natures. Using the imagery of light, Augustine argued that blinded by our own self-will we grope around in the darkness believing that we are free. Yet only when God offers the "gift" of divine favour (grace), can we freely pursue the spiritual good. Though he persecuted Donatists, Augustine himself envisioned a small assembly of true spiritual believers, enlightened by God, as the true Church. Late in his life he followed his own logic to the conclusion that God the Father had predestined some to be saved and some to be damned.[31] Augustine's views on sin and grace would have a profound effect on later Christian thought, particularly among the sixteenth-century reformers.

As the ancient Roman world continued to disintegrate in the West, individuals such as Benedict of Nursia (c.480–c.550) in Italy founded monasteries, communities of monks, whose rules included the dutiful copying of ancient manuscripts. Because of the Benedictines' efforts, critical writings of ancient pagan and Christian scholars survived. As time passed, however, the cultural environment that had produced the original works faded from memory, and the writings took on a monolithic character as enshrined sacred texts. The books of the New Testament and the Fathers of the Church, like Augustine, spoke with an authority no later writer could muster.

Medieval Christendom: Christian Empire and Papal Monarchy

In the centuries between the deposition of the last western Emperor in 476 and the outbreak of plague in 1348, Latin Christianity underwent a number of changes. The sixteenth-century reformers argued that medieval Christianity had mutated from its original form, and they unfavourably juxtaposed medieval innovations against the word of God embodied in the New Testament, the records of the primitive Church, and the writings of the Church Fathers. Developments in medieval Christianity did affect the practices of faith and the Church's structure in several ways: first by germanizing classical Christian beliefs; secondly by formalizing the schism between the Latin and Greek churches; thirdly by militarizing religious self-defence during the Crusades; fourthly

by galvanizing Church and state under the rubric of Christendom; and
finally by institutionalizing the religious authority of the popes in the
form of a papal monarchy. Before moving to the body of the text, let us
briefly examine these five developments.

The Germanization of Christianity

The Germanic tribes poured into the Western Empire in the fourth and
fifth centuries as both invited and uninvited guests, settling in among
their Latin neighbours. Several German tribes entered Imperial territory as Christians, though they followed a heretical form known as
Arianism, which did not accept the full divinity of Jesus or the Holy
Spirit. Arian Christian warlords harassed and persecuted Catholic
Christians. Other tribes, such as the Angles, Saxons, and Franks, came
into the Empire as pagans and soon Catholic Christian missionaries
sought to convert them. German tribal leaders, known as kings, embodied
the "luck" of the tribe and possessed sacral characteristics, so missionaries
devoted their efforts to converting kings, such as the Frankish leader
Clovis, who in 496 accepted Catholic Christianity along with his whole
tribe. The dramatic conversion and baptism of several thousand
Frankish warriors in one day, however, was only the first step in the
complex process of Christianizing Germanic beliefs, attitudes, values,
and behaviours.[32]

In order to make the new faith understandable to the converts,
Christian missionaries recast it in German cultural terms, accepting
Germanic political ideals and integrating aspects of Germanic folk
religions. For example, the kings claimed ultimate ownership of all lands
controlled by the tribe and cemented the loyalty of their retainers,
including churchmen, with gifts of land or precious metal, referred to
in the sources as benefices. Royal generosity entailed obligations from
the recipient, and "beneficed" churchmen became beholden to their lay
patrons. Likewise the German common folk, whose religiosity centred
on rituals that placated or manipulated forces in the physical and spiritual
world, accepted Christianity as a new and powerful set of ceremonies
and magical objects. Germanic moral or ethical responsibilities, however,
remained embedded in kinship obligations of honour and vengeance,
and the ethical fabric of classical Christianity carried little meaning.
Conflicts between the ethical expectations of kinship and of faith would
continue into the early modern era.

The schism between Latin and Greek Christianity

As Latin Christianity became more German, relations with the Greek-speaking Christians deteriorated. Ruled by the Emperor from Constantinople, the medieval Eastern Roman Empire became known as Byzantium. Here urban life, Imperial administration, and ancient religious culture survived. The emperors acted as head of both Church and state in a system referred to by historians as Caesaro-papism.[33] Nevertheless, what became known as the Greek Orthodox Church was never fully subservient to Imperial will. In key urban centres such as Alexandria, bishops claimed the title of patriarch, and exercised significant authority in religious affairs. Furthermore, monastic communities also operated as independent power-brokers, whose religious artefacts (icons) attracted widespread devotion among the faithful. Down to the ninth century, the Byzantine emperors convened ecumenical councils to address the endemic religious debates which plagued Greek Orthodox Christianity. The Orthodox patriarchs normally invited the pope to the councils, but they treated papal officials as poor cousins, whose claim to special authority was laughable. Under Emperor Justinian (*527–65) Byzantine forces attempted to reconquer Italy from the Germanic Ostrogoths, but he could only secure the southern half of the peninsula.

Beginning in 632, Islamic armies from the Arabian peninsula swept through Syria, Palestine, and North Africa depriving the Byzantine emperors of their richest provinces and the Orthodox Church of its leading patriarchs. Prior to 750 the popes had formally recognized the Emperor's authority in southern Italy; but as Byzantine influence waned, the popes turned to the Germanic Frankish Catholic kings as military and political partners. This Frankish–Papal alliance alienated the popes from the Byzantine Church and state.[34] For centuries Latin and Greek Christians had practised and understood their faith differently; political will and the memory of empire alone had held them together. By the end of the eighth century, however, the Empire was in shambles, and the will to cooperate had dissolved. The two churches went their own way until the mid-eleventh century when the papacy, in the throes of internal reform, again claimed full authority in all spiritual matters. In 1054, papal officials declared the patriarch of Constantinople a heretic and broke communion with him. Henceforth popes would dream of ending the schism and reuniting the two churches on papal terms, but the division endured and still endures.

The growth of Islam and the Crusading ideal

The dynamic spread of Islam following the death of the Prophet Mohammed in 632 was shockingly quick and extensive. By 711, Muslim armies had conquered an empire that stretched from central Asia to the Atlantic coast of Africa. They also controlled a number of ports on Europe's Mediterranean coastline, and most of the Iberian peninsula. The medieval Islamic empire produced a rich and sophisticated urban culture sustained by an elaborate trading network and religious toleration for Jews and Christians.[35] For our purposes, the Muslim presence created a formidable and alien enemy against whom Christianized Germanic warriors would direct their bellicose energies. In 732, Charles Martel, a Frankish warlord, defeated a Muslim raiding party at Tours in France, which earned him papal accolades as "defender of the faith". Soon the remnants of Christian kingdoms in northern Spain began an inexorable "holy war", the *Reconquista*, against their Muslim neighbours, which continued until 1492. The volatile mixture of faith and violence, epitomized by orders of warrior monks such as the Knights Templar, directed against an imagined dehumanized Islamic enemy, later characterized the Crusades, which began under the auspices of the reformed papacy in 1096. When the Crusaders stormed Jerusalem in 1099, they slaughtered every inhabitant in the city. For a time the Christian warriors were successful, but they eventually lost their edge, as Muslim counter-offensives regained the Holy Land.[36] By the thirteenth century, the crusading ideal itself had changed as popes invoked crusades against heretical Albigensians in southern France and political enemies on the Italian peninsula.[37] All in all the crusading spirit reflected a mix of piety and militancy that pervaded Christianity from the Middle Ages into the early modern era.

Christendom imagined: the Frankish–Papal alliance

The popes could draw warriors from all over Europe to participate in the Crusades by invoking the ideal of "Christendom", which had its roots in the Germanization of Christianity and in particular the Frankish–Papal alliance.[38] Since Clovis's conversion ecclesiastical officials had depended on his successors, the Merovingians, to defeat Arian and pagan rivals. Merovingian victories expanded the Frankish domain, but the dynasty followed the Germanic practice of divisible inheritance, resulting in fratricide and factional warfare. The kings relied on powerful warlords, headed by the *maior domus*, who was steward of the royal household, to rule effectively. Charles Martel held this title and in 732 brought prestige to his own family with his victory over the Muslims.[39] His son Pippin planned to depose the Merovingians but had no legitimate claim to sacral kingship. In 751, Pope Zacharias justified Pippin's coup with an archival forgery, the Donation of Constantine, which claimed to grant the pope the right to make and unmake kings.[40] Three years later when Zacharias's successor, Stephen III, requested assistance against his troublesome neighbours the Lombards, Pippin marched into Italy and subdued them. Pippin then cemented his compact with the popes through a benefice of land in central Italy, which became the core of papal territories in the peninsula.

The new Frankish dynasty, known in history as the Carolingians after Charlemagne, their most famous member, initiated a reform movement within the Church that established a template for ecclesiastical administration that lasted until the Reformation. Under the leadership of the Anglo-Saxon churchmen Boniface and Alcuin, the Carolingians ordered the construction of parish churches in the countryside, assigned priests trained to carry out sacramental duties in the parishes, and assessed a tithe, a tax of one-tenth on the parishioners' harvests, to support the local clergyman in his duties.[41] Boniface also sent missionaries eastward into Central Europe with the Carolingian armies to convert the defeated pagan tribes, often at sword point. As they had with the popes, the Carolingians granted to monasteries and bishops lands and rights along this religious and military frontier, establishing a powerful landed clerical elite in Central Europe.

As their domains grew, the Carolingians became increasingly dependent on the clergy to handle correspondence and record-keeping as traditional Germanic face-to-face administration became too difficult. The clerical advisors identified the expanding Carolingian Empire as the *imperium christianum* (Christendom), a concept they drew from Augustine of Hippo's *City of God*. Christendom fused Church and state and blended membership in both. Baptism made one both a Frank and a Christian, and forced conversions were essential for submission to Carolingian overlordship. Finally, on Christmas day 800, the pope crowned Charlemagne as Emperor of the Romans and chief Christian layman. Ultimately, Frankish Christendom failed to hold together and by the mid-ninth century the Carolingian Empire had collapsed. None the less, the concept of Christendom would take on new life under the auspices of a reforming papacy in the eleventh century.

Papal monarchy

The Carolingian political system disintegrated as a result of internal friction and external threats from Vikings, Magyars, and Muslims. Political authority soon devolved as peasants and towns folk turned to local warlords and their fortified castles for protection. In return the lords demanded labour service in their fields, which bound the peasants as serfs to the noble manors in a system historians have traditionally referred to as "feudalism".[42] In time, some lords amassed regional power-bases and assumed control over local ecclesiastical institutions, as Church benefices became personal possessions (*Eigenkirchensystem*). Bishops and abbots often fought side by side with their lay kinsmen and acted as feudal lords in their own right.[43] Lay appropriation of ecclesiastical appointments extended to Rome where magnate clans fought among themselves over the papacy and several pontificates ended in assassinations. In 955, Otto I, king of Germany, defeated the Magyar invaders and consolidated his authority over much of Central Europe. In 962, Pope John XII, hoping to forge an alliance against his rivals, offered Otto the Imperial crown in Rome. Otto, who had built his power in Germany by substituting royal patronage for local lay patronage over ecclesiastical benefices, sought to reform the papacy along the same lines and deposed John when he resisted. This act initiated a century of imperial involvement in papal affairs.

In the tenth century there were also signs of revival within the Church. Monastic communities, spearheaded by Cluny in Burgundy, reinstated the strict Benedictine rule. In order to minimalize lay influence in monastic affairs, the houses placed themselves under the protection of St Peter in the guise of his vicar (representative) on earth, the pope. The Cluniac reform movement nurtured a cohort of monks who were filled with zeal to revive the clergy as a distinct order and to separate the Church from local lay interference.[44] With this initial conservative agenda, the reform movement appeared as an ally to the German emperors; and in the mid-eleventh century, Henry III sought assistance from Cluny to undermine the Roman magnates' ongoing influence over papal affairs. Beginning with the pontificate of Leo IX (*1048–56), the reformers pushed for clerical celibacy and an end to the practice of simony – the purchase of ecclesiastical office – which contemporaries associated with lay control over clerical appointments. Leo and his successors also reorganized staffing for Rome's civic churches, whose benefice holders, the cardinals, traditionally came from local magnate families. The popes installed new cardinals drawn from a circle of Cluniac reformers and called on their expertise to help administer the Church.

In 1056, Emperor Henry III's untimely death left the six-year-old Henry IV as heir. In 1059, Pope Nicholas II (*1058–61) decreed that henceforth the college of cardinals would elect the pope, thus ending the Emperor's influence over the reform movement. As the next step, the popes completed their campaign against lay influence over clerical appointments by claiming the sole right to ritually install (invest) abbots and bishops throughout Christendom. By 1076, Pope Gregory VII (*1073–85) would clash with the now mature Henry IV over the investiture of the archbishop of Milan. In the ensuing conflict, Gregory excommunicated the Emperor and initially compelled Henry to submit, but the Investiture Controversy dragged on until the Concordat of Worms in 1122, which permitted nomination by those, including lay persons, who had rights over the benefice, while insisting on formal papal approval (provision) of the nominee.[45] The emperors had initiated reform within the Church, but the reformed papacy now claimed full authority over the Church and spiritual headship over all of Christendom.

The "Gregorian" reforms in the mid-eleventh century ushered in two centuries of expanding papal authority and power, culminating in the pontificate of Innocent III (*1198–1216). The popes refashioned themselves from vicars of St Peter to vicars of Christ, thus claiming to represent God on earth. Exercising their new authority, beginning in 1123 the popes called a series of ecumenical councils, without Greek participation, to spell out papal primacy in spiritual affairs. Furthermore, benefitting from imagined ties to the old Roman Empire embodied in the forged Donation of Constantine, papal officials followed Roman traditions that designated the ruler as the creator and guardian of the law. Roman law was written law, and papal lawyers compiled lists of decretals and canon laws promulgated by the popes before the councils, which defined proper practices in all aspects of Christian life. The popes dispatched legates (representatives) to various principalities, and the papal court became the seat of justice for disputes within Christendom.[46] In the process, the popes constructed a system of administration, prerogatives, and precedence that allowed them to exercise authority over the Christian clergy comparable to the power of any monarch over his or her subjects. The papal monarchy, like other medieval lay monarchies, was a hierarchical network of persons who owed ultimate loyalty and obedience to their monarch, the pope. Like other monarchs the popes claimed the right to appoint their subjects to important governmental posts such as bishoprics and abbacies, through papal provision, as well as the right to tax them and judge their transgressions. Unlike that of lay monarchs, whose authority over their subjects applied within a relatively coherent territorial block, papal power extended over influential and socially prominent individuals throughout Europe. Conflicts over the personal allegiances of powerful churchmen in England, France, and especially the territories subject to the Holy Roman Emperors of the German Nation would often sour medieval Church–state relations, but by 1300 the papacy's role as head of Christendom seemed unassailable.

The early modern reformers looked backward through Church history to determine the pure form of religion and Christian community they hoped to realize. Inevitably they would read the Bible in light of their own experiences, with the confidence that the Holy Spirit would guide them. The medieval Church had imagined its own reforms as true to the apostolic Church and informed by the Spirit, yet as in the fourteenth-century artworks, the imagined apostles wore contemporary clothing. While claiming affiliation with the old, any reformed church would be new and different. The Christian community had evolved from a tiny group of Jewish believers at odds with society to a rich and powerful institution integrally engaged in a system of social power that its ecclesiastical institutions and moral guidelines sustained. To reform such a structure would be unthinkable unless society itself faced a profound crisis.

Part I

The Warp: Threads of Reformation Histories, 1350–1650

1

THE LATE MEDIEVAL CRISIS, 1348–1517

During the four centuries covered in this study, Europeans lived under the murderous shadow of the plague. Between 1347 and 1350, an epidemic, later known as the Black Death, swept through Europe and killed perhaps one-third of its population. Imagine the effects of the frightening and unexplainable deaths of nearly two billion people in the course of two summers. The pervasiveness and scope of misery left the fourteenth-century chroniclers seeking moral explanations in human sinfulness and divine retribution. Long processions of penitent flagellants passed from community to community whipping themselves in hope of appeasing God's wrath and warding off plague through their expiation. Townsfolk blamed resident Jews for poisoning wells, even though they too were dying. Christian mobs murdered entire Jewish communities and burned their homes, yet the plague continued to rage. One could imagine, along with John of Winterthur, a Swiss Franciscan, that the Apocalypse promised in the Bible had begun.[1]

The European world didn't end in 1350, but it changed dramatically. Plague is a complex disease whose dissemination requires the presence of bacteria, fleas, and rodents. Endemic forms of plague exist in reservoirs among rodent populations throughout the world. Occasionally an epizootic disease among the rodents forces the plague-carrying fleas to find other hosts, including humans. Once plague has entered the human population, it spreads inexorably in great pandemics, series of cyclical epidemics covering vast areas, that can last several centuries.[2] In Christendom the Black Death began in the ports of southern Italy and spread like a slow but relentless brush fire across Europe. News of the calamity preceded the outbreak of the illness itself, and religious officials called for special services to ward off the catastrophe. Yet inevitably the disease came, for as the Florentine humanist Boccaccio noted, "all the wisdom and ingenuity of man were unavailing" to prevent it.[3] The initial outbreak struck rich and poor, clergy and laity, townsfolk and peasants. The epidemic's pathology left the survivors in shock yet relieved that God had relented in his punishment; but the disease, which was now endemic among the rat and flea populations in Europe, reappeared in the early 1360s. This second deadly assault of plague had a profound psychological and cultural impact whose effects were as devastating as the Black Death.[4] With the plague as a recurrent nightmare that would haunt Europe until 1721, late fourteenth-century Christendom faced a crisis marked by demographic stagnation, economic depression, endemic warfare, and schism within the Catholic Church itself.

The Late Medieval Crisis

Scholars have traced the roots of the late medieval crisis to conditions prior to the plague, when Europe was overpopulated, malnourished, and under-employed. Between 1000 and 1300 CE, the population had grown rapidly, and by the fourteenth century, perhaps 75 to 80 million people inhabited the continent. Given available agricultural technologies, Europe was "full", and many regions sheltered more inhabitants than they would at any time prior to the nineteenth century.[5] In the early Middle Ages, Europeans had lived in isolated settlements surrounded by dense and often intractable forests. Beginning in the eleventh century, the growing population cleared forests and drained marshlands, bringing new land under cultivation. By 1300, from nearly any steeple top in Western Europe, an observer could see church towers in all directions, each marking a settlement. The forests remained, but as grazing lands for domesticated pigs and as sources of lumber and firewood.

Most Europeans lived in villages and worked the land. As we have seen, when the Carolingian Empire disintegrated, the elites, both those who prayed and those who fought, asserted rights over the land, which they divided into manors.[6] Under the manorial system, the peasants (serfs) owed labour obligations on the lord's demesne in return for the physical and spiritual protection which the warriors and monks provided. During the twelfth and thirteenth centuries many lay and ecclesiastical lords moved away from direct management of their estates and leased out farms to peasant tenants. The former serfs commuted their labour duties to fixed payments in coin or kind and so gained some autonomy;

however, the emerging system of codified laws reinforced seignorial legal rights over the supposedly "free" peasants. Lords now collected fees for the use of manorial mills and ovens, for authorizing marriages, or for permitting a son to inherit a tenancy from his father. This new, more flexible form of feudal lordship allowed lords to rachet up demands in response to changing market conditions.

The system was exploitative, but the peasants were not simply hapless and passive victims. They treated the fields they worked as their own land, and the law awarded them some rights as tenants. Possession of a plough and team of oxen or horses elevated wealthier peasant house-holders to positions as village leaders, and in some villages all principal householders purchased citizenship and exercised communal rights.[7] Over much of Europe, peasant communes evolved as political agents in local life. Peasants also participated in market activities. As the population grew, grain prices rose, and many tenants benefitted from the increased value of their yields in relation to contractually fixed quit-rent owed on their lands. As a result, peasant communities became increasingly strati-fied with their own internal social and economic tensions, yet the funda-mental social gulf remained the distance between those who worked and those who, under the guise of lordship including ecclesiastical officials, benefitted from the fruits of the working peasantry.[8]

In the wake of increased population and prosperity, some villages and market centres evolved into towns, which received charters and privileges from the king or regional prince. Towns existed everywhere in Europe, but they especially clustered in dense commercial networks in northern Italy and the Low Countries (modern-day Belgium and the Nether-lands).[9] Traditionally scholars have juxtaposed the freer air of medieval towns against the servile rural world that encompassed them. According to this model, the peasants lived out their days constrained by limited technology and clouded by ignorance, while the walls that separated medieval towns from rural backwardness enclosed a free and politically active populace engaged in manufacturing and trade. Recent research, however, has shown that this dichotomy between town and country simply distorts historical conditions. Medieval towns emerged primarily to accumulate and distribute agricultural surpluses. Gradually these "peasant markets" erected walls and became permanent centres of both trade and handicraft production in household workshops. Most central markets exchanged food and manufactures in limited regional networks. Some cities, such as Florence or Augsburg, however, sheltered thousands of workers devoted to cloth production, and a merchant elite with agents in distant cities and customers who included royalty; yet even these manufacturing centres retained their ties to the regional agricultural economy. Town walls never circumscribed economic zones, for as many as one-fifth of urban residents engaged in part-time agricultural work, while rural craft production probably contributed as much to the volume of manufactured goods as urban workshops.

Towns were in fact embedded in "feudal" society. Urban ecclesiastical institutions, lay elites, and even the civic government itself held rights of lordship over neighbouring villages and peasants. Powerful extended families with ties to the regional nobility and expertise in long-distance commerce formed the urban elite.[10] Beneath them tradesmen and labourers organized themselves into guilds to regulate production, exchange, and wages. This urban middle class divided itself along strata of wealth and professional prestige. By modern standards European towns were small with only Paris sheltering in excess of 100,000 residents. On the whole, perhaps 10 percent of the population lived in towns, yet the concentration of wealth, political power, and education in urban settings gave towns much greater significance than their demographic weight warranted.[11]

By the end of the thirteenth century, Europe's growing population had reached a demographic ceiling. Despite improvements in agricultural technologies, in particular the shift from a two- to a three-field system, which increased the percentage of cropland under cultivation, the land could no longer feed everyone. Rural parents found it difficult to provide a livable legacy for their children. Forms of inheritance which favoured one child, such as primogeniture for the eldest son, or ultimogeniture for the youngest, left other siblings with few resources beyond their labour. Divisible inheritance turned livable holdings of fifteen to twenty acres into micro-plots which could not support families. The surplus of labour reduced wages, while grain shortages produced steadily rising prices. As the climate grew cooler and wetter after 1300, frosts and heavy rains triggered famine in much of north-western Europe between 1315 and 1317, which may have carried off 10 to 15 per cent of the population. The ensuing generation filled in the gaps, but dearth and hunger had become the norm for the vast majority of Europeans.[12]

When plague struck in 1348, it reduced the human pressure on resources, but it also strained familial, social, economic, and political relations. Soon institutional structures, inheritance patterns, systems of trade, and even the lord's ability to control the peasantry, came under stress because, in Western Europe at least, feudal social foundations assumed a large population and limited resources. The initial redistribution of wealth profited peasants, whose rents for tenancies fell, and skilled artisans, whose wages rose, as the late fourteenth century formed something of a "golden age" for commoners with more disposable income, available land, and political leverage than their ancestors or descendants. The initial social and economic burden of depopulation fell on lay and ecclesiastical lords, who responded by freezing wages at pre-plague levels and preventing tenants from moving to estates with better lease rates for land, but these measures failed.[13] As time passed, however, conditions for peasants began to deteriorate. Depopulation had altered traditional patterns of demand for market-oriented agriculture. Ironically, a series of good harvests in the last quarter of the fourteenth century triggered a prolonged slump in prices, which temporarily enriched the purchasing power of wage labourers but ruined those drawing income from farming. Peasants abandoned their fields and homes, while marginal soils reverted to pasture and woodland. In the German-speaking lands, perhaps a quarter of all villages ceased to exist.[14] In northern France and other turbulent regions, marauding armies drove the peasants out, but war and plague alone cannot adequately explain these abandonments.[15] Farming had grown unprofitable for many, and people quit to find better work.

The economic strains affected more than the poor alone. Ecclesiastical and lay landlords continued to feel the pinch as rent revenues from their tenancies shrivelled up, for the tenant farmers could not afford the old rates. Historians have argued that this crisis in revenues drove some lords to banditry and helps explain the endemic civil wars in fifteenth-century England, France, and elsewhere. Some impecunious lords mortgaged their holdings and rights, handing them over to civic governments or wealthy individual townsmen. The ploughmen, who had formerly been the social and economic backbone of the peasantry, also fell into debt to urban moneylenders and Jews. Peasants continued to work small to medium-sized plots of land, but the towns assumed increasing control over rural production and peasant labour, which exacerbated town–country antagonisms.[16] None the less, growing urban economic clout did not necessarily spell prosperity for all town dwellers. In many European cities, artisan householders lost their economic cushion and merged into the growing ranks of working poor, while wealthy guildsmen who had profited in the decades of crisis distanced themselves from their poorer neighbours and intermarried with older elite families. Civic governance became the prerogative of a small circle of oligarchs who saw themselves as rulers maintaining good order among their "subjects".

Good order and public peace were at a premium all over Europe in the fifteenth century. The kings of England and France had warred with one another for most of the Middle Ages, primarily over the English monarch's extensive territorial holdings in France. In 1337 rival claims over Gascony, Aquitaine, and Flanders initiated conflict between the French Valois monarchs and Edward III of England which plunged France into a devastating century of bloodshed. As the Hundred Years War drew to a close, frustration among English nobles over losses in France and the ineptitude of Henry VI touched off a power struggle in 1455, known as the War of the Roses, which divided the nobility and weakened the once proud English monarchy. In fifteenth-century Italy most of the great city republics fell into the hands of noble despots or ambitious mercenary captains, whose legacy of violence and duplicity would inspire Machiavelli's model of a successful prince. In the German-speaking lands of the Holy Roman Empire, dynastic struggles among the dukes of Bavaria, Luxembourg, and Austria over the Imperial throne combined with the expansionist policies of the dukes of Burgundy in the Rhine valley to disrupt peace and trade. Stronger states would eventually emerge from these struggles, but the wars' immediate impact was to weaken established authorities and undermine traditional loyalties.

Late medieval states functioned through networks of aristocratic families bound together by personal ties rather than through institutional structures. Royal councils, central and regional law courts, and fiscal chambers provided the skeleton of a state, but the human muscle that moved it responded to other stimuli than modern bureaucrats. Politics entailed a welding of private interest onto royal service. Officials treated their posts as personal property, allocated to them as members of a distinct and privileged class. They governed through a distribution of favours, both personal and official, and by calling in debts and obligations from clients. Devotion to a superior and generosity to subordinates were honourable and ethical traits. The members of this power elite envisioned themselves as the community of the realm, and they jealously defended the "public" interest, which meant their collective private rights. By the late fourteenth century nearly all leading ecclesiastical officials belonged to the ruling class by birth or ambition, and ties of blood, patronage, and class interest remained strong. Clerical education was a traditional pathway to governmental service, except in Italy where a new cohort of university-trained laymen, who modelled their political behaviour on ancient pagan statesmen such as Cicero, had emerged.

Over time, lay officials would gradually replace churchmen in royal councils everywhere.[17]

Throughout the Middle Ages, two theories justified political legitimacy. The first, hierarchical and rooted in Roman imperial law, saw authority descending from God through the pope, emperor, or king downward. The second, communal and rooted in Germanic conventions, grounded authority in mutual oaths sworn among relative equals. Both models spelled out a code of conduct for their adherents, though neither accurately depicted political reality. Communal assemblies generated hierarchies, and royal charters called on the community of the realm as often as on divine authority. The papacy, as self-conscious heir to imperial Rome, had nurtured the hierarchical model throughout the Middle Ages, but communal values legitimated the activities of many religious groups such as monasteries, parishes, and confraternities. Since the Gregorian reforms, lay rulers had struggled with popes and with the clerical elite within their territories over jurisdictional and property rights, with both king and pope asserting direct authority from God. As we have seen, in building the medieval papal monarchy, the popes had fashioned a centralized judicial and fiscal system that claimed authority over Europe's entire clerical population. As lay monarchical states grew and began to define their legitimacy on the basis of "national" myths, clerical leaders all over Europe faced difficult choices over whom they should serve. This clash of patronage, private interests, and loyalties would come to a head in the fourteenth century.

The Late Medieval Church

The image of Christendom, first articulated during the Carolingian era, informed religious and political discourse into the fourteenth century. In 1350 most Europeans recognized one spiritual leader, the pope, and this must be seen as the greatest achievement of the medieval Church. Only a few European regions lay outside of Christendom. In the southeast, the Balkan territories of the Byzantine Empire followed the Greek Orthodox Christian Church, whose spiritual and political leaders refused to recognize papal authority. In eastern Europe, Muscovite Russia also honoured Orthodox Christianity. In 1386 the conversion of the Grand Prince of Lithuania and his subjects to Catholic Christianity stretched the eastern frontier of Christendom to Kiev, where it would remain. Finally, in southern Spain, Granada formed the last remnant of the once great Moslem emirate of al-Andalus. Otherwise Catholic Christianity predominated, though pocket Jewish communities persevered under the shadow of extortionate protection fees demanded by political authorities and threats of collective violence from Christian neighbours.

In the broadest sense the late medieval Church encompassed all baptized Christians who recognized the pope as their earthly head, but for our purposes we will focus on the visible institutional structure, outside of which, according to Pope Boniface VIII, there was "no salvation or remission of sins".[18] Salvation for the Christian came first from baptism, a sacrament or ritual act involving water, oil, and prayers, which in Augustine of Hippo's imagery washed away original sin. Following the Fourth Lateran Council in 1215, once a Christian reached spiritual adulthood, canon law required at least an annual confession of sins to a priest, followed by reception of the Eucharist – bread, consecrated through rituals performed by a priest, that miraculously became the body of Christ. These two sacraments sustained a Christian in grace, literally a spiritual "gift" from God brought on by the salvation of Jesus Christ, which allowed a Christian full communion with God in heaven after death. Finally, the sacrament of extreme unction offered a last confession of sins, with prayers and anointing, which prepared the shriven soul of the dying Christian for judgement before God.[19] These sacradotal (grace-giving) acts were essential for salvation, and all of them, except baptism on rare life-threatening occasions, required a man sacramentally anointed into the priesthood to perform them. Among its members the late medieval clergy counted nuns, monks, hermits, administrators, and schoolboys; but the fundamental cleric was a priest responsible for the cure (care) of souls, who performed sacerdotal rituals. Most Christians received the crucial sacraments as members of a parish community, from their parish curate.

The parish (*parochia*) system had slowly evolved since its Carolingian foundation, and as with so many other medieval institutions it had acquired multiple functions. At its core was a "mother" church with full rights to baptize all parishioners. Since 1215 every Christian belonged to a parish, and the invisible lines of parish boundaries portioned out the landscape of Christendom. Not all churches had parochial status, and many parishes, particularly in England and Italy, included filial churches, with some sacramental rights, along with chapels, chantries, or other sacral sites. The medieval demographic growth had resulted in the foundation of frontier parishes and the subdivision of older parochial units, but the process was never systematic, so tensions among parishioners between the rights of the mother church and newer sacral centres, reinforced by communal disputes over other resources, often soured parochial relations.

The parish church itself normally comprised a choir or sanctuary, where the priest performed his sacerdotal functions, and the nave, where the faithful gathered to observe and hear the priest. Though local lords, as patrons, might claim the right to attend religious services in the sanctuary and often to be buried there, a railing or screen topped by a crucifix (rood) divided the church's two parts, visibly distinguishing clerical space from that allocated to the laity. Painted or carved images of Christ, Mary, and the saints covered the nave walls as teaching devices. Some churches sheltered side altars, called chantries, for endowed commemorative Masses for the dead. The bells in the tower attached to the church were rung to summon parishioners to services, sound the hours of the ritual day, honour the dead, warn the community of fires and threats, and ward off storms. Finally the walled yard around the church sheltered the cemetery, offered defensive protection for the living in border regions, and sometimes provided space for plays, celebrations, and church ales. Ecclesiastical law required all parishioners to attend parish services on Sundays and feast days. The people also came to receive the sacraments and to be buried. Religious sites covered the landscape, but the parish church was the nerve centre for collective spiritual life.

To maintain the building and the ritual objects associated with the sacraments and to sustain the curate with food and lodging, the community paid annual tithes, normally assessed at one-tenth of their crops. Parishioners sometimes delivered the grain, fruits, and eggs to the parsonage for storage in its barn or larder, but normally officials representing the tithe-holders collected the fruits directly at harvest. As with so many other aspects of feudal administration, tithe revenues, known as "temporalities", actually belonged to the patron, who reserved the right to appoint a priest as curate. Patrons were often church officials or monastic houses, but lay men and women sometimes held the right of patronage as descendants of the original parish founder or by acquisition of the rights through mortgage or sale. The system could become quite complex, with patronage rights and tithe revenues belonging to separate individuals or in some cases shareholders. Those who pocketed tithe revenues had responsibility for maintaining the sanctuary and sustaining the priest, but the alienation of tithe collecting from religious service opened the door for all sorts of irregularities as many patrons treated their rights as a source of revenue and were less than conscientious about making repairs or choosing priests. Patrons would grant their benefice to a clerical relative or promising university student, who in turn would use part of the income to hire a "mass-priest" as vicar. Absenteeism among benefice-holders was not uncommon, and pluralism (the holding of more than one benefice) was also widespread.

Lay interest and demand favoured resident priests, who could effectively perform the sacraments and other religious services (called "sacramentals") such as blessing crops and livestock, and despite absenteeism and pluralism most parishes had resident beneficed clergy. To cover for revenues skimmed off by patrons, parish priests often charged fees for services, to the frustration of their tithe-paying parishioners. Communities with chapels or filial churches paid tithes to the mother church, whose curate was supposed to visit the outlying sites for bi-weekly or monthly services and, most importantly, to attend the sick and dying to prepare their souls for the next world. Distance, age, and temperament sometimes resulted in irregular contact between the curate and these outlying communities. Village officials routinely petitioned to elevate their chapel or filial church to parochial status. Meanwhile a proletariat of unbeneficed priests celebrated commemorative Masses for the souls of dead parishioners at chapels and chantries financed by their surviving kin.[20] Overall the extractive nature of the tithe system created tension between supply and demand for religious services, and the misappropriation of revenues made many under-compensated clergymen fee conscious. The laity responded by criticizing the tithe system and by seeking to gain greater control over parochial revenues. Over the centuries, community members had provided additional gifts to support parochial activities, and the accumulated capital formed the church fabric. In the later Middle Ages local lay parish members known as church wardens assumed responsibility for the fabric.

While the countryside might be poorly served by priests, towns tended to be infested with clergy. Most cities had more than one parish whose religious and administrative structure resembled rural churches, but in urban centres personal piety and concentrated wealth resulted in significant numbers of endowed chantry altars, chapels, and commemorative Masses. Towns also housed religious communities such as monasteries and convents, as well as clerical administrators, especially in the cathedral towns which served as diocesan sees (capitals) for a bishop. Finally, urban educational institutions from grammar schools to universities were ecclesiastical bodies, whose administrators, teachers, and students claimed clerical status. While villages were lucky to have their own priest, in some urban communities one-tenth of the residents claimed clerical status.

After around 1100 all parishes belonged to a diocese under the spiritual guidance of a bishop. Episcopal sees varied in size, from immense dioceses such as Lincoln and Constance to the tiny bishopric of Ravello in Sicily, that stretched two miles at its widest.[21] In 1400 there were 263 bishoprics on the Italian peninsula but only 131 in much larger France. England, Scotland, and Wales combined had only thirty-three dioceses, one less than neighbouring Ireland.[22] The bishop was the "ordinary" who held all spiritual jurisdiction, though in most of Europe, except Italy where the dioceses were too small, the bishop exercised control over his see through archdeacons, archpriests, or rural deans, who presided over clusters of parishes in the bishop's name. In some areas deanery boundaries demarcated the original parish of the mother church.

The bishop's chief task was to be the liturgical head of his church. He should perform all of the sacerdotal rites required of a priest, along with the sacraments of confirmation for all Christians and holy orders to ordain the priests needed to meet the spiritual responsibilities of parish ministry in his diocese. As a result of the Investiture Controversy, clerics attached to the episcopal cathedral, known as canons, held the exclusive right to elect the bishop, yet everyone knew that powerful laymen would influence elections, and by the fourteenth century many bishoprics had become permanently associated with princely and noble dynasties. Canons of cathedral chapters were themselves normally members of elite families. Outside of the tiny Italian bishoprics, it was extremely rare for a parish priest to become a canon, much less a bishop. Day-to-day supervision and instruction of the diocesan clergy had never been an episcopal duty, and bishops had limited control over parochial appointments and normally accepted the candidates nominated by the various patrons.

Bishoprics were significant political institutions, and as with parish benefices, some men held more than one episcopal office. Within the Holy Roman Empire many bishops were territorial lords as well as ecclesiastical officials. In Italy urban oligarchic families dominated important episcopal offices, though here the bishops had less influence. In England, the kings granted diocesan sees to valued clerical advisors, and once appointed, English bishops often continued in royal service. In France, the monarch's supervision of episcopal elections was recognized by law.

Throughout Christendom bishops were seldom appointed for their religious merit, and many, saddled with governmental or familial responsibilities, resided far from their diocese. Thus co-adjutors or suffragans, bishops whose "dioceses" were located in former Christian towns under Moslem rule, performed the day-to-day judicial, liturgical, and administrative responsibilities of absentee bishops, such as ordinations, confirmation, and parish visitations.

Some bishoprics, such as the see of Toledo in Spain, held the distinction of primacy over others within an ecclesiastical province, and their incumbents were referred to as "archbishops". An archbishop had prestige and might exert leadership in his province, but the office was never designed to include specific authority over bishops. Archiepiscopal courts did play a role in adjudicating disputes between dioceses within the province or as a step in an appeals process to Rome. The traditional archiepiscopal synods of provincial clergy rarely occurred in the later Middle Ages, and bishops basically functioned independently within their diocese. The quality of orderly religious life depended on firm and sensitive episcopal administration, and effective governance varied from diocese to diocese and, within the diocese, from bishop to bishop. The more conscientious sought to reduce lay exploitation of benefices, absenteeism, clerical immorality, and concubinage. Nevertheless, given existing rights of appointment, bishops recruited only a fraction of their own parish ministry, while the vested interests of local elites in ecclesiastical affairs often mitigated efforts to discipline beneficed clergy and thwarted reform programmes. Moreover, monastic communities and religious orders involved in education and preaching operated throughout the diocese but outside of episcopal jurisdiction.

Since late antiquity, religious communities of men or women had cloistered themselves away from the world and worshipped together after making a profession to live under the guidance of a rule (*regula*). These monastic orders of "regular" clergy distinguished themselves from "secular" clergy, who lived in the world having neither professed nor entered a cloister. The oldest monastic order in Christendom, the Benedictines, traced their origins to the sixth-century rule of Benedict of Nursia. Benedictine rule required obedience to a patriarchal abbot and a routine schedule of prayer, chant, and work for the cloistered monks. In many communities the monks' central labour was copying and illuminating manuscripts, which did much to preserve classical Christian and pagan writings. Carolingian patronage and later pious donations resulted in many abbeys acquiring extensive tracts of land, so that as landlords with feudal rights, monastic communities were often at odds with their peasant tenants. The Benedictines had no centralized governance system, and the level of discipline in the houses varied. In earlier centuries frustration with lax discipline had spawned reform movements among communities, such as the Cistercians and Carthusians, calling for greater austerity and more centralized governance, but on the whole, houses maintained their independence. Originally founded in the countryside away from settled communities, many houses later attracted settlements during the medieval demographic expansion. In all, given the autonomy of houses, it is difficult to generalize about religious behaviour, social power, and political influence among Benedictines and their reformed branches.

Some regular clergy focused their ministry in towns, where they served as preachers and teachers. Among these orders, communities of mendicant (begging) friars took a vow of poverty requiring that they beg for alms to support their ministry. Among the mendicant orders the three most famous were the Dominicans, the Augustinians, and the Franciscans. Founded by Dominic of Calereuga in the early thirteenth century, the Dominicans practised corporate poverty until 1475, holding only their churches and friaries. Having begun as a movement to combat heresies, the Dominicans pursued education at emerging universities, wrote on theology, preached and administered confession, and served as prosecutors and judges for the Papal Inquisition. Representatives of the various houses met yearly at provincial chapters, which in turn sent representatives to the General Chapter at Rome. The Dominicans consistently supported papal authority in ecclesiastical policy and acted as arbiters of orthodoxy. Modelling themselves along the lines of the Dominicans, the Augustinian Hermits originated in Italy and received papal sanction in 1256. The Augustinians were closely associated with universities and urban preaching. Finally the Franciscans, founded by Francis of Assisi in 1209, competed with the Dominicans as educators, preachers, and confessors, and the rivalry between these orders often soured urban religious life. The Franciscans' commitment to the austere poverty of their founder was their strength and weakness, as disputes over the possession of churches and houses and even the quality of their habit (standard clothing) divided Franciscans. In the fourteenth and fifteenth centuries, attacks on clerical wealth associated with radical Franciscans nearly led to the order's dissolution.

Most religious orders had female houses, whose members also followed the rules set down by the founders. Down to the Gregorian reform era, Benedictine abbesses exerted significant authority over their houses and as landlords. By 1100, however, most found themselves yoked to a male monastery and under the supervision of its abbot. Some cloistered communities of women, such as the Poor Clares, sought to follow stricter rules of poverty along the lines of the friars, but gender biases prohibited them from engaging in public ministry such as preaching, associated with the mendicant orders. Convents provided families with a means to settle a younger daughter without a costly dowry, and some houses accepted novices only from elite families. Convents also offered their professed residents an opportunity to read and write, and the evidence from late medieval manuscripts suggests that many houses fostered sincere and profound spirituality. The male-dominated society outside the cloister, however, remained suspicious of women living without male supervision, and in their dealings with the outside world, nuns required male interlocutors.[23]

The bishop of Rome, as pope, served as titular head of this elaborate collection of ecclesiastical communities, jurisdictions, and institutions. The pope was also ruler of the Papal States, a significant territorial block in central Italy. This double role as religious leader and territorial prince created tensions in papal policy and bifurcated the interests of the several hundred officials who staffed the "curia" and handled papal governance, from issues affecting the spiritual commonwealth of Christendom to the mundane duties of tax collection, justice, and defence for the Papal States. The three branches of papal administration were the Apostolic Chamber, the Chancery, and the *Sacra Rota*. The Apostolic Chamber (*camera*) served as the papal treasury for Church revenues, but the Chamberlain (*camerlengo*) also supervised the appointments of all officials in the Papal States. The account books of the Apostolic Chamber recorded both "spiritual" and "temporal" income, and the treasurer maintained accounts for exchange of monies, for investments, and for credit with banking houses in Florence, Genoa, and elsewhere. The Chancery, meanwhile, handled papal correspondence on nearly all issues except those directly involving financial affairs. It also issued decrees under the papal seal, known as "bulls", from the Latin term *bulla* (seal). Papal bulls applied to all members of the Church and, under the principle of papal spiritual sovereignty, were inscribed as canon laws of the Church. The bulk of Chancery business involved individual cases, requests, forms or letters that did not become canon law. To interpret canon law the *Sacra Rota* served as the supreme court for all ecclesiastical cases that were appealed to Rome and as the sovereign law court for the Papal States. Canon lawyers and theologians staffed the *Sacra Rota*, and as with most tribunals in the fourteenth century, pursuing justice there proved an expensive and time-consuming endeavour. A fourth component of the papal court was the chapel whose members handled the liturgical duties connected with the pope's priestly, episcopal, and pontifical responsibilities.

Since the era of the Gregorian reforms, the College of Cardinals had assisted the pope: liturgically as Rome's beneficed civic clergy, administratively as curial officials, or diplomatically as representatives or legates to the leading courts throughout Europe. Those cardinals resident at Rome formed the consistory, which met two or three times a week to advise the pope on various issues. When a pope died, the cardinals assembled within ten days at the site of the death, as a conclave to elect a successor, who was more often than not a cardinal himself. A pope could ignore the consistory's advice as well as whatever promises he had made to the conclave to secure his election. Thus the role cardinals might play in papal governance varied dramatically, depending on the personality of the pope and loyalties among the cardinals. Nepotism was common as popes tended to trust their own kinsmen, and the consistory itself was often rife with familial factions among the cardinals' large households of retainers. Neither personal piety nor ordination to the priesthood were prerequisites to wear the red cardinal's cap.

The mix of worldly and spiritual interests which characterized ecclesiastical life from the parish to the papal court was not inherently problematic, provided that the clergy emphasized their spiritual ministry, particularly at the parochial level. For most Christians the pope and even the bishop were distant and vague figures who impinged on their lives only when local disputes brought parochial affairs to the attention of higher authorities. In the fourteenth and fifteenth centuries, however, a crisis at the top forced ecclesiastical officials to reconsider the unbridled power of the papal monarchy and the destructive effect of worldly interests on the Church's spiritual life. Proposed solutions to the crisis could have reformed and renewed the medieval Church. Their failure to do so, set the stage for the much more dramatic and divisive changes of the sixteenth century.

The Avignese Papacy

In 1300 thousands of Christians poured into Rome hoping to receive a plenary indulgence which offered complete remission of temporal

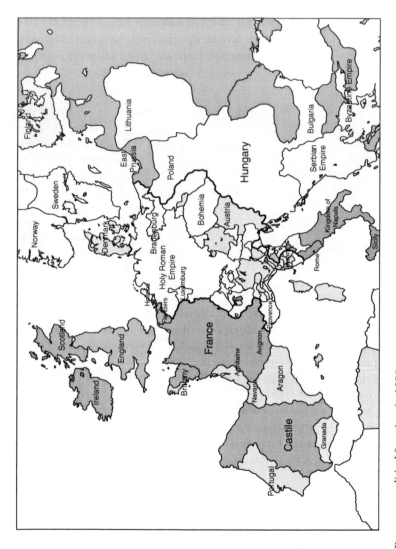

Map 1 European political frontiers in 1350

Note: Heavier line marks the boundary of the Holy Roman Empire.

punishment in Purgatory for all confessed sins. Rumours had promised such a grant, and popular thirst for it had attracted the pilgrims. Pope Boniface VIII (*1294–1303) eventually declared a Jubilee Year and offered the indulgences. The papacy appeared to be at the height of its spiritual power. Three years later on 7 September 1303, as he was preparing to excommunicate the French king, Philip IV, a body of French knights, joined by Boniface's Italian enemies, stormed the papal palace at Anagni in central Italy and imprisoned the ageing pontiff. The local militia soon rescued him, but he would die a short time later at Rome. The assault at Anagni culminated a protracted dispute between Boniface and Philip over royal power to appoint, tax, and judge the French clergy; and it exposed the papacy's basic weakness in a test of political wills.

The guiding principle of the Gregorian reforms had been to separate the clergy from lay influence, and under papal monarchy, all clerical men and women, though they lived within territories ruled by lay men or women, were to submit first to papal authority. Like other monarchs, the pope taxed his subjects, demanded that they bring their legal disputes to his courts, and asserted ultimate say through "papal provision" over all significant administrative appointments. Tensions existed between royal and papal demands on ecclesiastical officials, and the fact that the popes themselves were territorial lords in central Italy further muddied the situation. Most of the thirteenth-century popes had been Italians, who depended on bonds of familial and personal loyalty to govern their spiritual commonwealth and secular domains.[24] In principle, authority within the Church derived from the office rather than the incumbent's familial or social connections, for every bishop, prioress, abbot, and priest was theoretically dead to the world. Many ecclesiastical officials, however, held some feudal rights or personal property distinct from their benefice, and many Central European bishops were also territorial lords. The inherent tension between religious and secular concerns triggered sporadic conflicts between the popes and various monarchs; and papal involvement in Italian politics often compromised the popes' spiritual office. None the less, prior to Boniface's reign the Church had held its own.[25]

In arguing his case against Philip, Boniface VIII spelled out papal theocracy in a bull, *Unam Sanctam*, promulgated in November 1302. In it he asserted that there was only one Church, outside of which no salvation was possible; with only one head, who was Christ acting through his vicar, Peter, and Peter's successors, the popes. Two swords of power existed on earth, the temporal and the spiritual. The Church wielded the more important, spiritual sword; but even when brandishing the temporal sword, any king had to follow the guidance of the Church. Boniface reminded his audience that spiritual power exceeded temporal power in dignity and could institute temporal power and judge its transgressions. God alone judged the pope, and whoever opposed the spiritual power invested in the pope opposed God. The theocratic assumptions of *Unam Sanctam* reflected over two centuries of canon law, but Boniface could not enforce his words with military might.[26] The assault at Anagni ushered in a century and a half of crisis.

Ten days after the pope's death, the available cardinals gathered to elect a successor; but their initial choice, Benedict XI (*1303–4), died a few months later. At the ensuing conclave, factional wrangling split the cardinals and denied any candidate the required two-thirds majority. Months of stalemate followed until the electors turned to an outsider, Bertrand of Got, a Frenchman and archbishop of the English-controlled city of Bordeaux, who became Clement V (*1305–14). Following his coronation at Lyons, Clement paused on his journey to Rome at Avignon in Provence. Earlier popes had lived outside of Rome, and Clement often discussed completing his journey to the papal city. He and his successors, however, would remain at Avignon until 1377.[27]

For the Italians and particularly the Romans, the Avignese popes suffered as French puppets, and Clement's pontificate established the template. Among the first cardinals he elevated were nine Frenchmen, including four nephews, which produced a French majority in the College. Many of the new cohort had spent part of their career in Philip IV's service, and the king's influence over the curia was strong. Clement convoked an ecumenical council at Vienne in southern France in 1311, which effectively completed Philip's victory over Boniface by exonerating the pope's assailants and expunging papal judgements against the French king. Moreover, despite their absence from Rome, Clement and his successors actively pursued aggressive policies in the Papal States.

At the heart of the political turmoil in Italy lay the rivalry between Angevin (French) and Aragonese (Spanish) claims to the southern Italian kingdoms of Naples and Sicily, and papal affiliation with France immediately created allies and enemies on the peninsula. To defend the Papal States the Avignese popes hired mercenary captains (*condottieri*), whose troops battled Aragonese forces in central and southern Italy. John XXII (*1316–34) even called for a "crusade" against his political rivals, the Visconti dukes of Milan. The curia sought to intervene in every major political conflict in Europe, from the ongoing wars between England and France to the disputes among the German princes over the

Imperial throne, and in all these arenas the Avignese popes moved in sync with French objectives. The papacy had been highly politicized for more than a century, but in operating on the border of the most power- ful monarchy in western Europe, the curia appeared to lack autonomy, which weakened its influence as an "honest" power broker. All seven Avignese popes were native Frenchmen, and of the 110 cardinals they elevated, 90 were French. Despite routine promises to return to Rome, they assembled a complete curia at Avignon, where the papal household alone counted 500 members with each cardinal supporting his own retinue. Eventually, in 1348, Clement VI (*1342–52) purchased lordship over Avignon and the neighbouring county of Venaissin, and he and his successors transformed the former episcopal residence into a beautiful palace.

To support themselves papal officials charged fees on everything from marital dispensations to confirmation of a document. None of this was new, but the Avignese curia pursued fiscal resources with a ruthlessness that tainted all its activities with venal intent. For example, claiming "fullness of power" (*plenitudo potestatis*) the curia asserted rights of papal provision over all benefices within the Church, though in practice such authority could never supplant the rights of local patrons nor the trad- ition of episcopal elections. In the past, papal provision had only entailed confirmation of a properly elected candidate, who secured his post by paying for the official forms. The Avignese popes applied the new prac- tice of "reservation" to episcopal and abbatial appointments, by which the popes "reserved" occupied benefices for particular candidates, who then moved into the post on the death of the incumbents. Office seekers had to petition the curia, usually in person, for posts and paid fees to secure an anticipated benefice. Papal reservations disrupted local systems of ecclesiastical appointment throughout Christendom, antagonized traditional patrons, and created tensions between benefice-holders and their vulturine successors.

The Apostolic Chamber at Avignon also collected a variety of trad- itional taxes, all of which had begun as gifts but in time had become obligations. Once a year the curia could assess *servitia*, which equalled one-third of the first year's income for any benefice. In 1306 Clement V created a new tax called "papal annates", by demanding the first year's income from all vacant benefices in the British Isles. In time these fees, along with the charges for reservations and provisions, created the impression that high ecclesiastical offices were for sale, and the cost of appointment meant that benefice-holders, once in place, needed to exploit the resources of their coveted positions to recoup their investment. Papal officials also collected forced donations called "subsidies" from clergy in various regions of Christendom to finance military ventures in the Papal States. Except for annates, the Avignese popes did not create these taxes, but they made them obligatory, systemized their collection, and spent them on activities far removed from pastoral care. The Avignese papacy's average annual income hovered around 200,000 gold florins, a level which was far less than that of the leading contemporary lay monarchs; but for those who visited Avignon, the papal court seemed avaricious and opulent. Gradually a reservoir of animosity built up against the efficient curial bureaucrats.

The Great Schism and the Council of Constance

The Avignese popes often promised to resettle in Rome, and Urban V (*1362–70) spent three years in Italy attempting to secure peace, only to return to Avignon disillusioned. His successor, Gregory XI (*1370–8), died at Rome while visiting the Papal States. Following canon law a conclave of sixteen cardinals (11 Frenchmen, 4 Italians, and 1 Spaniard) assembled at Rome to elect Gregory's successor. Civic leaders petitioned them to choose a Roman, as crowds surrounded the chambers. In the charged atmosphere the electors settled on a compromise candidate, the archbishop of Bari, who was an Italian with ties to the French rulers in southern Italy. Though an outsider, Urban VI (*1378–89) had some experience at Avignon, and the cardinals felt they could manage him. Urban, however, imagined himself a reformer, and his attacks on the cardinals' lavish lifestyles and their retinues quickly soured relations within the curia. The bulk of the papal court fled to Anagni, repudiated the "forced" election of Urban, and chose Robert of Geneva as Pope Clement VII (*1378–94).

Disputed conclaves, anti-popes, and schisms had occurred in the past, but the dual elections in 1378 ushered in an unprecedented crisis in Church governance – the Great Schism (1378–1417). Urban VI at Rome and Clement VII at Avignon both claimed apostolic succession, fullness of powers, jurisdictional and administrative rights, and the symbolic "keys" to salvation. Christendom fractured into two "obediences". Urban retained the allegiance of the Emperor and much of the Holy Roman Empire, northern and central Italy, England, Scandinavia, and the eastern monarchies of Hungary, Poland, and Lithuania when it embraced

Roman Catholic Christianity in 1386. The Avignese curia drew obedience from France, Naples, Scotland, the duchy of Savoy, and later the kingdom of Castile. Some states, such as Aragon, remained neutral, with royal officials administering the kingdom's churches in the interim. Though insisting on the heretical nature of his opponent's status, each pope cautiously limited his administrative reach to the regions under his obedience, except for border territories such as Austria and south-western Germany, where multiple candidates to benefices often held rival papal provisions and reservations. Nevertheless, the schism threatened the legitimacy of all ecclesiastical business. For example, when the city of Erfurt sought to combine its mendicant schools into a university, officials hedged their bets and expended the time and money to secure provisions from both curia.[28] A unified Church formed the cornerstone of Christendom, and the Great Schism prompted repercussions within every diocese, cathedral chapter, monastic community, and important family in Europe.

Christian leaders hoped for reunification with the death of each pope, but the contending cardinals feared losing their status and power and so elected successors, Boniface IX (*1389–1404) for Urban at Rome and Benedict XIII (*1394–1417) for Clement at Avignon, thwarting expectations that one or the other party would back down. As the crisis dragged on, representatives from the rival curia attempted to negotiate a settlement requiring the resignations of the popes and the consolidation of the two colleges in conclave for a new election. Under canon law, however, the cardinals were powerless without papal approval, and the rival popes refused to resign or to call a general council which might have produced a settlement.[29] By 1400, more and more intellectuals and ecclesiastical leaders were calling for a general council with or without papal approval to resolve the schism and reform administrative abuses. These "conciliarists" asserted that under normal circumstances the pope governed the visible Church but under special circumstances the universal Church, as the body of Christ, could act in its self-interest and convene a council against papal wishes. The schism, conciliarists argued, had produced a crisis "in head and members" that required extraordinary measures to preserve the universal Church. In 1409, cardinals from both curia summoned a general council at Pisa with widespread support from lay rulers, especially the Emperor Sigismund, attracting several hundred prominent ecclesiastical leaders. Hoping to bring unity, the participants deposed the popes at Avignon and Rome and elected the archbishop of Milan as Alexander V (*1409–10). The deposed papal claimants, however, refused to relinquish their rights, so now there were three curia, three sets of cardinals, and three obediences. Traditional papal claims of moral and spiritual leadership sounded false and shrill throughout divided Christendom, as papal authority reached its nadir.

The conciliarists continued to advocate an assembly of ecclesiastical leaders to resolve the schism but recognized that they needed a pope to summon it. Finally, in 1414, the Pisan successor to Alexander V, John XXIII (*1410–15), a mercenary and lifelong libertine, convoked a council at Constance (1414–18). The Emperor Sigismund had prodded John to assemble the council after his efforts to reconquer the Papal States ended in disaster. The choice of the southern German town weakened the Italian influence at the council's sessions, and political consider-ations remained paramount throughout the assembly. The conciliarists argued that the Church was a *res publica* (republic), and the reformers drew on the civil law traditions which were growing in prominence in the Italian states, along with the communal model of sovereignty in which authority rested in the people and was conferred to their elected leader.[30] Such views directly threatened papal monarchy, and the pos-sibility of extensive institutional reforms seemed imminent. Thousands of ecclesiastical and lay leaders converged at Constance in search of insti-tutional unity, reforms of abuses, and a resolution of debates over faith.

Unity first required an end to schism through the deposition of the three popes and the election of a new, single leader. Realizing that he couldn't control the council and hoping to discredit it, John XXIII fled Constance in late February only to be escorted back as a prisoner. In April 1415, to secure its right to act, the council issued the decree *Haec Sancta*, which stated that the assembly had "authority immediately from Christ; and that all men of whatever rank or position, including the pope himself are bound to obey [the council] in matters concerning the faith, the abolition of the schism, and the reformation of the Church of God in its head [the papacy] and members".[31] The following month the council tried John XXIII for simony and deposed him. He accepted the judge-ment and ended his days as a cardinal. The Roman pope, Gregory XII (*1406–15), finding himself without political allies, approached the council with a request that, if the assembly allowed him to convene it and accepted the decrees of his pontificate, he would resign. On 4 July 1415, Gregory stepped down and also donned a cardinal's hat.[32] The recalci-trant Avignese pope, Benedict XIII, never recognized the council which eventually deposed him in 1417. His lay supporters having abandoned him, Benedict was held under protective custody in a Spanish castle.

Following Benedict's deposition a special conclave of cardinals and representatives of the "nations" (regional churches) among the clergy assembled at Constance, elected a Roman aristocrat, Oddo Colonna, as Pope Martin V (*1417–31). The cardinal-deacon was promptly ordained a priest, consecrated as a bishop, then crowned pope. The schism had ended, and reform could begin.

With unity secured, the council turned to disputes over faith, in particular the frequency and form of the laity's reception of the Eucharist. A growing devotion to the consecrated body of Christ and a desire among many lay folk to receive the sacrament regularly in both forms, as consecrated bread and wine, challenged the earlier, thirteenth-century trend of infrequent lay communion limited to bread alone. Desire to receive communion under both "species" (bread as body and wine as blood), known as Utraquism, had inspired a radical reform movement among the Czech-speaking Bohemians led by Jan Hus. The Hussite movement, centred at Prague, deeply troubled Emperor Sigismund, who hoped for a reconciliation between Hus and ecclesiastical authorities and had offered Hus, and his colleague Jerome of Prague, safe passage to the council. At Constance negotiations with Hus quickly broke down, and the Czech reformers were condemned and executed as heretics. Their "martyrdom" triggered a revolt in Bohemia, which we will explore in the next chapter, but the council believed it had defended true faith against undisciplined dissenters and that Hus had chosen heresy rather than submission. The Council supported other lay reform movements, such as the Brethren of the Common Life, in part because these movements accepted established authority and offered no direct threat to religious unity.

With the consolidation of the three curia, the conciliar reformers sought to bring order to papal fiscal practices, to reform blatant abuses, and to restore a spiritual aura to papal policies.[33] The council attacked a broad range of oppressive dues, taxes, and fees whose use had grown as the papacy experienced a decline in traditional revenues at the expense of the growing fiscal appetites of the monarchical states. Despite strongly worded legislation against these "simonical" practices, the council failed to reform most abuses. In an effort to bring order to the college of cardinals, curial policies and papal conclaves, reformers at Constance reduced the number of cardinals to between eighteen and twenty-four with an absolute maximum of thirty. In addition, to prevent the domination of the college by French or Italian prelates as had occurred earlier, the reformers called for broader distribution of "national" origins so that no nation had a two-thirds majority for a conclave, and proposed alternating "national" origins for the popes. In one of the most significant conciliar decrees, *Frequens* (1417), the council attempted to put constraints on the head of the Church by requiring the regular convocation of ecumenical councils. The next was to occur in five years, then seven, and then every ten years. Finally, to ensure that future popes complied with the reforms, the council called for papal capitulations – a set of promises sworn as a kind of contract between the newly elected pope and his electoral conclave. Martin V accepted these constraints. The conciliarists hoped that future popes would honour their promises and, if not, that conclaves would have the legal means to force compliance.

Renaissance Papacy and the Failure of Conciliarism

Over the next century Martin V and his successors re-established papal autonomy under the shadow of conciliar constraint. By the 1450s the popes had circumvented the requirement for regular councils and delayed or ignored promises made at their electoral capitulations. Once again they began to stock the college of cardinals with Italian relatives. In contrast, the papacy found its control over the selecting and supervising of clergy north of the Alps sharply curtailed, and with this shrinking influence came a continued reduction in revenues. The papacy's fiscal base increasingly depended on feudal dues and taxes in the Papal States, and thus papal officials focused attention on their worldly resources and worldly affairs. This increased entanglement in Italian secular affairs demoralized the Renaissance papacy for many.

The drift away from conciliar reform occurred gradually. Martin V (*1417–31) initially honoured the demand for frequent councils and convoked an assembly at Pavia in 1423. Political tensions in Italy, however, forced the council's transfer to Siena and prevented Martin's attendance. The assembly soon dissolved. Reform still seemed possible, and Martin followed *Frequens* again when he convened a new council at Basel in 1431 shortly before his death. It would be the only council after Constance to meet outside Italy, and it would prove the most troublesome. Problems began with the election of Martin's successor, Eugene IV (*1431–47), who had no desire to cooperate with the conciliarists. Though the council formally opened on 23 July 1431 with high expectations, Eugene IV soon dissolved it and summoned his own assembly at

Florence. The confrontation between pope and council divided the college of cardinals, where only six of twenty-one favoured Eugene's actions, and most secular leaders endorsed the council at Basel, which refused to disband and carried on its business. The pope and the council sent rival embassies to Constantinople with the aim of negotiating a rapprochement with the Greek Orthodox Church. The Hussites from Bohemia sent a negotiating team to Basel to hammer out a settlement, which Eugene's curia would not authorize. The conciliarists attempted to complete the administrative reforms begun at Constance, outlawing the practice of papal reservations of benefices and abolishing annates, but these reforms would only have effect where the council's competence was recognized. Meanwhile Eugene's anti-council migrated from Bologna, to Ferrara, to Florence, and eventually to the Lateran palace, where it dissolved in 1443 having failed to secure a binding agreement with the Greek Church or to supersede its rival at Basel. Ultimately the conciliarists at Basel deposed Eugene in 1439 and elected their own pope, Felix (*1439–49), positing that a duly convened council was superior to the pope and that Eugene had no power to transfer it. Schism had returned, but few had the stomach for it. When Eugene IV died in 1447, his successor Nicholas V (*1447–55) negotiated settlements with the council's political patrons, particularly France. In 1449, having lost the leverage of secular support, the council's anti-pope resigned, and the council dissolved itself after formally electing Nicholas. The short-term crisis had ended.

Henceforth, Renaissance popes ignored further requests to convene regular councils. Pius II (*1458–64) reclaimed sovereignty with his bull *Execrabilis* (1460), which asserted papal superiority over any council. *Frequens* ceased to carry force, and no council would meet until 1511 when several renegade cardinals gathered at Pisa to attempt to depose Julius II (*1503–13). Julius's successor, Leo X (*1513–21), would call his own council at the Lateran palace, and in 1516 this Fifth Lateran Council asserted in the decree *Pastor aeternus* that the popes had authority over all councils, including the right to convoke, transfer, and dissolve them. *Pastor aeternus* effectively ended the conciliar reform movement. The conciliar model of Church governance would survive as a spectral alternative to papal autocracy, and reformers, including Martin Luther, would advocate a general council to bring about reform. When such a council finally convened at Trent in 1545, however, its members faced a radically different religious and political environment in which a unified ecumenical consensus on issues of reform and faith was no longer possible.

The councils had failed to reform the papacy in part because they remained irregular bodies dependent on papal convocation. The reformers at Constance had sought to strengthen the college of cardinals so that its members could use their role in regular curial administration, and their potential leverage at electoral conclaves, as a more permanent counterweight. Unfortunately the vision of a potent body of cardinals drawn from among Europe's leading churchmen failed to materialize as the college soon became a profoundly Italian body in which familial political interests played a key role. As early as the pontificate of Calixtus III (*1455–8), the majority of new cardinals were Italian, with French and Spanish churchmen, whose monarchs had a deep interest in Italian politics, comprising the next largest contingents. Decrees at Constance sought to limit papal nepotism, and the first six popes following Constance appointed "only" eleven relatives. Beginning with Sixtus IV (*1471–84), however, the next five popes elevated twenty-four kinsmen.[34] Family interests and dynastic politics became paramount, as epitomized in the career of one "nephew", Cesare Borgia, the natural son of Alexander VI (*1492–1503), who was elevated to the college in 1493 then released from clerical status in 1498 in order to fashion a hereditary duchy in the Romagna. In all, five nephews became popes with two powerful Italian dynasties, the della Roveres from Siena and the de' Medicis of Florence, arrayed in opposition against the Catalonian Borgias.

In this factional atmosphere the death of a pope triggered power struggles within the conclave, among rival candidates, in which family feuds and regional interests played the dominant part. At the conclave of 1471, among the eighteen electors only three were non-Italians, and in 1484 only four of twenty-five. To avert potential deadlock, candidates offered bribes to secure the needed two-thirds majority. Each new pope publicly submitted a formal capitulation, promising to initiate crusades, to work in harmony with the consistory, and to further reforms, but between 1417 and 1517 none delivered on these promises. The cardinals, who benefitted personally from the status quo, found it difficult if not impossible to force changes. So through negotiation, deception, and bribery, the Renaissance popes defused the conciliar movement, secured their authority over the curia, and held off substantive reforms.

Over the course of the fifteenth century the papal curia increasingly came to resemble an Italian princely court. In part this was due to papal weakness outside of Italy brought on by the separate "concordats" negotiated with secular rulers of France, Spain, and England, which granted these monarchs extensive powers over their subject churches.

The circumstances varied from kingdom to kingdom, and control over the territorial church often resembled a tug of war, for example in France, where the struggles resulted in seven different official protocols between 1418 and the Concordat of Bologna in 1516 that finally placed the Gallican Catholic Church formally under royal control. The loss of influence over emerging "national" churches pinched off the flow of revenue from papal provisions, taxation, and judicial fees and forced the Renaissance popes to draw from their limited temporal resources as rulers in the Papal States, while endemic warfare in Italy eventually drove them to borrow heavily and ultimately to sell ecclesiastical offices in their bureaucracy.[35] Cash-strapped monarchs all over Europe sooner or later would resort to venality, the sale of offices such as judgeships to the highest bidder, but the sale of administrative offices in the papacy reeked of simony.

Italian politics operated under the shadow of French and Aragonese claims in southern Italy and Sicily. During the fifteenth century the age of the small and fiercely independent medieval communes in northern and central Italy slowly gave way to larger regional states dominated by *signori* such as Visconti and later the Sforzas at Milan, or by the urban oligarches who controlled nominal republics, such as Venice or Florence. The French–Aragonese conflict divided these regional states into rival alliance systems and factionalized the magnates within each territory. The popes as elected rulers of the largest single Italian state were critical players in this political drama, and prominent Italian families sought representation in the curia and, if possible, control over the see of Peter. Papal elections punctuated shifts in the balance of power on the peninsula, and spiritual qualities were often counterproductive when it came to effective papal leadership. Some popes saw themselves as defenders of Italian interests against the foreign influence of France and Spain. Nicholas V (*1447–55) had tried to secure an Italian defensive alliance through the Peace of Lodi of 1454, but not all Renaissance popes were peacemakers. Sixtus IV (*1471–84) intrigued in the Pazzi conspiracy in 1478 in which an assassination attempt against Lorenzo de' Medici was orchestrated during Mass at the Florentine cathedral. Several popes faced assassination plots themselves. Alexander VI's (*1492–1503) political machinations plunged Italy into a destructive round of wars during which his successor, Julius II (*1503–13), earned a reputation as a talented and ruthless general. The Italianization of the papacy and the deepening engagement of the Roman curia in the power struggle for hegemony on the Italian peninsula ultimately weakened papal authority in religious matters, both on the peninsula and beyond the Alps.

As members of wealthy and powerful aristocratic families, Renaissance popes such as the humanist Pius II (Aeneus Silvius Piccolomini) and the Venetians, Eugene IV and Paul II, brought aristocratic tastes to the curia. By the mid-fifteenth century, papal architectural and artistic patronage had begun in earnest and would bear full fruit in the early sixteenth century with Michelangelo's painting of the Sistine Chapel and the construction of St Peter's Basilica. The grandeur and artistry of these projects did much to beautify Rome but little to improve papal finances or religious life. By the beginning of the sixteenth century, it was clear that reform from above was highly unlikely.

The fifteenth-century Church was fully integrated into the systems of political and social power throughout Europe. Factional disputes, violence, and snobbery seemed distasteful in men and women of God and would inspire anticlerical literature and art. It is easy to read pent-up anger in this anticlerical criticism, but much of this literature focused on reform rather than radical change. Some scholars have argued that people mocked and poked fun at the Church in poems and during Carnival burlesques because they were familiar and comfortable with it. People took the Church for granted and "wore it lightly".[36] Throughout fifteenth-century Europe lay folk desired increased participation in ecclesiastical affairs at all levels of society, from royal involvement in reform movements to local lay participation in religious confraternities and third-order movements.[37] Tensions between lay demands for spirituality and clerical supply would play a key role in turning reform into Reformation.

The late medieval Church was resilient, and the Reformation was not inevitable. The papacy had weathered decades of schism when two, then three, rival popes claimed spiritual authority over all Christendom. The expense of sustaining multiple courts and, after 1417, increasing papal involvement in volatile Italian politics had stimulated the papacy's fiscal appetite at a time when lay princes were also undertaking the expensive first steps of state-building. Lay princes found in the Church a wealthy and privileged estate in need of closer supervision, though clergy and lay folks with a stake in the old Church resisted reform to protect vested interests. Earlier the plague had prompted increased pious donations and religious exercises among surviving commoners, but as the economy soured, their poorer descendants grew frustrated with the cost of salvation and the real or imagined unholiness of its purveyors, the clergy. It was into this mix of anticlericalism and earnest piety that the Reformation preachers brought their message. If Church leaders had maintained closer and more cooperative ties with lay rulers and officials, then the reform movements would probably have had limited impact. Unfortunately Church officials continued to fight with kings and princes in Italy – where it seemed every major ruler had some interest – and elsewhere. Thus political ambition had driven a wedge between the popes and their potential religious allies, and it would be nearly impossible for Church authorities to rally secular support to suppress religious reform movements that enjoyed the backing or tolerance of lay rulers. In the end even where Reformation movements failed, the popes would lose their religious authority to Catholic princes and kings. The growing influence of monarchical states in ecclesiastical affairs was a principal precondition for the European Reformation, which then completed the shift of religious power into the hands of state officials.

2

RESISTANCE, RENEWAL, AND REFORM, 1414–1521

In October of 1414 a university professor and popular preacher travelled to the council at Constance under a guarantee of safe conduct offered by the Emperor, to discuss his views on the Church. There Jan Hus was arrested, tried, and executed as a heretic without ever having the opportunity to articulate his call for reform. A century later in the spring of 1521, another university professor and popular preacher travelled to the Imperial Diet at Worms under a guarantee of safe conduct from the Emperor, to discuss his views on the Church. Martin Luther was aware of Hus's fate, but unlike Hus he was permitted to speak. Luther's refusal to recant put him at risk, but he managed to escape and, while in hiding, to sustain and further his movement. The different fates that these reformers faced had less to do with their message than with the profound shift in Church–state relations during the intervening century. This chapter will plot the changes in Europe's political landscape in the era between Hus and Luther and examine the various calls for resistance, renewal, and reform.

In Chapter 1 we learned that the Church was fully integrated into the late medieval European political and social power structures. Ecclesiastical corporations administered vast landholdings and claimed extensive revenues from pious endowments and tithes. Late medieval religious practices were diverse and pluralistic, while ecclesiastical administration was divided and often factionalized. Despite papal claims to universal authority, a series of concordats and local reform initiatives were transforming Christendom into a federation of regional churches, and further pluralizing religious practice. Throughout the Middle Ages reformers had pushed for greater accountability in ecclesiastical life because they cherished their faith and loved the Church. After its development in the 1450s, the printing press gave calls for renovation and reform new impetus, raising awareness among reform-minded individuals of the commonality of the problems that troubled them, sharpening the critical imagery of an insensitive and money-grubbing Church, and heightening the rhetoric of immorality and divine retribution. By 1500, potential reformers could reach a broad audience quickly, but the question remained whether they could sustain a movement in the face of powerful vested interests committed to the status quo.

The late medieval Church was an old institution with roots in the Carolingian era. Even the dramatic Gregorian reforms were already four centuries old. Ecclesiastical wealth had always been unevenly distributed, and over the centuries this fact had generated many calls for divestment or at least accountability. The expense of sustaining multiple courts and, after 1415, increasing entanglement in volatile Italian politics would further arouse papal fiscal appetite and worldliness. Though clerical elites and lay patrons had a stake in the Church's traditional privileges and revenues, princes offered new avenues for power and ambition, which weakened opposition to princely appropriation of ecclesiastical resources for dynastic needs. In the changing political environment, clerical privileges came increasingly into question, and the popes' ability to marshal lay support against their critics steadily diminished.

When Hus travelled to Constance, the assembled churchmen were struggling to end decades of schism by restructuring ecclesiastical governance and clarifying acceptable practices and beliefs. The reformers at Constance needed religious unity, and Hus's views seemed to put that goal at risk, so they silenced him. Rather than ending his movement, however, Hus's execution triggered an uprising which would transform Bohemia's Catholic Church into a breakaway Hussite Church resilient enough to defend itself against direct military assault. Meanwhile, the failure of the decrees promulgated at Constance to reform the Church "in head and members", along with the politicization of the Renaissance papacy, undermined further efforts at internal reform. Luther could trace the genealogy of his protest to Hus, but Luther's message resonated across a different political and ecclesiastical landscape.

Reform, Dissent, and Heresy

From the outset, Jesus's followers quarrelled among themselves about how best to serve his message and mission. In the Introduction we saw how Catholic Christianity emerged after centuries of religious discord to predominate, though not monopolize, Christian beliefs. The integration of the Church into the Roman state under Constantine and his successors made Catholic Christianity Rome's official religion while transforming other paths of faith into politically destabilizing threats. The close association of heresy with political disorder thus emerged early in Church history. As the Empire fell, bishops and other ecclesiastical leaders fought to preserve the Roman Catholic religious and political system against Germanic Arian Christians, pagan warlords, and Moslem raiders. Down to the eleventh century, however, references to internal heresies in the Latin West were rare, in part because the Church itself had pluralized as Christianization of the pagan Germans depended so much on local initiative, which entailed Germanization of Christianity.

With the onset of the Gregorian reforms, heresy as a manifestation of political and ideological dissent returned.[1] Some scholars have seen the development of medieval reform and heresy as a dialectical process, in which the Church and the heretics engaged in a competitive conversation over faith, correcting and goading each other. From this perspective distinguishing reform from heresy was central to constructing the medieval Church.[2] Moreover, many medieval heresies drew support from the socially and politically dispossessed while advocating reforms that threatened established lay powers. Eventually, Church and state would unite to suppress their critics, as ecclesiastical authorities stigmatized heresy as a disease infecting the body of Christ, and lay officials responded by cutting out infected members with violent persecution.

Beginning in the eleventh century, inspired religious reformers attracted small groups of followers to purer forms of Christianity as they understood it, often living in common like monastic communities but without seeking or receiving official sanction. For some, inspiration turned to violence. Peter of Bruis's disciples smashed altars and crucifixes and beat priests.[3] Many other reform movements turned to dissent targeting the Church's growing wealth and political involvement, and these trends were most obvious in the towns, where the richest and poorest members of medieval society came in direct contact. Around 1170 a moneylender from Lyons named Peter Waldo experienced remorse over his usury – the sin of lending money at interest. He gave away his wealth and adopted the apostolic life (*vita apostolica*) of a wandering preacher, building widespread support among the poor. Peter contrasted the poverty of the apostles as recounted in his vernacular New Testament with the opulence of the contemporary Church. By the time of his death in 1205, the Waldensian movement had attracted papal scrutiny and eventually condemnation, yet despite steady repression Waldensian enclaves survived down to the sixteenth century in remote valleys of the French Alps.[4]

Not all advocates of apostolic poverty became heretics. In the 1190s Francis of Assisi, a merchant's son, left home to live as a hermit, though he soon acquired a circle of devoted followers. Francis insisted that his associates accumulate no earthly goods, but unlike the Waldensians, the Franciscans and their sister group the Poor Clares backed away from open criticism of clerical wealth and received papal sanction in 1210. Francis would become a saint, whose cult was particularly cherished among commoners, but he left a complex legacy regarding apostolic poverty within his order and within Christian life. Radical Franciscans, called Spiritualists or Fraticelli, publicly criticized clerical wealth and faced sporadic persecution for their dissent.[5]

Some heretics, such as the twelfth-century Cathari, combined criticism of the ecclesiastical order with a model for a completely separate religious community.[6] Support from local elites in parts of southern France and northern Italy allowed the movement to flourish for a time. The Cathari embraced a dualistic, Manichaean version of Christianity in which Satan ruled in the world while God controlled spiritual forces. The Cathari organized belief networks under leaders called "perfects", who through dietary and physical self-discipline mastered their earthly bodies and achieved spiritual purity. Most Cathari were not perfects, nor did they expect to be. The movement thrived due to the apparent merit of the leadership and the strength of its political allies. Suppressing the Cathari required political force. When Cathari at Toulouse murdered a papal legate in 1208, Innocent III summoned a crusade against them and established an inquisitional tribunal to hunt them out and prosecute them. The Cathari threat thus created the judicial machinery that the late medieval and early modern Church would use to subdue other heretics, dissenters, and would-be reformers. By 1243 the capture of Montségur effectively broke the Cathari's political infrastructure, but pockets of believers continued to appear before inquisitorial courts up until 1320.[7]

Having suppressed the Cathari, inquisitors turned their attention to university students and professors with dangerous ideas, as well as to illiterate non-conformists and popular expressions of anticlericalism. Permanent judges drawn primarily from the Franciscan and Dominican orders manned this special tribunal, which travelled from region to region at the invitation of local authorities. The inquisitors granted a month's grace, during which those who came forward to admit their heretical beliefs and recant received light punishments. Others against whom accusations existed were then summoned to appear. The accused could neither call witnesses nor confront their accusers. If individuals admitted their faults, they often survived. Relapsed heretics or those unwilling to recant faced torture and ultimately corporal punishment administered by lay authorities. Through the Inquisition, Church and state worked hand in iron glove to suppress opposition.

During the fourteenth century many Christians viewed outbreaks of famine and plague as signs of divine judgement. Anger against ecclesiastical wealth and privilege resurfaced among Franciscan spiritualists and led the Avignese popes to threaten to disband the order. In northern Italy followers of Dolcino di Novarra waged a religiously inspired guerrilla campaign, desecrating churches and murdering priests.[8] Perhaps the most significant fourteenth-century critic of the institutional Church was the English philosopher John Wyclif (c.1329–84). Echoing back to the fifth-century Donatists, Wyclif drew a distinction between the invisible Church of true Christians and the visible and fallible historical institution. Only true Christians were righteous with God; and if bishops and priests ceased to be in a state of grace, Wyclif argued that they should be deprived of their offices. He went so far as to identify the pope, whether in Avignon or Rome, as the Antichrist, Satan's minion on earth and leader of the unholy. For Wyclif the visible Church had no authority in and of itself; only the Bible as the Word of God should be the guide to Christian doctrine and practice. Wyclif translated the Bible into English to provide true Christians with personal access to its guidance.

Building on his emphasis on spirit and word, Wyclif denied that priests, good or wicked, could turn bread and wine into the true body and blood of Christ through the ritual of the Mass. Wyclif believed that Jesus was only present at communion in spirit, and not bodily due to some miracle of sacerdotal power.[9] In challenging the sacramental foundation of clerical privilege and power, Wyclif appealed to powerful lay patrons, who sheltered him from England's ecclesiastical courts. Emboldened, Wyclif criticized sinful lay officials, who in his view merited no obedience. This call for "godly" magistrates and churchmen threatened to undermine the political fabric of the kingdom, a fear nearly realized by the great Peasants' Revolt of 1381. Wyclif spent his declining years under house arrest, but his ideas circulated in manuscript as did copies of his vernacular Bible, spawning a movement called the Lollards, or "prayer mumblers". The Lollards believed that scripture was the only true guide to Christian faith and that it must be read by the individual believer. Armed with God's Word, they attacked clerical celibacy, indulgences, transubstantiation, and pilgrimages. The Lollards, most of whom lacked Wyclif's social status and patrons, were regularly prosecuted as heretics in the English courts. After 1410, however, they ceased to comprise an organized movement, and "Lollard" became a catch-all tag for any accused heretic.[10]

Meanwhile on the continent, especially in the Rhine valley, individual mystics faced accusations of embracing the heresy of the Free Spirit, which probably existed only in the minds of the inquisitors. According to their accusers, Free Spirits believed that through meditational reflection one could experience a mystical union with God while still on earth, comparable to the soul's spiritual union in heaven. Individuals who experienced this mystical union would no longer require the ministrations of the sacramental Church and, in fact, could violate moral law without committing sin.[11] Official concerns over the prevalence of this movement derived in part from the spread of pious mystical literature composed by women, such as Marguerite Porete's *Mirror of Simple Souls*, and the often distorted reading of such texts by male judges. Anxious lest Marguerite's union with Christ might be understood carnally, the Inquisition at Paris burned her as a relapsed heretic in 1310. Efforts to suppress the "Free Spirit" movement soon shifted to Beguine houses – communities of middling and lower-class women leading collective lives of chastity, work, and prayer but without formal rules or the status of wealthier convents, which increasingly required costly dowries from their novices. Beguine houses often supported themselves by weaving cloth, which brought them into competition with male guilds. Their transgression of established boundaries of gender and class made the Beguines vulnerable; but though some of them probably held unorthodox views, there was no Free Spirit movement. Nevertheless, inquisitors closed Beguine houses in many towns.

One other thread of late medieval spirituality often brought individuals to the attention of the Inquisition: millennial dreams.[12] Jesus's earliest followers expected the imminent second coming of Christ, which would take place in an historical drama of anticipatory signs, vivid punishments for the wicked, and a triumphal elevation of the righteous. Apocalyptic (expectant) visions drew on scriptural sources in the Book of Daniel and the Book of Revelations. These scriptural texts predicted a reign of the Antichrist for a thousand years, a millennium, sometimes followed by a thousand-year reign of Christ on earth, before the end of the world. The transition from the dominion of the Antichrist to that of Christ would be violent and unprecedented, with the conversion of the Jews to Christianity as a harbinger. Many millennial prophets read the signs of the second coming in dramatic political events, and after 1348, in outbreaks of plague. Millennialism was not inherently heretical, and most of those awaiting the second coming did so patiently and peacefully. Some preachers and visionaries, however, called on believers "to make ready the way of the lord" by destroying the forces of the Antichrist, which, if associated with the Church or political elites, could draw the wrath of the authorities. It was in this environment of expectancy, dissent, and repression that the Hussite movement surfaced.

John Hus and the Hussite Movement

Many scholars view Jan Hus (1369–1415) and the movement associated with him as derivative of Wyclif and the Lollards.[13] Wyclif's ideas certainly influenced Hus and the Hussites, but Bohemia's complex political context, the Hussites' resilience, and their diverse and sometimes radical views, argue that Hussitism was much more than Central European Lollardry. The emergence of the Hussite Church in Bohemia coincided with papal recognition of territorial Catholic Churches through concordats. What made the Hussite Church's establishment unique and significant was the role played in it by men and women from the lower rungs of the social order and its ability to resist the coordinated efforts of lay and clerical authorities to suppress it. Let us examine briefly the political and religious background of the reform movements in Bohemia, Hus's career, and the turbulent history of the fifteenth-century Hussite Church.

The kingdom of Bohemia formed a key political block within the Holy Roman Empire, and following the elevation of its ruler Charles IV (*1346–78) as Emperor, Prague, its capital, became a significant administrative and commercial hub with its own university. The rich Bohemian Church was polarized between a wealthy, German, and mostly urban clerical elite and impoverished, rural, Czech-speaking parish priests. Under the Avignese papacy, the Bohemian Church had become a ready source of papal revenues and a reservoir for papal provisions. The Avignese popes favoured Germans for higher ecclesiastical appointments, which angered the Czech nobility who had traditionally controlled regional patronage rights. Charles IV restored the balance for a time, but his incompetent son Wenceslas IV (*1378–1419), who would eventually be deposed as emperor, lacked his father's political acumen. The papal schism further exacerbated tensions between the Germans who favoured the Avignese claimant and the Czechs who recognized Rome. To circumvent papal provision, Czech nobles privately sponsored endowed preacherships, whose incumbents, such as Conrad Waldhauser and Jan Milič, began to use the pulpit to rail against clerical abuses in terms strongly seasoned with anti-papal sentiments. Waldhauser answered for his criticism at Avignon, but Milič helped found an independent yet orthodox Bohemian reform movement.

The marriage of Wenceslas to an English princess fostered an exchange of scholars and manuscripts between Oxford and the Charles University at Prague, which brought Wyclif's ideas into circulation in Bohemia. Wyclif's criticism of the institutional church and the call for good Christians to ignore unrighteous officials struck a cord among Czech teachers and students. His views on the Eucharist also found adherents. In 1408 a popular professor, Jan Hus, was appointed as preacher at one of Prague's largest privately endowed chapels, and he used his pulpit to spread Wyclif's ideas, as Hus had come to appreciate them, in Czech. The ensuing debate split the university, and nearly all of the German students and teachers left Prague in protest. The Pisan pope, John XXIII, condemned Hus, but the young reformer refused to be cowed. King Wenceslas ordered him to leave the city. Banished to the countryside, Hus composed a critical tract against the Church, which, divided into three obediences, lacked the unity to quiet this critic. Meanwhile, among the urban artisans and rural peasants, Wyclif's social and religious message as presented by Hus and others led to a popularizing and radicalizing of the reform programme. Priests began to say Mass in Czech in barns, without vestments or precious vessels, in clear imitation of the primitive Church as understood from scripture translated into Czech. To further break down the distinction between clergy and laity, radical priests began to share communion with the laity under the two "species" of bread and wine (Utraquism). When the reformers gathered at Constance, they summoned Hus to attend and answer the charge of heresy. Wenceslas, who hoped to placate the Emperor, his half-brother Sigismund (*1410–37), assured Hus that the Imperial safe conduct would protect him.

Hus believed that the council would welcome his views and clear his name; instead he was questioned regarding heretical ideas attached to

Wyclif, condemned along with a lay associate, Jerome of Prague, and burned at the stake. The council further outlawed the use of the cup by lay folk. The martyrdoms of Hus and Jerome of Prague, along with the condemnation of Utraquism, galvanized the Czech reform movement. As betrayers of reform, Sigismund, Wenceslas, the council, and its pope, Martin V, became enemies to Hus's supporters, while lay participation in frequent Utraquist communion reinforced solidarity among Hussites. When the ageing Wenceslas outlawed the lay cup in Bohemia in 1419, he precipitated rebellion in Prague and in the countryside. In October the Hussites drew up the Articles of Prague, which demanded communion of bread and wine for the laity, freedom of vernacular preaching in Bohemia, removal of churchmen from secular offices, and the clergy's submission to civil law. Wenceslas's death that same year transferred the kingdom to Sigismund, but the Hussites refused to accept the Emperor's authority, throwing his representatives to their deaths from a window of the royal castle. With the "defenestration" at Prague, religious and political rebellion merged.

Sigismund responded by marshalling an army and invading Bohemia. The Hussites, under the brilliant military leadership of Jan Žižka, repelled every attempt to subdue the movement by force. Žižka relied heavily on soldiers from the Hussites' radical popular wing, who regularly assembled for religious services on a hill near Prague, which they called Mt Tabor. The Taborites rejected everything in Catholic liturgy and doctrine that could not be found in the Bible. They repudiated the cult of the saints, Purgatory, indulgences, and prayers for the dead. They denounced transubstantiation and recognized only baptism and communion as sacraments. All religious services were in the vernacular, and they elected their own priests.[14] Meanwhile, the more moderate Hussites centred in Prague garnered support from the Czech nobility and restricted their reform agenda to the Articles of Prague. When the council of Basel offered to negotiate peace with the Hussites in 1431, the movement split, and the moderate Utraquists defeated the outnumbered Taborites in a murderous battle. The Taborite remnants, however, would survive in scattered cells called brotherhoods (*Unitas Fratrum*), sheltered in rural Bohemia under the protection of sympathetic nobles. By 1436, moderate Hussites had negotiated a settlement with officials at Basel that restored the Hussites to membership in the Church while permitting Utraquist communion, but Pope Eugene IV refused to ratify this compromise. Eventually, a political settlement between the Emperor and the Bohemian nobility allowed the unsanctioned Utraquist

Church to survive, marking the first permanent fracture in the *Respublica Christianae*.

Popular Piety and Reform

Calls for reform did not always imply dissent and conflict. Late medieval religion satisfied most people by spiritualizing rites of passage, codes of behaviour, and the temporal rhythms of life. Christian faith was probably stronger and more widespread in the fifteenth century than in earlier centuries, and reform-minded preachers such as Geiler von Kaysersberg and John Colet could rely on an informed audience among the lower clergy, petty officials, merchants, master artisans, and tenant farmers, who shared in criticism of clerical unholiness and indifference but who continued to practise traditional corporate and personal acts of piety. Furthermore, during the fifteenth century "observant" movements within the major monastic and preaching orders sought to revive the founding spirit of these communities. These reformers did not seek to undermine existing ecclesiastical structures or religious practices; rather they sought to renew them with religious energy.

Contrary to traditional Reformation historiography, recent scholarship suggests that fifteenth-century Christianity was not in a state of crisis and decay awaiting a Reformation.[15] What gave the late medieval Christian faith its vitality was its diversity. Its imagery, metaphors, and rituals were open to multiple readings, and many lay folk expressed their faith through rituals and beliefs more or less syncretized into official practices. This polyglot Christianity provided a flexible enough world view to meet the spiritual needs of most believers. The sacred and profane were interconnected in every way; thus objects such as the Eucharist and relics, and hallowed sites such as pilgrimage shrines, possessed or focused spiritual power.[16] Attending official liturgical services, especially the Mass, was a passive act for the laity, but the Church also sanctioned rituals that offered individuals and groups the means to negotiate with the sacred, while at the edges of the official liturgy "sacramentals" – various rites and benedictions, usually reinforced by holy objects – helped individuals ward off or recover from calamities. Personal access to spiritual assistance in the struggles of daily life empowered Christians and widened the frontier zone between official teachings and lived faith. Believers understood their relationship with God, Mary, or the saints as contractual. If parading Mary's image through the streets could help ward off an epidemic,

the community promised to honour her in some special way in return.
Failure to prevent harm, however, could lead to the desecration of the
image. In the economy of the sacred, there were obligations on both
sides.

Christians made sense of the relation between sin and grace and conceptualized Jesus's life and mission by humanizing spiritual associations
in terms of kinship, the fundamental human connection. In customary
law the wrongful act of an individual required satisfaction for the
injured party by the kin of the perpetrator, and peace could only be
restored if the compensation offered was comparable in weight to the
original offence.[17] Adam's original sin offended God, and the law of satisfaction required the sacrifice of a man–God, Jesus, the son of Adam and
of God, whose suffering and death would carry sufficient weight to satisfy
the initial offence. Jesus's humanity and his historical kindred fascinated
late medieval Christians, and the passion and human suffering of Christ
was a central theme in their spirituality. The high point of the official
calendar was Holy Week, especially Good Friday, which commemorated
the passion and death of Christ. The miracle of the Mass brought Jesus,
as God made flesh, to the altar to be presented to the faithful at the elevation
of the consecrated bread (the "host"), and fascination with Christ's real
presence generated a rich lore of bleeding hosts and nurtured "holy
anorexics" who lived on the Eucharist alone.[18] In late June, near mid-
summer's eve, the new and highly charged feast of Corpus Christi (the
body of Christ) was celebrated with processional displays of the consecrated host.[19] The Franciscans fostered devotion to the passion of Jesus
through the creation of the fourteen stations of the cross, which plotted
the events of Good Friday, while pious artists carved crucifixes with the
tortured human image of Christ's suffering and death. Traditions lacking
scriptural foundation also integrated Jesus into a pseudo-historical
kinship network, as cousin to John the Baptist, whose mother Elizabeth
became Mary's sister. The extended family also included Mary's mother,
Anne, who often appeared in paintings and prints with Mary and the
infant Jesus. As son of God, Jesus's significant human ties were feminine,
but devotion to the step-father, Joseph, was also on the rise.

Sacramental rituals practised in the late medieval Church spiritualized
the rites of passage of birth, marriage, and death. Baptism incorporated
the child into the Christian community, reinforcing or expanding the
linkages of blood and affinity through the fictive kinship of god-parenting.
In urban settings, families chose godparents to strengthen bonds of
patronage and clientage, while rural nobles often chose peasant godparents

to remind their offspring of duties to their serfs. God-parentage, as spiritual kinship, circumscribed boundaries of incest, which it required papal dispensation to cross. During the rite of baptism, the priest asked for the child's name. One barometer of the spread of Christian piety was the growing practice of choosing a saint's name to provide a spiritual patron for the child, and members of Jesus's extended family were particularly popular.

Marriage allowed potential enemies to make peace by weaving together kinship networks, thus, choosing appropriate partners was a significant act of familial politics. During the fifteenth century, the Church sought to curb some of the traditional contractual and sexual rituals associated with marriage and eventually to define a marriage ceremony in church as a sacrament. Nevertheless, many weddings still occurred without priestly involvement. The tension between familial interests and ecclesiastical policy was clearest in the issue of parental consent. The Church recognized the promise between two adults as sufficient for the union, which deeply troubled parents for whom a carefully negotiated match secured family honour and fortune as a legacy for the next generation. Ultimately, fear of magical spells against the groom's sexual potency, animated by envy, encouraged more and more families to seek the priest's blessing, especially of the rings, as prophylactic magic.[20]

The rites of passage surrounding death also reinforced spiritual and secular kinship. The body normally remained with kin overnight, with the local priest supervising burial the following day. By participating in the funeral rites the deceased's family fulfilled their spiritual obligation for their relative's soul. Even in Purgatory, where the soul served out the suffering required to achieve satisfaction and union with God, the living kin had responsibility, through prayers and the acquisition of indulgences, to honour their filial obligations. Moreover, the dead physically lay in communal graveyards attached to the church or beneath the church itself, and they might play tricks on the living who failed to meet their obligations.[21]

Medieval Christians also plotted time in daily, weekly, and annual liturgical cycles.[22] Religious time governed diet by circumscribing periods of fasting and feasting, regulated work patterns by honouring Sundays and holy days with rest from labour, and affected rhythms of conception by advocating sexual abstinence during the penitential seasons of Advent and Lent. Monks were the first Europeans to live by the clock, with the seven hours of the Divine Office dividing the day's activities from Lauds in the pre-dawn hours to Compline following the evening meal. Pious Christians who wished to pursue a holier life could observe this rhythm of prayer in books of hours, with meditational passages drawn from the Divine Office. The weekly cycle of church life revolved around liturgical worship on Sunday, a day specifically dedicated to God, during which work and commerce ceased. Parish services included Mass, catechetical instruction, and collective prayers, though conflicts between the parish priest and village tavern-keeper for patrons were commonplace. Saturdays were dedicated to the Virgin Mary, while Fridays were associated with Good Friday and honoured by abstaining from meat, though fish could be eaten. Finally, the Christian liturgical year combined the Roman solar calendar, which determined the celebration of Christmas, with the Jewish lunar calendar, which placed Easter, with its historic ties to the Jewish Passover, on the first Sunday after the first full moon after the vernal equinox. The rituals associated with the birth, death, and resurrection of Christ, from Advent in early December to Ascension and Corpus Christi in June, comprised the festive half of the liturgical year, while the other half, "ordinary time", was punctuated by local saints' days. If liturgical cycles split the year in half, most Christians measured it in four seasonal parts, beginning with the Annunciation (25 March), the feast of John the Baptist (24 June), the feast of St Michael the Archangel (Michaelmas, 29 September), and Christmas. These ritual passage points for the seasons preceded Christianity, but the medieval Church had covered the pre-Christian agricultural rites with a Christianized veneer.

R. N. Swanson has argued that the late medieval Church succeeded in bringing an official view of Christianity, as articulated at the Fourth Lateran Council, to the people.[23] Since the council's reforms in 1215, the expansion of education and the relative standardization of diocesan administration, including visitations, at least allowed conscientious bishops to ensure that parishioners had good priests. Itinerant preachers drew large audiences, and lay patrons often endowed permanent preacherships. The popularity of preaching demonstrated an intellectualizing of faith, shifting from something one practised to something one believed, but the demand for professional preachers also spoke of the poverty of the sermons offered by the beneficed parish clergy. In the fifteenth century the mendicant orders produced a flood of preaching manuals and confessional guides to aid pastors. Furthermore, evidence of the widespread outpouring of orthodox lay piety in the fifteenth century suggests that the model of lay Christian life imagined at the Fourth Lateran Council had been realized, but in successfully stimulating pious demand, ecclesiastical officials failed to ensure an adequate and qualitative supply. As lay men and women came to understand their faith, they sought fuller participation and influence in local religious life, which laicized late medieval Christianity. Through calls for elections of parish priests, the formation of religious confraternities, revitalization of local cults, and personalized pious endowments, lay folk wanted more control over how they practised their faith. Popular demand led to a vulgarization of some aspects of spirituality, such as the market for indulgences and relics, but it also reflected the growing influence of lay officials over Church business.[24] To a degree this shift was "anticlerical" in that it challenged clerical privilege, yet its impetus came from faith not alienation.

Perhaps the clearest and most significant example of this trend was the *Devotio Moderna*, a cluster of individuals and groups of pious lay men and women that flourished in the Lower Rhine valley between the time of the Black Death and the Reformation. Founded by Gerard de Groote (1340–84), a cleric who renounced his offices, the movement observed his principles – that religion should be simple, devout, and charitable. Groote's followers formed lay communities known as Brethren or Sisters of the Common Life. They pooled their resources and lived together through shared work, prayer, and the reproduction of pious literature.[25] In theology and religious practice the movement was unoriginal, but it produced numerous devotional works such as Thomas à Kempis's *Imitation of Christ*. Designed as a set of short reflective meditations, the *Imitation of Christ* called the reader to live simply, deny the world, and obey superiors. The Brethren distrusted the subtle scholastic learning favoured at universities and offered in its place their own boarding schools. These schools provided an early education for many humanists and some later reformers, but they did not advocate direct attacks on ecclesiastical authorities nor offer a reformed model for religiosity. The Brethren and Sisters of the Common Life were one example of hundreds of pious lay foundations, which hinted at the vitality of fifteenth-century Christianity rather than its decay.

Humanism, Renaissance, and Reformation

As late medieval European society became more commercially integrated, and expanding governments required the recruitment of regiments of notaries and scribes, education became a vehicle for lay social mobility.

Throughout the Middle Ages, the Church had monopolized schooling, but burgeoning civil society demanded non-clerical intellectual skills. First in Italy and later throughout Europe, a new form of elementary education centred on the study of the liberal arts, such as philology, rhetoric, and history, the *studia humanitatis*, offered learning laced with moral injunctions drawn from classical pagan authors but cloaked in Christian ethics. This educational programme created a new normative code of common values that seemed to the adherents to have been reborn from classical moral philosophy. Historians have long associated this Renaissance of classical learning with the Reformation.

Both the Renaissance and Humanism are nineteenth-century neologisms created by scholars who sought the national, secular, and cultural roots of modern Europe. Jacob Burckhardt's monumental study *The Civilization of the Renaissance in Italy* envisioned Italy in the age of the Renaissance as the birthplace of modern individualism, by which he meant self-consciousness. For Burckhardt the secular and egotistical self-awareness of Renaissance individuals informed both brutal politics and high art. He drew a sharp line between medieval and Renaissance values, paving the way for later historians to discover a comparable chasm between medieval Christianity and the Reformation.[26] Nineteenth-century German educators had earlier coined the term "humanism" (*Humanismus*) to describe the emphasis placed on Greek and Latin classics in their contemporary educational system. Burckhardt traced the roots of humanism to Renaissance Italy and attached to it secular, even anti-religious, values which constituted in his view a new and distinctly modern philosophy that glorified the individual and the attractions of earthly life.

Current research has challenged Burckhardt's model.[27] Medieval scholars had always cherished the classics, even pagan literature, but in the commercial cities of northern Italy, men working in contractual law and seeking a professional edge turned to authors such as Cicero and Quintilian for stylistic models and rhetorical flourishes. The clerical faculties at Italian universities belittled humanistic studies as elementary, but humanism came to provide a practical educational foundation for those active in secular affairs. The pagan authors wrote on history, moral philosophy, and rhetoric, and these texts inspired Italian humanists in conceptualizing and moralizing civic life. None the less, though Renaissance humanists read the same books, copied stylistic patterns, and corresponded with one another, they never formed a coherent school or programme.

The circle of participants remained relatively small until the development of the printing press suddenly and dramatically changed the relation
between readers and texts. For the first time "critical" editions could be
drawn up, with a standardized text and common reference points. For
the humanists printing made possible wide-scale access to classical texts
for interpretive discussion among participants in a "republic of letters".
Initially humanistic studies were conducted in Latin with an ancient
Roman cultural backdrop, but the appearance of a Greek refugee
community in Italy following the collapse of the Byzantine Empire in the
1450s made classical Greek available to a broader audience. In time,
humanistic education in Latin and Greek formed the common intellectual
coin of Italy's ruling elite including papal officials.

Humanistic scholarship attracted intellectual pilgrims to Italy to study
with the best teachers, and by 1500 humanists could be found north of
the Alps in almost every major political and intellectual centre, even
penetrating university curricula. Northern humanists read the standard
classical authors, but many were clerics, who directed their classical
philological interests to scripture. These "Christian" humanists hoped to
recover the original inspired apostolic text and to use their methodology
to re-educate fellow churchmen. New polyglot bibles that juxtaposed the
"original" Hebrew and Greek texts with a revised Latin translation
employed clusters of scholars, such as those assembled under the supervision of Cardinal Ximénes de Cisneros at the university of Alcalá in
Castile.

Humanism was not inherently reform-oriented nor amenable to
reformation, and these issues are perhaps best explored in the career of
the most famous Christian humanist: Desiderius Erasmus of Rotterdam
(c.1466–1536). The son of a priest, Erasmus took minor orders, becoming
a cleric but not a priest himself. He depended on the hospitality and
generosity of friends and patrons along with piecework wages as a proof-
reader for several printing houses to support his scholarship and writing.
Erasmus produced an enormous body of published works on a whole
range of topics. He had the intellectual scope to compose a full Greek
text of the New Testament with a new Latin translation and extensive
notes to justify the alterations. Erasmus encouraged pious lay folk to
study scriptures, mocked monasticism and clerical corruption, and
composed a dialogue between Pope Julius II and St Peter in which the
warrior pontiff failed to convince his Apostolic forebear that he, Julius,
deserved to enter heaven. None the less, Erasmus gave a positive assessment
of human nature. He embraced the classical belief that understanding of

the good would generate the ethical desire to do good, and thus one could achieve a moral life through learning. This assumption that learning would foster piety, and that education grounded in careful reading of the classic pagan and Christian texts could properly direct humans to do good, epitomized the agenda historians have associated with Christian humanism. Clearly Erasmus was a critic of the distances between contemporary religious principles and practice, and he accumulated enemies among the conservative intellectuals in the Church. He had numerous admirers too, but he never built a party among the republic of letters. Finally, since he wrote primarily in Greek and Latin, his criticisms and witticisms reached only a small intellectual audience.

Luther's calls for the reform of Christian values led Erasmus at first to see the reformer as a kindred spirit, but by 1524 the two men were publicly at odds over the question of human will, which Erasmus saw as free to pursue God while Luther viewed it as free only when submissive to God's will. As for other Christian humanists, key reformers such as Huldrich Zwingli (1484–1531) and Philip Melanchthon (1497–1560) had pursued humanist studies early in their careers, and among the men in German-speaking Europe identified as humanists, more than half of the generation born after 1480 (135 out of 243) embraced the Reformation.[28] Was there a connection? Humanists formed a small intellectual elite whose insistence on purity in learning drove many to reflective, esoteric, and often self-centred scholarship. Erasmus and many others essentially worked with the biblical texts, but Lorenzo Valla and Conrad Celtis studied the Jewish Cabala and the mystical Greek writings of Hermes Trismegistris, which offered secret insight into the mind of God though little to cultivate piety or moral Christian behaviour. As a self-conscious elite, humanists called for renewed piety while mocking the excesses popular piety encouraged, and their assumption that cultivation of the mind led to ethical goodness deflected the standard Christian assumption that cultivation of the spirit was the path to right living. Humanists taught statesmen, and some, such as Thomas More, served as statesmen, but in the end humanism was a method of scholarly study and never a programme, so when reformers with a programme came along, all the humanists could do was choose to join or resist.

Fifteenth-Century Monarchs and their Churches

As lay piety was becoming increasingly localized, and printing uncovered and cultivated "national" markets for vernacular literature, princes and magistrates secured a freer hand in ecclesiastical affairs within their subject territories. At the height of the papal monarchy, Innocent III had successfully claimed feudal suzerainty over kingdoms and principalities, but by the fifteenth century the only region outside of the Papal States which recognized the pope's feudal overlordship was the southern Italian kingdom of Naples. The overshadowing of the Avignese papacy by the French kings had weakened papal authority in much of Europe, and schism had only furthered the decline by providing rulers the leverage to choose their pope. Lay officials had participated at Constance, and the bishops had voted as "nations", representing regional churches. In the wake of the council, papal claims over provisions of benefices, clerical taxation, and ecclesiastical jurisdiction throughout Christendom were forfeited, as popes ratified a series of concordats with secular rulers, granting them wide-ranging control over their territorial churches.[29]

During the fifteenth century many Western European monarchs increased their authority over their subjects and fashioned new instruments for accumulating revenues and enforcing order. Secular control over ecclesiastical affairs and revenues formed an important aspect of enhanced state power. Earlier claims of imperial suzerainty by the Holy Roman Emperors faded from political discourse at the same time that papal universality had begun to wane. Contemporary writers, when referring to what we might call "the state", often used the phrase *status regis et regni*, the state of the king and kingdom, emphasizing the close personal association between the two. By the fifteenth century a new term, *respublica*, suggested a state separate from its ruler's identity, but most early modern theorists still conceptualized the state as the property of its sovereign ruler.[30] Some historians have argued that the consolidation of royal power over subjects set the foundation for national identity and consciousness, but fifteenth-century "nations" remained intellectual constructions, while most kings found themselves ruling a linguistically mixed conglomerate of territorial pieces with different laws and separate governments. This lack of centralized administrative organs also characterized many fifteenth-century "national" churches, and princely sovereignty over them would slowly bring coherency to diverse and sometimes factious ecclesiastical corporations.

The fifteenth-century English Church, for example, comprised a morass of institutions held together by royal supervision. The bishops and principal abbots sat among the peers in the parliamentary House of Lords, and control over clerical appointment, secured by the Statute of Provisors of 1351, was essential to royal authority, while the Statutes of Praemunire of 1353, 1365 and 1393 sharply limited the cases that could be taken from English ecclesiastical courts to Rome on appeal. Fifteenth-century English kings appointed all bishops, regularly taxed their clergy, and used parliamentary legislation to circumscribe clerical immunities. That the papacy did not offer a concordat to the English Crown was partially due to the existing scope of royal claims.[31] Pope Martin V had attempted to recover some influence, but by the mid-1430s the curia accepted the situation, only requiring formal approval from Rome for the consecration of English bishops, though the ceremonies took place in England. Relations between the English kings and the papacy were normally harmonious, for papal will had limited influence over the English Church.

In France, royal leverage over the kingdom's ecclesiastical affairs traced its ancestry to Philip IV and the Avignese papacy. The Hundred Years War between the French and English claimants to Philip's legacy, however, had mitigated the effective exercise of royal will over much of the kingdom, including its ecclesiastical institutions. In order to raise income and rally support for their cause, the Valois kings had offered concessions to the clerical "First Estate" at assemblies, known as the Estates General, that brought together the kingdom's elite to discuss issues of governance. During the Great Schism, moreover, the leading French churchmen had met in synods, with royal approval, to plot collective strategy. Thus the fifteenth-century French upper clergy had established traditions and institutions for a "national" Gallican Church, which could negotiate in its own interests with pope or king. In the 1430s the Valois claimant, Charles VII (*1422–61), was slowly securing the military advantage won by the inspiration of a visionary peasant girl, Joan of Arc, while Pope Eugene IV faced a renegade council and anti-pope in Basel. Gallican churchmen exploited the circumstances to secure the Pragmatic Sanction of Bourges in 1438, which curtailed both papal and royal authority over the French Church, by restoring capitular elections for all bishops, abolishing annates, and restricting appeals to Rome. The Pragmatic Sanction marked a highpoint for the fifteenth-century Gallican Church and held force in the kingdom until the Concordat of Bologna in 1516, when Francis I (*1515–47) effectively recovered royal control over ecclesiastical affairs at the expense of the French clergy and the pope. Henceforth, the king hand picked the kingdom's 114 bishops and archbishops as well as over 880 abbots and abbesses. Given the resilience of provincial legal traditions, the concordat did not apply everywhere, but royal control of the French Church would effectively dull the edge of ecclesiastical reform movements.

The fifteenth-century Iberian peninsula comprised four Christian kingdoms, Portugal, Castile, Aragon, and Navarre, along with the small Muslim state of Granada. The Aragonese kings also ruled in Sicily and had claims to Naples, so papal relations with them were highly politicized. For example, King Alfonso V (*1416–58) withdrew his support for the council of Basel when Pope Eugene IV promised to recognize the king's claims to Naples and to grant Alfonso full rights over the Aragonese Church. In 1469 the marriage of Ferdinand of Aragon (*1479–1516) and Isabella of Castile (*1474–1504) paved the way for the dynastic union of those kingdoms a decade later. The union of Spanish crowns preserved the distinct laws, estates, and privileges of each kingdom, though with its population and resources Castile would be the dominant partner. Castilian soldiers paid from Castilian taxes completed the *Reconquista* of Granada in 1492, and later Spain's empire in the Americas would be ruled as an extension of the Castilian crown.

Ferdinand and Isabella's territorial churches also functioned independently of one another. In 1478 the devout Isabella petitioned Rome to establish the Castilian Inquisition to investigate the orthodoxy of *Conversos*, descendants of Jews who had converted under force during the pogroms of the late fourteenth century. Jealousies and residual prejudice had led to accusations of backsliding among *Conversos*, and the Inquisitions in Castile and later in Aragon earned a reputation for aggressive thoroughness in policing faith, as the first grand inquisitor, Tomás de Torquemada, authorized nearly 2,000 executions. Under Ferdinand and Isabella's patronage, Spanish Catholicism experienced an internal revival spearheaded by Cardinal Ximénes de Cisneros (1436–1517), a Franciscan ascetic who was Isabella's personal confessor and, as archbishop of Toledo, primate of the Castilian Church. Cisneros supported Observant movements among the monastic and mendicant orders and supervised the reform of many religious houses. He invited the Observant Franciscans as teachers to the new university at Alcalá, where the cardinal patronized a coterie of humanists including several *Conversos*, whose trilingual abilities aided in his programme of biblical analysis and criticism of the Vulgate text, leading up to the publication of an orthodox polyglot Bible. Cisneros later served as Chancellor of Castile and ruled there as regent from Isabella's death in 1504 to 1517. Sixteenth-century Spanish Catholicism operated independently of papal supervision. It combined devout piety, a rigid sense of purity, and Castilian militancy into a dynamic force that would animate ongoing Catholic reform efforts and the militant counter-reform against Protestantism.

Elsewhere in Europe local and regional estates retained substantially more independence than in these western monarchies. In some cases dioceses in Austria, such as Salzburg and Passau, were administered by foreign prince–bishops. In the composite kingdom of Scandinavia, the centralizing efforts of the ruling Danish monarch faced resistance from Swedish and Norwegian elites including the bishops and influential abbots. In other cases, such as the Netherlands, Poland, or Hungary, the nobility drew on familial ties with the upper clergy to build a common front against royal inroads into local rights and privileges. The Church could serve both as a tool for centralization and as a guardian of particularism. Nowhere was this double role more evident than on the Italian peninsula.

As Machiavelli would counsel in *The Prince*, a ruler's chief duties revolved around war, and as rulers of the Papal States, the Renaissance popes took such advice to heart. Protracted warfare in Italy would absorb papal interests during the first decades of the Reformation and embitter the rivalry between the leading Catholic dynasties, the Habsburgs of Spain and Austria and the Valois of France, at a point when concerted effort could have easily defeated Protestant forces. Since the late thirteenth century, the Angevin branch of the French royal family and the Aragonese monarchs had both laid claim to the kingdom of Naples, whose feudal overlord was the pope. When the last Angevin claimant died in 1481, his rights were bequeathed to his royal Valois cousins. The French kings also held title to the duchy of Milan through a fourteenth-century marriage contract with the Visconti dukes, whose line had died out in 1447. Any ruler who controlled both Milan and Naples could dominate Italy and threaten the political security of the Italian princes, including the pope. When Charles VIII of France invaded Italy in 1494 to lay claim to Naples, he initiated decades of warfare, throughout the peninsula, with the Aragonese kings, first Ferdinand and then his successor Charles, who by 1519 ruled over the Spanish kingdoms and the Habsburg domains in the Netherlands, as well as holding the title of Holy Roman Emperor. Accounts of the diplomatic flip-flopping of the Italian principalities and republics, combined with the military campaigns, battles, sieges, political murders, and local feuds precipitated from the French–Aragonese power struggle in Italy, make enthralling reading, but for our purposes the papacy's active participation in the Italian wars further tarnished its spiritual standing, diplomatically bound its hands at key junctures, and politicized all decision-making regarding internal reforms or appropriate responses to external critics.

In 1527 the Catholic Habsburg claimant, Charles V,[32] secured Spanish interests on the peninsula by sacking Rome. For decades the papacy's political entanglements in Italy would restrain its involvement in the religious debates in Germany triggered by Martin Luther's call for reform.

Luther as Reformer

Traditional accounts of the Reformation begin with a university professor, Martin Luther (1483–1546), nailing 95 theses for public debate to a church door at Wittenberg on 31 October 1517. This apocryphal story reflects traditional accounts among Church historians that focus on Luther as essentially a theologian, and on the Reformation as essentially a theological struggle. In addition, some have presented Luther's theology as a complete and coherent whole rather than an evolving and some-times contradictory product of intense polemical fighting.[33] Luther's innovative understanding of the centrality of faith in Christian life and his willingness to broadcast his insights gave people an opportunity to re-evaluate their own relationship with God. The diverse individual responses of Luther's audience eventually created distinct paths to faith, and that process is just as significant as Luther's role as instigator. Luther had the charisma and energy to trigger reform, but, as we will see, he could not control the course of events, nor, in the long run, the nature of his own reformation.

Martin Luther, the son of a well-to-do peasant miner, was born in Eisleben in Saxony and raised in the small town of Mansfeld. With his father's encouragement, Luther took up the study of law at Eisenach. In 1505 following a dramatic conversion experience, Luther withdrew from legal studies and entered the Observant Augustinian convent at Erfurt. By his own admission the new monk was obsessed with his personal salvation and overzealous in his pursuit of faith, confessing his sins daily for fear of dying unshriven. Luther embraced the ethos of late medieval piety and worked tirelessly to find assurance of his righteous relationship with God, but without avail, for he could sense no guarantees of God's grace from his personal efforts. In 1508 Luther was recruited to teach theology at the new university at Wittenberg, founded in 1502 by the duke-elector of Saxony, Frederick the Wise. As Luther lectured on Paul's epistles between 1513 and 1518, he came to realize that Jesus's suffering and death had provided all the satisfaction that one needed for salvation. This merciful gift of salvation through the sacrifice of God's Son overcame Luther's anxiety over God's judgement. Christians did not need to struggle to prove their faith through constant pious acts; they only needed faith in God's love and mercy. This radical new view of faith provided the theological foundation for the anticlerical criticisms embedded in his ninety-five theses.

Since the Great Schism, popular preachers, would-be reformers, and papal critics presented the Church as an institution driven by fiscal appetites, with the papacy as the chief glutton. After 1450, printing presses disseminated these ideas and images to a broad audience in "fly-sheets" and wood-cuts.[34] Unlike the kings in England, France, and Spain, the Holy Roman Emperor held few rights over the Imperial Church. In fact neither the Emperor nor any prince could appoint bishops, whose elections traditionally alternated month by month between the papal curia and the cathedral chapters. Nevertheless by 1500 Imperial princely families had secured the inside track to episcopal appointments for those positions critical to their dynastic interests. The mix of money, family interests, and power-brokering essential to any "successful" epis-copal election politicized papal involvement in Imperial affairs, where the popes appeared as meddling foreigners. Under the Concordat of Vienna in 1448, the Imperial princes recognized papal rights to annates, a payment equalling the first year's revenues from the benefice, in exchange for their own right to tax their territorial clergy. Under this system Imperial ecclesiastical elections worked smoothly when money flowed to all interested parties, and the election that triggered the Luther affair demonstrates the process. In 1514 the 27-year-old Albert of Brandenburg was elected cardinal-archbishop of Mainz. This young Hohenzollern prince already held the bishoprics of Magdeburg and Halberstadt, yet he received papal dispensations for his youth and pluralism when he promised prompt payment of his annates and a special gift toward the construction of St Peter's Basilica in Rome. Albert borrowed heavily from the Fugger banking house in Augsburg to meet his obligations, and Pope Leo X (*1513–21) authorized the sale of indul-gences in Albert's territories, so that his subjects' piety might pay off his extraordinary debts.

Though a pious and avid collector of relics, Luther's prince, Frederick the Wise, refused to allow Albert's indulgence-sellers to enter Saxony. When a notoriously persuasive salesman named Johannes Tetzel set up business near the borders of the electorate and attracted many pious Saxons, Luther railed from the pulpit against indulgences and eventually offered to defend his criticisms in open debate. Whether he posted his ninety-five theses or not, their contents soon became public knowledge. The theses, composed in academic Latin, reflected Luther's new views on the centrality of faith for salvation and the fruitlessness of human efforts to achieve satisfaction through works, in particular by purchasing scraps of paper to remit sins. Of greater immediate importance, the theses implicitly criticized the pope and the clergy's role in salvation, and when they were published in November without Luther's consent, trouble ensued.

Printing provided Luther a vast and ready audience which Hus could not have imagined. Many of Luther's early writings appeared in short, pithy vernacular pamphlets which could be quickly and cheaply produced and widely distributed. Luther became the publishing industry's first best-selling author, whose name on the cover could quickly sell out a press run. Printers pirated his works or inserted his name as the author of other anticlerical writings. In response, Tetzel and others wrote diatribes against Luther and the "Martinists", and a pamphlet war ensued as tracts for and against Luther appeared all over Germany. Luther had stirred up an already rich stew of anti-establishment sentiment, particularly among the better educated lower clergy in the German-speaking lands. Though not all agreed with Luther or appreciated his new theological perspective on faith, they rallied to him.

The archbishop of Mainz, frustrated because the controversy threatened his ability to meet his debts, sent a copy of the theses to the papal curia, where officials directed the matter to the head of the Augustinian order. Dominican inquisitors at Rome also studied the theses and detected heresy in their assault on papal power. In October 1518, under a promise of safe conduct, Luther met the papal legate to Germany, Cardinal Cajetan, while the Imperial Diet gathered at Augsburg. Realizing the danger in Luther's ideas, Cajetan demanded that Frederick surrender Luther to Rome for judgement, but the Saxon electoral-duke refused. When Emperor Maximilian I died, in January of the following year, Luther's fate became inextricably bound to the election of the new Emperor.

In the early sixteenth century the Holy Roman Empire of the German Nation was a fragmented federation with over 500 semi-autonomous jurisdictions that extended over northern Italy and much of Central Europe under the theoretical suzerainty of an elected Emperor. Imperial territories constituted four estates (seven "electors", dozens of lay and ecclesiastical princes, more than sixty Imperial free cities, and hundreds of Imperial knights) all of whom, no matter how small their domains, claimed a degree of autonomy embodied in the phrase "immediacy to the emperor". Since 1348 the king of Bohemia, the margrave of Brandenburg, the count Palatine, the duke of Saxony, and the archbishops of Cologne, Mainz, and Trier had held the title of electoral princes and chosen the new Emperor. Each election drew the interest and potential candidacy of Europe's leading monarchs, and the electors leveraged their vote to extract concessions from the successful candidate through a formal capitulation. The electors, princes, and cities also claimed the right to participate at Imperial Diets, where they met in separate houses. The Diets functioned like meetings of the United Nations, involving negotiation as much as legislation. When the Diets ended, any agreements between the estates and the Emperor were published as a "recess" (*Abschied*), which then functioned as law for the members. The Empire lacked an independent military force, a judicial system, and a means of taxation, so emperors depended on their own territorial revenues and dynastic resources (*Hausmacht*) to govern. Maximilian I's (*1493–1519) push for centralized institutions had met with some success at the Imperial Diet of 1495, which established a Common Penny Tax that eventually failed, and an Imperial Chamber Court (*Reichskammergericht*) that endured.

When the electors met in June of 1519 at Frankfurt, Francis I of France sought to block the candidacy of Maximilian's grandson, Charles of Ghent, who through his mother had already become king of Castile and Aragon and now through his patrimony could lay claim to the Imperial throne. The potential combination of Charles's territories and titles would nearly surround France. Francis advocated Luther's protector, Frederick of Saxony, as a rival candidate, but the duke declined because he lacked the *Hausmacht* to perform the duties of office effectively. After drafting a stringent capitulation to safeguard their territorial prerogatives, the electors settled on Charles, who was in Spain at the time. The new Emperor became Charles V, and his election made his family, the Habsburgs, the most powerful dynasty in Europe.

The election temporarily placed the "Luther affair" on the back burner, and Luther spent the respite studying scripture and Church history. His research convinced him, as it had Wyclif and Hus, that spiritual truth lay in the Word of God and not in the visible Church. The ecclesiastical hierarchy, canon law, papal bulls, and even rituals and liturgy should all submit to a scriptural test. Thus armed, Luther engaged in public debate with Johann Eck of Ingolstatt in July 1519. Eck drove

Luther to question papal authority openly and then, by demonstrating Luther's ties with Hussite ideas, cornered the hot-tempered reformer into condemning the Council of Constance. Luther's advocacy of scripture over the traditions of the Church clearly echoed the heretical Wyclif and Hus, and on 15 June 1520, the papal bull *Exurge Domine* condemned forty-one of Luther's propositions as heretical. The curia ordered his books to be burned and granted Luther two months to recant or be excommunicated. On 10 December 1520 outside the city gates of Wittenberg, Luther and his supporters ritually burned canon law books, papal decretals, and the bull itself. Up to this point Luther's charisma, energy, and faith along with the steadfast support of his lay protector had spared him arrest and execution.

Between the promulgation of the bull and Luther's rejection of it, he published three famous tracts which were critical to the articulation of his theology, his ecclesiology, and his programme for reform: *Address to the Christian Nobility of the German Nation* (August 1520); *A Prelude on the Babylonian Captivity of the Church* (September 1520); and *The Freedom of a Christian Man* (November 1520). In these tracts he followed the implications of justification by faith and the unrivalled authority of scripture to their logical conclusion in terms of the Christian community. Luther argued that the sacramental priesthood should not be a privileged and separate caste, for their activities had little to do with true faith and often lacked scriptural precedence; instead all true Christians could claim priestly status. Because the Word, the source of faith, was a free gift of God's mercy, the community of the faithful functioning in harmony with the New Testament were true priests. Luther argued that the contemporary Church was out of harmony with God's Word and had continually failed to reform or renew itself, so he called on German princes and magistrates to reform the Church by virtue of their political office. The concordats between the papacy and the European monarchs had conferred authority over ecclesiastical institutions within their kingdoms to the lay rulers. Luther encouraged the Imperial lay leaders to exercise that authority without a concordat in order to undertake religious reform.

Luther's vision of this reform rested on three pedestals: justification by faith; the authority of scripture alone; and the priesthood of all believers. From his first days as an Augustinian friar, Luther was deeply concerned about grace and salvation. For Luther human beings were by nature sinners, depraved and corrupt. Only God's mercy and grace could free them from their sinful natures. The Church claimed that individuals achieved grace by participating in the sacraments. Luther believed, however, that since human nature was corrupt, participation alone could not bring grace. Traditional piety also assumed that individuals acquired grace through good works, such as pilgrimages, acts of charity, or even prayers. Again Luther pointed to sinful human nature and argued that pious acts were insufficient. Any murderer could go on pilgrimage; the act itself was not enough. Good Christians would indeed perform good acts because, Luther argued, the gift of grace achieved by Christ's sacrifice animated true Christian charity and fostered an ingrained disposition (*habitus*) toward good works among the faithful. Thus faith led to Christian behaviour, not Christian behaviour to faith.

Luther had originally viewed God's justice, *justitia*, as judgement, and had worked hard to avoid that judgement. Through his reading of Paul, Luther came to see *justitia* as God's mercy, God's gift of faith. In a series of sermons delivered and printed in 1518 and 1519, Luther first defined Christian righteousness with the phrase "justification by faith alone". Justification means "to make righteous", and it derives from Augustine of Hippo who, as you may recall, also saw grace as God's free and undeserved gift. For Augustine as for Luther, moral achievements, no matter how impressive, could not justify someone, only faith in God's mercy could do that. Given human nature, only through God's mercy could inherently sinful individuals turn from sin, so faith alone justified the Christian. This truly innovative perspective short-circuited the entire sacramental system of late medieval piety.

In the pamphlet *A Prelude on the Babylonian Captivity of the Church*, Luther articulated what he meant by "the priesthood of all believers". He noted that clerics represented the Christian community but only through their ministry or service. The clergy and the institutional Church were not a separate, distinct order. The spiritual church of true Christian believers ordained ministers to a delegated function, thus the visible Church, the clergy, was subject to the invisible body of the faithful. In Luther's words, "every baptized Christian is a priest in God's sight and is not dependent on another for the reception of divine grace". The resolution of his personal spiritual dilemma brought Luther to this revolutionary conception of faith and ministry, but in publishing his beliefs Luther fuelled a storm of controversy that eventually brought him before the Imperial Diet at Worms.

The man in position to do something about Luther was the devout twenty-one-year-old Emperor, Charles V, who though he had held the title for nearly two years was making his first trip to Germany to meet the assembled estates at Worms. The Emperor was firmly orthodox, favouring the religious reforms already underway in the Spanish Church, yet he was quite comfortable with moderate critics such as Erasmus. Furthermore, Charles V's political interests in Italy put him at odds with the pope. On 18 April 1521 he personally asked Luther to recant, who refused and left the diet. Charles V honoured his promise of safe conduct, and Luther, though eventually declared an outlaw and heretic, escaped into hiding.

Luther's defiant stand at the Imperial Diet of Worms ended the personal phase of his protest and call for reform. Hus's execution had broadened his movement and paved the way for a military confrontation between the Hussites and Imperial forces acting in the interests of the popes. Luther's escape paved the way for a similar confrontation between "evangelicals" – Christians committed to reordering the world on the foundation of God's word – and Catholic and Imperial authorities. The Hussites succeeded in defending their fledgling church within the confines of Bohemia. In 1521, thanks in part to the printing press, Luther's evangelical followers were scattered across the German-speaking world. If Catholic authorities sought to suppress the reform movement with force, the repercussions would shake the Empire's existing religious and political order to its foundations.

3

EVANGELICAL MOVEMENTS AND CONFESSIONS, 1521–59

With hindsight the division of medieval Christendom into several Christian churches appears as the inevitable outcome of Martin Luther's dispute with Rome, but for the early reformers, their audiences, and their opponents, the trajectory of events was far from clear. Initially the "Luther affair" triggered debate among theologians, but the implications of his new view of faith soon affected all Christians and threatened the privileged place of the clergy. In an age of vernacular printing in which reading was a public act, Luther's emphasis on the Word of God, coined in the catch-phrase "scripture alone" (*sola scriptura*), opened the floodgates of popular enthusiasm for reform and induced the percolation of new ideas from below that would fuel the "evangelical" (scripture-based) movement throughout the 1520s. In the enthusiasm of the moment, many believed that God was directly intervening in history, and Luther along with others saw the unfolding events as a sign of the coming Apocalypse. The dynamic imagery of the "last days", with its violent struggle between the saved and the damned, took on a harsh reality when thousands of peasants and artisans rose in rebellion in 1524–5. Their defeat ended the first and radical phase of the evangelical movement, and in the wake of the Peasants' War, those magistrates and princes who still favoured Luther's message assumed greater control over reforms in ecclesiastical institutions and practices. By the 1530s popular enthusiasm had mostly waned, and the Reformation became a struggle among political authorities to determine the belief and practices of their territorial churches.

This chapter will centre on the traditional decades covered in classic accounts of the Reformation era, from the 1520s to the 1550s. In 1520 Catholicism remained the official faith in nearly all of Christian Europe. By 1550, cells of Protestants of all stripes existed in most European territories, and many regions officially recognized the Lutheran Augsburg Confession or the Zwinglian Helvetic Confession. Though an ecumenical council had gathered at Trent to iron out religious truth, it was animated by a fierce Catholic reaction to Protestant beliefs and overshadowed by political rivalries among Catholic princes. By 1559 the Reformation had clearly become a political affair. This did not mean that individuals, including princes, made choices in faith only for politically expedient reasons, but rather that political factors would frame the effects of personal choice and regional religious identity. To carry our story from Luther to the broader political realm, we need to begin at Wittenberg.

Reform at Wittenberg and the Spread of the Evangelical Movement

Luther's protector, Frederick the Wise, arranged for the reformer's abduction during his return to electoral Saxony from the Diet at Worms, and for nearly a year (May 1521 to March 1522) Luther hid in disguise in the ducal castle at Wartburg. For Luther this was a period of personal doubt and depression, while for his supporters at Wittenberg, Luther's absence left a vacuum in leadership that Andreas Bodenstein von Karlstadt (c.1480–1541), a fellow professor, boldly stepped forward to fill. Claiming to follow Luther's vision, Karlstadt exercised his Christian freedom by redefining local liturgical practices and the role of the priesthood. These new definitions hinged on the nature of the sacraments.

Luther had earlier argued that only two sacraments, baptism and the Eucharist, possessed scriptural foundations; and "sacramentalist" debate, particularly over the nature of the Eucharist and the ceremonies surrounding it, quickly separated the evangelical reformers from Catholics and would eventually divide the reformers themselves. As we have seen, in Catholic tradition transubstantiation, the miraculous changing of the substance – i.e. the inner reality, but not the outer appearance – of bread and wine into the body and blood of Christ through the words and actions of the priest, was the keystone to the clerical order; for although the miracle occurred through God's power, only a sacramentally ordained priest could perform the ritual. The Latin liturgy, the elaborate priestly vestments, and the infrequency of lay communion, limited to the consecrated host, highlighted the distances between the clergy and laity in this central act of faith. On Christmas day 1521, Karlstadt said Mass without vestments, pronounced the words of consecration in German rather than Latin, and following Hussite practice, offered bread *and* wine to the congregation. That day in other churches at Wittenberg, traditional Masses and Eucharistic services took place. Wittenberg's citizens and students could now choose their form of worship and, in doing so, their partisan allegiance.

The next day Karlstadt announced his betrothal to Anna von Mochau, the sixteen-year-old daughter of a poor nobleman. In the 1520s parish priests throughout Europe lived with housekeepers who were in fact wives, though ecclesiastical law declared them concubines and their children bastards. Challenges to clerical celibacy were prominent in humanistic critiques, and Luther himself had identified celibacy as a papal accretion without scriptural basis, in his *Address to the Christian Nobility* (1520). The reformers' offensive against enforced celibacy offered the prospect of legitimate dignity to priests and their families. In electoral Saxony as early as May 1521, individual priests began to marry in defiance of ecclesiastical law, and the non-sacramental celebration of Karlstadt's wedding on 19 January 1522 became another occasion to flaunt his disrespect for the established order. Karlstadt's reform programme moved quickly, and on 25 January Wittenberg's magistrates approved a new ecclesiastical ordinance proposed by Karlstadt, which featured a simplified communion service, a common chest for the poor, restrictions against begging and prostitution, and the purging of images from civic churches.[1]

As with other aspects of the new church order, the removal of images legitimized earlier acts of iconoclasm (the ritual desecration of religious art) carried out by Luther's followers, first at Wittenberg's Augustinian monastery and later elsewhere. The magistrates' decision called for orderly removal, but some enthusiastic reformers broke into civic churches and chopped up wooden statues and crucifixes and burned the pieces. This new round of iconoclasm coincided with the arrival at Wittenberg of the first harbingers of the socially disruptive potential of personal interpretations of scripture. The pastor at nearby Zwickau, Thomas Müntzer (pre-1491–1525), advocated a radical model for the community of faith, which inspired members of his congregation to ecstatic visions. The "Zwickau prophets", led by the weaver Nikolaus Storch, held private religious services where women preached and members claimed to have conversations with God. The group opposed sacramental baptism for infants because they argued that only adults could fully understand the commitment of faith.[2] With Karlstadt, Müntzer, and Zwickau's prophets, the voices of reform in electoral Saxony had become cacophonous, and among the "Martinists" there was no visible leader to control the profusion of tongues. On 6 March 1522, Luther returned to the city to police his own church, to organize the liturgy, and to expel those who had gone too far. Within days of his arrival Luther delivered a series of sermons against Karlstadt's innovations, discouraging the new practice in which lay folk handled the consecrated bread and wine, calling for a return to fasting and private confession, and condemning iconoclasm. Luther argued that, before changing rituals, reformers must first thoroughly preach the Word to give people time to internalize the message and come to faith on their own. In April Luther met with Storch and his associates and afterwards dismissed their prophetic powers as the devil's work.

Having slowed the pace of reform and discounted the beliefs of the radicals, Luther devoted the following months to completing his German translation of the New Testament and to an examination of ecclesiastical institutions and liturgical practices. In April 1523, at the request of the Saxon town of Leisnig, Luther crafted a new Church ordinance, *The Ordinance of the Common Chest*, which urged reapportionment of municipal ecclesiastical revenues to pay a preaching minister, who would be elected by the congregation, and to finance Christian social welfare. To counter those advocating the forcible dissolution of monasteries, Luther proposed that monks be free to choose another occupation or to leave for another house, while the buildings themselves should be turned into schools, endowed from monastic revenues. He also called for bishops and abbots to surrender their land-holdings and incomes for the common good. Throughout electoral Saxony individual communities, including Zwickau, adopted the pieces of Luther's developing model. Though Duke Frederick was unwilling to authorize this first ordinance officially, he did not suppress the innovations.

The term "Lutheran" was initially applied to Martin's supporters as a pejorative smear. They referred to themselves as "Martinists", then later as "evangelical Christians" to lay claim to the "good news" of the Gospels, which soon became a dividing line in community after community. Either you supported reforms justified by the Gospels or you opposed them. Learned theologians in large urban churches and itinerant "hedge preachers" in the countryside spread evangelical ideas, some drawn from Luther, others not. Everywhere the Word of God appeared to challenge religious, social, and political order. In some communities smouldering sentiments of anticlericalism fed on the evangelical message and triggered attacks against parish priests, or iconoclastic destruction of church property. More and more people refused to pay tithes. The early evangelical movement combined "strong religious fervor, impatience, militancy, and turbulence". Luther had restrained those forces at Wittenberg and elsewhere in electoral Saxony, but the movement was spreading so quickly that individual participants had to draw their own conclusions on how to revive the Gospel "as salvation and as ethic".[3] Eventually evangelical enthusiasm triggered violence and repression in towns and in the countryside.

Reformation Contested: the Rural World and the Peasants' War of 1524-5

The early evangelical movement reinforced anticlerical sentiments at all levels of society and raised the cry for confiscation and disbursement of ecclesiastical wealth, while leaving open the questions of how and to whom. In 1523 a band of Imperial knights, faced with deteriorating social circumstances due to declining profits from lordship and the increasing prominence of firearms in warfare, gathered under the leadership of Franz von Sickingen (1481–1523) and the humanist Ulrich von Hutten (1488–1523), who had called for "a war on priests". The ensuing "knights' war" against the electoral archbishop of Trier had the outward appearance of an anticlerical campaign, and Sickingen justified what amounted to glorified brigandage on religious grounds, but the impetus came from personal animosities and economic desperation. Eventually the Swabian League of Imperial Cities crushed the renegade knights, but the war exposed the fragility of public peace in the Empire and the potential threat posed by armed evangelical Christians to ecclesiastical states and properties.

Since the mid-fifteenth century, organized peasant resistance, such as the *Bundschuh* uprisings in the Upper Rhine valley, had threatened all lords, both ecclesiastical and lay, as well as urban efforts to control rural hinterlands.[4] Worsening social and economic conditions, brought on in part by rising prices and efforts by feudal lords to extract more revenue from their tenants, angered peasants and artisans who envied the commoners in the Swiss Confederacy, where the rural communes recognized no lords. The threat of "turning Swiss" racheted up social and political tensions, especially in south-western Germany.[5] Into this environment, the evangelical emphasis on the authority of scripture alone, and the call for the priesthood of all believers, resonated among the common folk, who internalized the reformers' message as divine judgement against existing feudal relations. Religious reformation ignited social war. The Peasants' War of 1524–6 was a nest of local rebellions triggered by local grievances, which blended frustrations with economic exploitation by elites, anger at clerical wealth and lordship, personal animosities, envy, and evangelical inspiration. The "Gospel of social unrest", a call to bring "Godly law" and social justice to the world, would become the religious glue that held the various peasant bands together for a time.[6]

Since the early 1520s evangelical preachers active in the countryside around Zurich had advocated the abolition of tithes, and encouraged iconoclasm and violence against priests. In April 1524, subjects of the abbey of St Blasien in the nearby Black Forest refused to pay feudal dues or tithes. By June other bands had formed in the Upper Swabian districts of Lupfen and Stühlingen, drawing up grievance lists to present to their lords. Meanwhile the rebels occupied St Blasien and sacked several convents, with the support of contingents from Zurich's hinterland. In October, Thomas Müntzer, who had left Zwickau, inspired a successful urban revolt at Mühlhausen in Thuringia under the banner of divine justice. By early 1525 the pockets of resistance inspired other rebel groups in the Klettgau, in Lower Alsace, and in the mining districts of the Austrian Tyrol. In Upper Swabia dozens of individual bands merged under the leadership of Ulrich Schmid, who, with the assistance of evangelical preachers from the imperial city of Memmingen, consolidated 300 individual charters into the *Twelve Articles of Memmingen* (January–February 1525), which became a template for manifestos drafted by other peasant armies, now calling themselves "Christian Assemblies" or "Christian Unions". In March, Müntzer proclaimed the "Eternal League of God" at Mühlhausen. As the bands grew and consolidated, the level of violence increased. Peasants in Franconia destroyed castles and seized the episcopal city of Wurzburg, whose bishop fled for his life. The Black Forest band successfully besieged the town of Freiburg im Breisgau, while other forces captured the bishop of Speyer and pressured the electoral archbishop of Mainz and the electoral count Palatine to endorse reform programmes. By early May 1525, the social and religious order of south-western Germany appeared to be teetering.

The restoration of feudal authority came quickly and ruthlessly. In rapid succession the pro-Lutheran landgrave Philip of Hesse and Catholic duke George of Saxony[7] crushed peasant bands at Boblingen (12 May) and Müntzer's forces at Frankenhausen (15 May). On 17 May 1525 Duke Antoine of Lorraine massacred the Alsatian peasants near the town of Saverne after they had signed a truce with him. The victorious princes rounded up hundreds of suspects for torture and public execution. In all, perhaps 100,000 rebels, including Thomas Müntzer, died in battle or on the scaffold. The Peasants' War was a crossroads for the German evangelical movement. Enthusiastic reform from below, seeking to restructure Christian society through godly law, was soundly defeated. Horrified evangelical leaders, such as Luther, now turned to the princes and civic magistrates as the only possible agents for godly order and religious reform.

Not all of the "radical" reformers died in the bloodbath that ended the Peasants' War. What George H. Williams has called the "radical reformation" survived among hundreds of individuals who followed personal visions of spiritual Christianity and gathered in small cells under the shadow of persecution.[8] Consoled by faith, these individuals and groups pursued distinct, self-righteous paths, often fighting among themselves as much as against the authorities. Most insisted that they, as true believers, formed a spiritual church separate from the world, whose membership derived from direct spiritual contact with God, an experience that filled them with the self-confidence and peace needed to endure fierce persecution. For these spiritual Christians, no earthly agency delivered God's grace; neither sacraments, sacramentals, nor even scripture.

In February 1527, an assembly of radicals drew up seven "articles of faith" at the village of Schleitheim near Schaffhausen in Switzerland. The Articles of Schleitheim included opposition to infant baptism, rejection of oaths, excommunication by shunning, and refusal to bear arms. Their advocacy of adult baptism earned them the label "Anabaptists" (re-baptists), and authorities applied the name indiscriminately to groups that agreed on nothing else except adult baptism. The Anabaptists' association with the German Peasants' War (many early members had participated) and the denial by some of private property, traditional family structures, and oath taking, an act which bound all polities together, made the Anabaptists dangerous to civil order.

Evangelical and Catholic officials reacted with aggressive persecution, executing over 600 Anabaptists between 1525 and 1533 and often burning them even if they recanted. Many Anabaptists still harboured desires to realize God's kingdom with the sword, but increasingly they embraced pacifism and found refuge either as Swiss Brethren in individual households in the Alpine highlands or among larger communities in Moravia, a kingdom attached to the Bohemian throne where tolerance of religious pluralism had roots in the Hussite wars. By the 1540s the Bohemian Anabaptists had settled into tightly organized multi-family brotherhoods, first advocated by Jakob Hutter, in which work and wealth were shared in common, and the Hutterites would continue to flourish there until the mid-seventeenth century.[9]

Other Anabaptist groups understood their persecution as the worldly church of the Antichrist's assault on the true spiritual church of Christ, and they expected an imminent apocalyptic transformation to establish a new spiritual Jerusalem on earth. For a time Melchior Hoffman convinced many that Strasbourg would be the site, but his imprisonment there in 1533 dispersed his followers. Hoffman had earlier preached in the Netherlands where he had attracted many converts, who would gravitate to the episcopal city of Münster in Westphalia in early 1534, after the conversion of the city's reformer Bernhard Rothmann to Melchiorite Anabaptism appeared to presage the second coming of Christ. Jan Matthijs, a charismatic baker from Haarlem who had settled at Münster, predicted the triumphal event for Easter Sunday. Word of this prophecy convinced thousands of people from all walks of life to pack their possessions and trek to the city. The scale of this response suggests widespread sympathy for spiritual Anabaptism. Neighbouring authorities turned back most of the trekkers, but at least 2,500 reached Münster and radicalized the community. The potential threat of this New Jerusalem led the bishop and the region's lords to besiege the city, and when Easter passed without incident, Matthijs sacrificed himself on a suicide sortie against the bishop's army. As the siege dragged on, his successor, Jan of Leiden, communalized all supplies and enforced polygamy. Recent scholarship has suggested that these radical innovations were only partially applied, and driven primarily by the pressure of the siege, but the implicit threat to the social and familial order of the Anabaptist Jerusalem would haunt the movement and its persecutors for decades.[10] Episcopal troops eventually stormed the city in June of 1535 and executed the surviving leaders. Despite the bloodbath at Münster, Anabaptism in the Netherlands would survive in scattered pockets, eventually consolidating behind the pacifist leadership of Menno Simons to flourish under tolerant Dutch authorities.

The Reformation Negotiated: Urban Reformations

The early evangelical movement spread quickly in the German-speaking towns. For the reformers, the urban setting provided a concentrated audience, quickly accessible to both preaching and pamphlets. Civic evangelical parties, in turn, could immediately confront the political authorities as fellow citizens rather than distant lords. Luther was never a self-conscious urban reformer nor did his writings demonstrate particular sensitivity to civic culture, but by 1522 he was instituting religious changes at Wittenberg based on a model for Christian society derived from scripture. His growing reputation ensured that his ideas were widely disseminated in print, while other civic reformers, inspired by Luther, preached the evangelical message from numerous urban pulpits. By 1523 over a dozen Saxon towns had taken the first steps towards reform, and advocates had reached Nuremberg in Franconia and Augsburg in southern Germany, from where the message quickly spread throughout the urban trading network.

Everywhere, pamphlets and fly-sheets mocked the papacy and other ecclesiastical institutions. Meanwhile, endowed preachers such as Huldrych Zwingli at Zurich, or evangelical missionaries such as Thomas Müntzer, addressed sympathetic audiences in large urban churches and open squares with slogans that juxtaposed a new Christian community of faith against the "faithless" Church. In Constance and Basel evangelical agitation helped drive out resident bishops, but everywhere the reformers' demand that the clergy submit to civic law appealed to municipal officials frustrated with clerical legal immunities. Reformers also advocated that churchmen marry and join a guild, which would "domesticate" priests and, hopefully, bring undomesticated women such as nuns, clerical concubines, and prostitutes under a new moral and patriarchal order.

Scripture served as an all-purpose yardstick to justify various social and political grievances, and popular preachers eventually provoked confrontations, first with ecclesiastical officials but eventually with municipal authorities. Some cities expelled the preachers, but religious and factional divisions within civic regimes often thwarted decisive action and allowed the public debate to continue. In many communities women openly preached and actively defended evangelical preachers, but women's public involvement demonstrated to male officials the disorder implicit in unregulated religious debate.[11] Ultimately, civic regimes had to resolve the controversy; and though the magistrates may have seen themselves as patricians, whose social status gave them the right to rule, effective governance depended to some degree on popular assent. In order to preserve public peace, municipal officials had to address the demands of the evangelical faction or risk internal unrest, while somehow avoiding external interference from neighbouring Catholic powers.

The short-term solution followed at Erfurt, Nuremberg, Memmingen, and Constance was to buy time with "scripture mandates", which required all parties to confine themselves to scripturally sanctioned practices; but eventually the magistrates had to define what these would be. If the evangelical party gained sufficient communal support, civic officials often stage-managed public disputations which "resolved" the issue in favour of reform, but the volatile mix of reforming enthusiasm and social animosity remained. In northern Germany at Rostock and Lübeck in 1531, evangelized citizens organized special committees that inspected the regimes' fiscal records and correspondence, expelled patrician incumbents, and elected new officials from among the guildsmen. In 1533–4 at Hanover the entire regime was expelled and a new constitution formalized the coup. In southern Germany civic elections brought new and ambitious evangelical men into formerly restricted branches of government, but constitutional changes were limited. For the towns outside northern Germany, the Peasants' War had been a critical social juncture for many civic reformations. Popular pressure had done much to drive the early reform movement, but the peasants' crushing defeat drove surviving radicals underground. At Schwäbisch Gmund and Wangen, the war ended budding evangelical movements; in other towns, such as Memmingen, it delayed implementation; and nearly everywhere threats of further unrest stiffened opposition among municipal authorities. After 1525, municipal regimes in southern and central Germany strove to regulate the pace and direction of civic reformations, and their strategies must be understood as a reaction to the evangelical movement's unruly first phase.

In Luther's writings, civic leaders found an emphasis on human sinfulness and the need to submit to God's authority. By assuming control over the local churches, lay magistrates sequestered divine authority under civic law, and Nuremberg and several other cities turned to Luther for guidance, even though he offered no specific model for a Christian civic community. Meanwhile Martin Bucer at Strasbourg and Huldrych Zwingli at Zurich had proposed such prototypes and sought to realize them in their respective communities. Like most evangelicals, both had initially been inspired by Luther, but unlike Luther, both were essentially urban reformers. They were comfortable with the vocabulary of urban corporate values embodied in the civic norms of peace, unity, and commonweal. In the wake of 1525, moreover, their models for sacral civic society were hierarchical and firmly governed by godly magistrates.

Municipal authorities had haphazardly begun to abolish the old ecclesiastical order before 1525, but in the following decade they approached reforms carefully and systematically. Both Luther and Zwingli spoke out in favour of caution, and traditional forms of worship faded slowly. Civic officials moved most aggressively against the privileged civic monastic communities, confiscating revenues, secularizing buildings, and expelling monks and friars. Female convents proved more difficult to close. For example, the nuns of St Clara's convent at Nuremberg, who came from the leading civic families, were allowed to die out gradually, and at Ulm several houses survived under the patronage of local patricians and nobles.[12] Those images and church vessels which had survived iconoclastic riots were also quietly removed from churches. Even then not all towns embraced the reforms. Corporate interests and ecclesiastical patronage in cities such as Cologne quieted the reformers' message.

Having swept away the old clerical corporations, civic reformers and magistrates plotted new forms of worship for the civic churches. By 1530 the German evangelicals were called Protestants, but their common name masked internal feuds as three rival camps compiled formulas of belief or "confessions". Luther's supporters signed the Confession of Augsburg, while Bucer rallied the South German towns of Strasbourg, Constance, Lindau, and Memmingen under the banner of the Tetrapolitan (four-city) Confession, and Swiss Protestant cities followed Zwingli's leadership. By requiring reformed ministers and public officials to swear adherence to one of these documents, civic regimes maintained the appearance of internal consensus, but securing public peace required tolerance and patience. Historians still debate over how many citizens believed or even understood the tenets of their civic church, but evidence from Strasbourg suggests a significant degree of general knowledge and informed lay confessional parties until the end of the sixteenth century.[13]

In addition to defining proper faith, officials replaced the Eucharistic Mass with daily sermons and periodic gatherings for the Lord's Supper. Except for Anabaptists, nearly all Protestants preserved some ritual re-enactment of the Eucharistic sacrament. These services brought the citizens together as a sacral community, but the bitter dispute between "Lutherans" and "Zwinglians" over what the faithful actually received with the bread would eventually force civic officials to define communal faith explicitly. Magisterial control entailed supervision over the city's ministers as well as the civil replacements for the ecclesiastical organs of moral oversight and education: the marriage court and the schools.

Regimes also assumed the charitable functions of the medieval religious communities, including hospital care, the supervision of orphans, and poor relief. In short, urban reformations consolidated the authority and enhanced the power of civic regimes, and gradually Protestant leaders constructed their new sacral society, one marked by hierarchy, respect for authority, and social discipline.

Zwingli and the Swiss Reformation

The term "Schwitzerland" came from the canton of Schwyz, whose peasant communes banded in 1291 with other "Forest Cantons" to form the Swiss Confederacy. Over the next two centuries neighbouring towns and individual rural communities swore oaths and joined this association. Initially the Confederacy grew within the Holy Roman Empire, but wars with Emperor Maximilian I led to a legal separation from Imperial institutions by 1500. The Swiss reputedly honoured no lords, yet the leading towns of Zurich, Lucerne, Berne, and Basel exercised lordship over their hinterlands, and even rural communes such as the Grey Leagues (Grisons) held feudal rights over other Swiss villages.[14] By the early sixteenth century the fragile economies of the high alpine valleys could no longer support the growing population, and villages recruited companies of pikemen from among their households to generate income as mercenaries for the various warring powers in Italy. The cantons held diets (*Tagsatzungen*), which met irregularly to address matters of mutual interest, but individual cantons and even communes within cantons exercised a broad degree of self-governance that often put them at odds with one another.

As we have seen, Zurich's reform movement had contact with radical reformers of the Peasants' War and the urban Reformation. The city's reformer, Huldrych Zwingli (1484–1531), was born in Wildhaus, a village in the Toggenburg district of Zurich's hinterland, the son of a well-to-do peasant who served as chief district magistrate. Zwingli studied at Basel and Berne and later matriculated at the universities at Vienna and then Basel, where he received a Master of Arts degree in 1506. He entered the priesthood that same year and served as pastor of Glarus until 1516. As pastor he ministered to his parishioners in a Swiss mercenary unit in Italy and witnessed the carnage at Marignano. Zwingli returned to become pastor at Einsiedeln, a significant Marian shrine, where his growing reputation as a preacher led Zurich's city council to recruit him in 1519 as *Leutpriester*, the people's priest, at the city's principal church, the Great Minster. Zurich was a wealthy city of 6,000 inhabitants, in the sprawling diocese of Constance. In making the appointment, the magistrates had ignored episcopal rights, and Zwingli's reforms and the city's push for religious autonomy would feed off one another through the next critical decade.

Though influenced by Luther, Zwingli came to his evangelical convictions from his own personal commitment, developing divergent views on the sacraments and Church–state relations. In his new post Zwingli soon abandoned the traditional liturgical cycle, to preach systematically from the Gospels.[15] For Zwingli scripture offered lucid and irresistible truths that had been obscured by the Church's innovations. What was needed, he argued, was a return to evangelical primitive Christianity, and he called on Zurich's magistrates to realize his vision of a pure Christian community. In October 1522, Zwingli renounced his clerical benefice and accepted a purely civic appointment more closely binding his leadership with magisterial authority.

Henceforth, Zurich's reformation would evolve through a series of public debates adjudicated by the magistrates. The first, on 23 January 1523, between Zwingli and episcopal representatives from Constance, addressed sixty-seven propositions. Zurich's officials invited representatives from the other cantons, but only Schaffhausen and Berne sent observers. Zwingli attacked papal authority, the nature of the Mass, Purgatory, prayers to the saints, and devotion to images. The bishop's men found themselves required to justify these from scripture alone rather than from ecclesiastical tradition. The magistrates declared Zwingli "victorious". Despite protests from the bishop, papal officials never excommunicated Zwingli or the city, for the curia was unwilling to alienate an important reservoir of mercenaries.

Time and again Zwingli carefully articulated arguments against sacramental practices and ecclesiastical institutions, but he was unwilling to act on his own principles when they challenged Zurich's magistrates. For example, though he preached against Lenten fasting in 1522, he declined to join a group of followers who ate sausage against the prohibition of civic authorities. The potentially radical thrust of Zwingli's theology sharply segregated the spiritual and sensual worlds, in contrast to late medieval views of their mutual interpenetration. His opposition to images, his view that baptism was a spiritual relationship not dependent on the pouring of water or other outward signs, and his insistence on the spiritual rather than bodily presence of Jesus at communion, all hinged on a clear separation of sensual and spiritual experience. Zwingli's church was an invisible congregation of the faithful, but he envisioned civil magistrates as essential protectors for his church against the threats of the visible world.

Unfortunately for Zwingli, many of his followers saw themselves as members in a spiritual community that in matters of faith should obey neither the visible Church nor lay authorities. Zwingli's attack on images, at the first debate, triggered iconoclastic incidents in Zurich and the villages under civic jurisdiction that the reformer was unwilling to condone.[16] When disgruntled villagers spoke out against the city's continued collection of tithes, Zwingli responded with a carefully reasoned treatise that men could not live in society without laws and constraint. Moreover, despite Zwingli's public statements against the Mass, Zurich's churches continued to celebrate the Eucharist with traditional services. Facing popular pressure to accelerate reforms and formulate a new Church ordinance, the magistrates staged a second public debate in late October 1523, which "resolved" to retain tithes and established sacraments and to remove images peacefully. The "defeated" advocates of further reform began meeting secretly under the leadership of a patrician named Conrad Grebel. On the basis of their understanding of scripture and Zwingli's own distinction between spiritual and visible truths, they publicly protested against infant baptism, which forced another disputation between Zwingli and Grebel on 17 January 1525, resulting in the latter's defeat. Several days later the defiant Grebel re-baptized sixteen followers then fled to the countryside. Finally, in November 1525, Zwingli and Grebel revisited the issue, after which the "Anabaptist" leadership were imprisoned or exiled.

In the ensuing months, against the backdrop of the Peasants' War, Zurich's magistrates with Zwingli's guidance finally instituted a new Church ordinance. They secularized the canton's monasteries and used the income to establish a common chest to finance a new school system and poor relief. Then on Easter Sunday they abolished the Mass, substituting a communion service of both bread and wine, shared from a table with words of blessing rather than consecration. Zwingli rejected the belief that the Mass replicated Christ's sacrifice through the miracle of transubstantiation, instead claiming that Christ was only present spiritually in the heart of the believer. For Zwingli, believers and unbelievers consumed merely bread and wine, but for the faithful who gathered in communion to commemorate the Last Supper, participation reinforced faith in the spiritual presence of Christ within each believer.

There was no miraculous presence of body and blood. This emphasis on the "spiritual presence" of Christ through communion would alienate Zwinglians from both Catholics and Lutherans.

Zwingli's civic reform programme resonated among many South German reformers, and he developed a close friendship with Martin Bucer at Strasbourg. After 1525 Zwingli helped facilitate the introduction of reformations in the Swiss cities of Basel, Berne, Schaffhausen, and St Gallen, always working closely with local lay officials. Other cantons such as Lucerne and the original "Forest Cantons" disliked Zurich's meddling in their affairs and expelled or sometimes executed Zwinglian missionaries. By 1529 Zwinglian and Catholic coalitions had divided the Confederacy, and war was narrowly avoided by a battlefield truce drawn up at Kappel. Two years later when Catholic forces staged a surprise campaign against Zurich, Zwingli joined the civic militia and was killed on the battlefield. Eventually the warring parties signed a religious peace, which granted the right of Zwinglian cantons to retain their religion but prohibited further evangelical proselytizing. The Swiss Confederacy became the first European state to accept confessional plurality. In the wake of Zwingli's death, Heinrich Bullinger assumed spiritual leadership at Zurich and in 1536 would play the lead role in drafting the First Helvetic Confession, which guided the Swiss reformed churches for several decades.

Reformation Secured from Above: the Protestant Political Community

Following the Peasants' War, Luther also turned to lay authorities to usher in gradual reform from above. Frederick the Wise had never officially sanctioned liturgical changes but had simply tolerated them; thus neighbouring Saxon parishes might follow Catholic or evangelical models or a hybrid mix. Frederick's successor, John (*1525–32), supported Luther more actively, ordering the German Mass throughout the electorate in January 1525. After trial visitations to rural communities around Zwickau and Eisenach exposed all sorts of "superstitious" practices, Luther composed a German order of service, which was printed and distributed to all parishes. The reformer also convinced the elector to appoint a commission of lay councillors and theologians to supervise future visitations, and this committee evolved into a permanent ecclesiastical council (*Kirchenrat*) with responsibility for administering the territorial church. Luther redefined the former parish system into community-based congregations, and the ecclesiastical council appointed pastors and readers for each. Luther also created consistories – local committees of pastors and lay officials that supervised moral disciplinary issues for clusters of from six to fifteen congregations, and he assigned church wardens and deacons to handle church finances and poor relief. Luther's model took time to implement and was not fully functional until 1542, but it would become the template for other Lutheran territorial churches. At every level, Church and state worked together.

For many princes conversion to Lutheranism offered a means of incorporating the Church's wealth and administrative resources into the apparatus of governance, which immediately increased princely power at the expense of local authorities. In East Prussia, Albert of Hohenzollern, the Grand Master of the Teutonic Knights, dissolved the crusading order in 1523, married, and then secularized his domains as an hereditary duchy. Prussia and Brandenburg-Ansbach were the only principalities to initiate reform measures prior to the Peasants' War, but in 1526 the rulers of Hesse, Braunschweig-Lüneburg, Braunschweig-Grubenhagen, Mecklenburg-Schwerin, Mansfeld, and Anhalt-Köthen joined the ranks of reformed territories. Landgrave Philip of Hesse implemented his own model of ecclesiastical administration, and in October 1526 he convoked a synod at Homburg that granted autonomy to local congregations to elect pastors and bishops. Luther opposed this plan, and Philip eventually acquiesced. Slowly a party of Imperial principalities and cities rallied around Luther, and at the Imperial Diet of Speyer in July 1529, they delivered a protest against a Catholic effort to overthrow a recess (decision) of an earlier Diet, which left religious decisions in the hands of territorial political authorities until the convening of an ecumenical council. Those associated with the document acquired the name "Protestants". Having set themselves against the Emperor, the question remained whether Protestants could develop a common religious programme.

Luther's reduction of the seven Catholic sacraments to two meant that these two, baptism and the Eucharist, assumed unprecedented importance among evangelical reformers. As we have seen, "radical" Anabaptists had challenged the views of Luther and Zwingli, as well as traditional Catholic practice, regarding infant baptism and would suffer persecution for their beliefs. Differing interpretations of the Eucharist would prove even more intractable and divisive. Many reformers, including Bucer and Zwingli, denied transubstantiation and argued that communion brought together the faithful in a ritual commemoration of Christ's sacrifice on the cross. Catholics believed that the body and blood of Christ became miraculously present in the elements through the ritual of the Mass no matter what the spiritual state of the priest or the parishioner, while for those who saw communion as a metaphor to remind believers of Christ's spiritual presence in their lives, no miracle was necessary, just faith in God's mercy. Luther called this view "sacramentarian", and against it he claimed that Christ was bodily present in the bread and wine, not through priestly sacerdotal powers but rather through a mystery whose meaning and power rested with God and which replicated the mystery of God made flesh. Luther's Eucharistic theology came to be known as "consubstantiation" because the bread and wine maintained their original substances while also becoming the body and blood of Christ. The theological differences were subtle, but increasingly for Luther the critical distinction lay between consubstantiation and the sacramentarian communion.

As more and more magistrates and princes rallied to the Protestant cause, they wanted a Eucharistic compromise to ease the way to political union. Philip of Hesse attempted to bring the leading evangelical theologians together to resolve the growing polarization between Luther's and Zwingli's interpretations, but the Marburg Colloquy (conference) of October 1529 only highlighted the distances between the two camps, and ended in disagreement. Afterwards Luther with Philip Melanchthon's assistance drew up a list of accepted beliefs (a confession) at Augsburg in 1530, which included consubstantiation. In response, Zwingli drew up his own confessional document, while Strasbourg's reformer Martin Bucer fashioned a rival, sacramentarian confession, adopted by Protestants at Strasbourg, Constance, Memmingen, and Lindau. The divisions among the Protestant religious leaders were now public. Facing a military threat from Charles V, who had temporarily ended his wars in Italy, and internal confessional divisions among Protestants, Philip of Hesse and John of Saxony invited the Imperial Protestant states to the town of Schmalkalden in Thuringia in December 1530, where seven princes and the cities of Bremen and Magdeburg formed a defensive alliance whose members subscribed to Luther's Augsburg Confession.

With the formation of the Schmalkaldic League, Lutheranism became the dominant form of Protestantism in Germany. Theological debates and infighting would continue during the 1530s, and Protestant churchmen and politicians soon gravitated into the two confessional camps: Lutherans, who accepted the real – if mysterious – presence of Christ at the Lord's Supper; and the "Reformed" sacramentarians, who envisioned only the spiritual presence of Christ among the believers sharing communion. The Lutheran party, centred in northern and eastern Germany, had its theological base at Wittenberg and political strength secured by the Schmalkaldic League. For the predominantly South German "Reformed" movement, Zurich served as ideological centre under Zwingli's successor Heinrich Bullinger, while Strasbourg, under Martin Bucer and Jacob Sturm, directed political activities.[17] In 1534 divisions among the Protestants surfaced when Duke Ulrich of Württemberg converted to Lutheranism and recaptured his duchy with the assistance of the Schmalkaldic League. The Lutherans expelled the Emperor's Catholic officials who had administered the sequestered duchy, and the move threatened to embroil the Empire in religious war. It also strained Protestant relations, for the sacramentarian Bucer had helped negotiate the duke's conversion, but the princes of the Schmalkaldic League insisted on Ulrich's sanctioning the Augsburg Confession. By 1540 Württemberg was a Lutheran state.

To secure a common defensive front, Bucer and Melanchthon attempted to find a Eucharistic middle ground, but Luther balked at compromise. As the military pressure increased, one by one the South German "Reformed" cities made their confessional peace with the Lutherans. Bucer signed a personal concord at Wittenberg in October 1536, which affirmed infant baptism and Luther's interpretation of the Lord's Supper in vague terms, though Strasbourg would officially retain its Tetrapolitan Confession until 1598. Nevertheless, by 1537 nearly all South German reformers were within the Lutheran camp, though conflicting interpretations of the Eucharist alienated Lutherans from Swiss reformers and remained a source of contention among Lutherans until the Formula of Concord in 1580.

Within the principalities and cities that recognized the Augsburg Confession, the break with Catholicism required the restructuring and reorganization of the institutional Church, including the establishment of instruments to police and discipline Christian life. Protestant states expected married clergy, which allowed many former priests to marry their concubines. Wherever possible, authorities closed monasteries and convents and confiscated their revenues to support religious education. Some former monks joined the Protestant parish ministry, while resettlement for released nuns was more complicated. State officials assumed authority over ecclesiastical properties, revenues, and services such as poor relief. Luther's model for a German liturgy came to predominate in Protestant churches, which needed a supply of vernacular German

Lutheran bibles and service books. With Luther's encouragement, Church officials conducted parish visitations and established local consistories to supervise them and to punish immoral behaviour, marital disputes, violations of Sunday worship, drunkenness, and even name-calling. Everywhere the new system subordinated ecclesiastical institutions to secular governance and increased the state's direct involvement in daily life, as the prince assumed traditional episcopal rights and prerogatives.

Medieval Catholicism was practised; but Protestant confessions emphasized understanding through preaching and the reading of scriptures. Having discovered an unlearned and superstitious countryside, Luther and other reformers composed catechisms, which were printed and distributed to parish ministers for use in teaching children the articles of faith and doctrine. Indoctrination became a key objective for Protestant Church officials. Secondary schools and seminaries would eventually spring up in connection with territorial universities to standardize clerical training. Until then Luther composed manuals of pastoral advice and sermons, which local ministers might plagiarize or parrot to ensure at least that some of the official message reached the people. Despite these efforts, Gerald Strauss and others have argued that the commoners were slow to accept and internalize reformed religiosity and that Lutheran leaders themselves saw their initial efforts as a failure.[18]

Reforms and Evangelical Movements in Northern and Eastern Europe

The Scandinavian monarchies were the first kingdoms to break with traditional Roman Catholicism in response to Luther's movement. In 1397 the League of Kalmar had brought together Denmark, Sweden, Finland, Norway, and Iceland into a dynastic union centred in Denmark, under which the regional components retained their separate institutions and estates. In 1460 the North German duchy of Schleswig-Holstein joined this conglomerate. It required deft leadership to balance the various political interests, and Christian II (*1513–23) lacked the touch, provoking regional opposition movements against his policies. In November 1520 Christian's massacre of eighty lay and ecclesiastical opponents among the Swedish aristocracy ignited a successful rebellion led by Gustav Vasa (1496–1560). In 1523 the exasperated Danish royal Council (*Rigsrådet*) deposed Christian in favour of his uncle, Frederick I (*1523–33). Regional differences and political factors would play a significant role throughout Scandinavia's reformations.[19]

By 1520, Lutheran tracts and itinerant Lutheran preachers were in circulation in the Baltic basin, and German-speaking enclaves within Scandinavian towns provided the seedbeds for the early evangelical movement. In 1521, Duke Christian of Schleswig-Holstein, King Frederick's son, converted to Lutheranism. With the guidance of the Wittenberg churchman Johann Bugenhagen, Christian pushed the duchy's religious reform gently along, allowing priests to marry and retain their posts, tolerating closet Catholicism among nobles, and delaying implementation of a Lutheran Church ordinance until the last Catholic bishop died in 1541. At that point, Christian assumed supervision (*cura religionis*) over the duchy's territorial church and its revenues and demanded a loyalty oath from all ministers.

In Denmark the irascible Christian II had flirted with evangelical ideas to threaten the kingdom's clerical elite prior to his deposition. His successor, Frederick I, while sympathetic to Lutheranism, found himself politically dependent on conservative lay and ecclesiastical officials in the *Rigsrådet*, so rather than forcing reforms, he cautiously limited his policies to tolerating fledgling evangelical congregations in Danish towns. Frederick's death in 1533, however, triggered a rebellion among pro-Catholic nobles and churchmen, which his son and successor, Christian III of Schleswig-Holstein (*1533–59), quickly suppressed. The new king then turned to the Danish estates (*Riksdag*), where the lower nobility and towns were more sympathetic to Protestant views, to introduce Lutheran reforms, confirmed by the Royal Church Ordinance in 1537. The following year Denmark joined the Schmalkaldic League and embraced the Augsburg Confession. None the less, Christian allowed Catholic monasteries, convents, and cathedral chapters to survive under the protection of aristocratic patrons tied to the old church, and focused instead on building an educational infrastructure to train an effective reformed parish ministry. Spreading the new faith proceeded slowly and for decades Catholic residues such as high altars, side chapels, shrines, and holy images remained part of church architecture and the landscape of Danish faith.

The Swedish Reformation was even more protracted, with little or no popular support outside of Stockholm prior to the 1560s. The rebel King Gustav I (*1523–60) never personally embraced Lutheranism. With his fragile position on the usurped throne, Gustav needed the approval of the Swedish estates to secularize some ecclesiastical properties in 1527, and the nobles shared in the windfall revenues. Committed Swedish evangelicals such as Olav Pedersson and Lars Andersson pushed for a Lutheran territorial church, as independent of civil authority as possible, but at the *Riksdag* of Örebro in 1539, the estates granted Gustav full control over the, as yet, unreformed Swedish Church. Peasant resistance thwarted efforts to institute new religious practices, while local lay elites controlled clerical appointments and ecclesiastical revenues. In this diffuse political environment, Catholic bishops and Lutheran superintendents functioned side by side. Sixteenth-century Sweden had no Church ordinance and would not sign the Augsburg Confession until 1593.

In Eastern Europe political fragmentation gave room for religious dissidents and evangelical radicals to manoeuvre but also prevented the establishment of territorial churches. The sprawling kingdom of Poland comprised three distinct regions: Little Poland (around Cracow); Great Poland to the North; and the Grand Duchy of Lithuania.[20] The Polish Diet (*Sejm*), encompassing the magnates and lower nobility (*szlachta*), elected Poland's king and circumscribed royal power within noble interests. Pocket German communities in the towns, along with the secularized Hohenzollern duchy of East Prussia, served as centres for Lutheran ideas, but German Protestantism made limited inroads among the Polish and Lithuanian intellectuals, churchmen, and nobles. In the 1540s Calvinist cells sprouted up in some towns, and in the countryside where sympathetic nobles protected them. Religious freedom became closely associated with noble rights and privileges, and reformed members of the nobility confiscated Church properties and revenues on their estates. Following the death of Sigismund II (*1548–72), the last Jagiellon monarch, the *Sejm* secured noble religious liberties in the royal capitulation negotiated with the Catholic Henri of Anjou (*1573–5). Throughout, noble liberties and self-interest determined the course of the reform movements in Poland.

The kingdom of Hungary was also ruled by a Jagiellon monarch, Louis II (*1516–26). His defeat and death fighting the Ottoman Turks at the battle of Mohács in 1526 effectively divided Hungary into three parts.[21] The Ottomans held the southern half and would push inexorably northward to Buda on the Danube in 1541. To the north-east, the province of Transylvania recognized János Zápolya I (*1526–40) as king, while the Hungarian estates in the north-west elected Ferdinand, Habsburg duke of Austria and brother of Charles V, to rule them. Hungary was a war zone throughout the sixteenth century, where Muslims, Slavic Orthodox, Catholic, and various Protestant communities coexisted in relative religious peace. As distant rulers of a strategic frontier province, neither the Sultan nor Ferdinand tinkered with the Catholic hierarchy or institutions. Meanwhile Hungarian Christians gradually abandoned Catholic worship as the percentage and diversity of Protestant believers steadily grew.

Finally, in Bohemia, the territorial estates, comprising the nobility and civic magistrates, had administered the Utraquist Church since the Hussite era through officials known as *defensores* who monitored the central consistory, set organizational and theological guidelines, controlled parish properties, and supervised priests. Some nobles also sheltered congregations of Bohemian Brethren, descendants of the Taborites, on their estates. In the 1520s and 1530s Lutherans evangelized the German Catholic communities in the towns and mining centres and developed close ties with the Bohemian Brethren. The Lutheran movement also stimulated a reformist wing within the Utraquist Church. Louis II Jagiellon had also ruled in Bohemia, and following Mohács, Ferdinand of Austria (*1526–64) became Bohemia's elected king. His ongoing campaigns against the Turks preserved the Bohemian estates' leverage in religious affairs, provided they supplied him with soldiers and material for the war effort. When Protestant forces clashed with Ferdinand's brother, the Emperor, during the Schmalkaldic War (1545–7), sympathetic Utraquists, Bohemian Brethren and German Lutherans rebelled against their king, only to endure a crushing defeat that resulted in executions, exile, and the confiscation of properties. Ferdinand's triumph was only temporary, but the first effort to integrate Hus's and Luther's movements in Bohemia ended in failure.

Early Reform Movements in France and Geneva

Lutheranism initially grew within the politically fragmented Empire, and then spread through dissemination in vernacular German. Evangelical movements which sprang up in political settings outside the German-speaking world drew on Luther's inspiration but required their own political and cultural impetus. The Concordat of Bologna (1516), contracted by Pope Leo X and Francis I, gave the French king extensive control over what amounted to a separate Gallican Catholic Church and left him little incentive to reform it. Just the same, political considerations connected to Francis's ongoing wars with Charles V in Italy and the Netherlands resulted in religious mood swings, from support of the Emperor's Protestant opponents in Germany and tolerance within France, to bouts of persecution. As early as 1521, theologians at the

university of Paris, the Sorbonne, condemned Luther's writings, but in
the diocese of Meaux, efforts to improve the clergy, simplify the liturgy,
and preach regularly from scriptures flourished under Bishop Guillaume
Briçonnet and his vicar-general, Jacques Lefèvre d'Étaples, both of
whom benefitted from the protection of Marguerite of Angoulême
(1492–1549), the king's sister. This elite circle of reform-oriented intellectuals remained orthodox, though among their students, Guillaume
Farel would become a leading Protestant. Francis's defeat and capture
by Habsburg forces at the battle of Pavia (25 February 1525) produced
a Catholic reaction that triggered the break-up of the Meaux circle,
whose leaders sought shelter at Marguerite's court or in exile. The king's
return in 1526 ushered in another period of tolerance, which came to
an abrupt halt following a 'pro-Lutheran' sermon delivered by the
Sorbonne's rector, Nicholas Cop, in November 1533, and the posting of
placards (posters) the following October, which attacked priests and the
Mass. Dozens of Protestant sympathizers were burned, while a coterie of
others, including Lefèvre d'Étaples, Cop, and a young protégé named
Jean Calvin, chose exile.

Calvin (1509–64) grew up as a lawyer's son in a humanist environment
at Noyon and was only eight when the Luther affair began. Following his
father's wishes, Calvin pursued humanistic legal studies at Paris and
graduated in 1531, shortly before his father's death. By that time Calvin
had already joined the pro-reform group in Paris and had helped Cop
draft his sermon. When royal reaction to the Placard Affair threatened
the Parisian reformers, Calvin followed Cop to Basel, a famous centre for
publishing and humanism that had recently instituted a civic reformation
along Zwinglian lines. The young refugee deeply felt the separation
from his "native soil" and envisioned himself achieving France's spiritual
reform as an exile. In 1536, shortly after arriving in Basel, he published
the first of many editions of his most famous work, *The Institutes of the
Christian Religion*, a sprawling summary of his theological views that he
regularly enlarged to reflect his deepening understanding of faith and life.

In the summer of 1536, following his book's appearance, Calvin had
begun planning his return to France when Guillaume Farel invited him
to Geneva, a border town near France with 10,000 inhabitants, politically dominated by its resident bishop and the neighbouring duke of
Savoy. At Geneva, religious reform was a vehicle for the civic regime's
independence from episcopal rule. From the outset, the neighbouring
Swiss canton of Berne had supported Geneva's rebellion militarily and
had aided its religious reform movement by sending Farel in 1533 to

mould the civic Church along Zwinglian lines. Farel coaxed Calvin into settling in Geneva as a preacher and teacher to assist in organizing the civic Church. Immediately, Calvin and Farel pushed for a new Church ordinance designed by Calvin that granted legal authority to the clergy to excommunicate sinners. Geneva's magistrates insisted on the Zwinglian Bernese system, which left such authority in their own hands, and eventually banished the troublesome Farel and Calvin in 1538.

Calvin spent this second exile at Strasbourg, where he worked under the tutelage of Martin Bucer with the refugee French Protestant community. Bucer arranged for Calvin's marriage to an Anabaptist widow and offered guidance in negotiating the intricacies of urban politics. Calvin felt at home at Strasbourg and reluctantly accepted an invitation to return to Geneva following the overthrow of his political enemies. On his return he immediately composed new ecclesiastical ordinances, which Geneva's magistrates accepted with amendments. For the next fourteen years, Calvin relentlessly pushed for his unadulterated model of religious governance and navigated the factional see-sawing of civic affairs. Meanwhile Geneva's social topography rapidly changed, through the influx of refugee printers, nobles, and merchants from France, who brought economic prosperity and broader cultural horizons while polarizing civic life. By 1555, growing French predominance at Geneva led to the electoral defeat of Calvin's principal opponents among the magistrates. The triumphant Calvin purchased Genevan citizenship in 1559 and directed its church until his death in 1564.

As a reformer, Calvin accepted the authority of scripture over tradition and saw the true Church as a spiritual community of God's chosen saints, juxtaposing the true spiritual Church against the corrupt visible Church. Calvin also denied Catholic transubstantiation and Lutheran consubstantiation, arguing for the sacramentarian spiritual presence at communion. Theologically, Calvin's *Institutes* emphasized God's absolute power and humankind's irremediable sinfulness in the "theatre of the world". Though humans belong to God and have a duty to seek God, Calvin denied the power of human will to freely pursue or achieve salvation. Drawing from Augustine of Hippo, Calvin believed that the spiritual community of Christians, the "elect", were justified by God's gift of faith; but unlike Luther, Calvin drew no comfort from God's mercy, for election was always in doubt. God willed that His chosen, the saints, face an internal struggle against human weakness and an external struggle against Satan's machinations in the world, so that life became endless spiritual combat within and without, until God's final judgement.[22]

Calvinism demanded righteous living in ways that Lutheranism did not, and it regulated social life in ways that late medieval pluralistic Catholicism had not. To win the war against Satan in the world, Calvin sought to instil godly public discipline by placing tremendous legal authority in the hands of a consistory comprised of ministers and Church elders. This purely ecclesiastical body assumed disciplinary responsibilities independent of the state. Every citizen, godly and damned, must obey the laws of the Old Testament and law of Christ. To ensure discipline, Calvinism fashioned a political culture which granted the "righteous" authority over others.

Calvin fashioned the Genevan Church as a shelter for spiritual refugees, an incubator for training missionaries, and the nerve centre for a far-flung network of religious cells. Refugees of conscience flocked to Geneva, which became a European centre for printing and the spiritual model of a righteous "city on a hill". As French Protestantism grew in strength, the Gallican Church and the king increased the pressure against religious dissidents. Under the shadow of the stake, lawyers, notaries, doctors, and petty local officials who sympathized with "Reformed" Protestant views attempted to hide their faith by outwardly conforming to Catholic practice. Calvin chastised them as "Nicodemites" and advocated open commitment to the Reformed faith by the elect, under the direction of Genevan-trained ministers. By the early 1550s French Reformed congregations, sheltered by local notables, began to establish consistories. These seeds, scattered in Paris and the provincial towns of France and nurtured from Geneva, would sprout after 1559, producing a religious and political crisis for the kingdom.

Evangelical Reform and the Church of England

Two tendencies dominate literature on the English Reformation. One side argues there was no Reformation but rather a series of political decisions which separated the institutional Church from the papacy for primarily political reasons. Other scholars attempt to draw every possible connection, from Wyclif through the Lollards, to the emergence of evangelical cells, to prove the presence of an underground dissident movement which would animate religious change from below. Whether initiated from above or below, under the Tudor monarchs (1485–1603) a dynamic relationship between religion and politics resulted in the formation of a distinct English Church whose proper rites and structure would be contested into the eighteenth century.[23]

Scholars have long assumed that the Lollard movement provided the social base for English Protestantism, but recent detailed analyses see the movements as discontinuous. Early sixteenth-century Lollardry survived in tiny cells among the rural middling classes. By 1520 Luther's works had come to England and inspired an early evangelical movement among clerics both at the University at Cambridge and in London. The most prominent reformer in these circles was William Tyndale (c.1494–1536), who presided over a group that included later Protestant leaders such as Hugh Latimer (c. 1485–1555) and Thomas Cranmer (1489–1556). When ecclesiastical officials discovered them, these "Lutherans" were forced to recant or face exile. Tyndale fled to Germany to publish an English translation of the New Testament to be smuggled into England. Until 1529, however, English lay authorities, directed by the humanist Chancellor Thomas More, effectively silenced religious reformers.

In 1529 Henry VIII (*1509–47) faced a domestic crisis with broad political implications. His father, Henry VII (*1485–1509), had sought to secure the dynasty's fragile claim to the throne through a marriage alliance with the Spanish monarchs. Honouring his father's dying wish, Henry VIII had married his older brother's widow, Catherine of Aragon, in 1509, fought a costly and disastrous war with France in 1512–13, and fruitlessly sought to marry his own daughter Mary to Charles V. By 1527, desiring a legitimate male heir, Henry sought to end his marriage to the ageing Catherine and wed a courtier named Anne Boleyn. Henry approached the papacy for an annulment, which he realized would anger the Habsburgs. Unfortunately Charles V's recent victory in Italy against papal forces made it impossible for the curia to comply with Henry's wishes. Frustrated, Henry racheted up the pressure by sacking Thomas Wolsey, archbishop of Canterbury and papal cardinal-legate. The king then summoned Parliament to secure legislation against clerical absenteeism and pluralism and to reduce further the scope of ecclesiastical courts. Henry arrested then pardoned a number of high churchmen after extorting a stiff fine levied against the kingdom's churches. By May 1532 Henry had outlawed papal annates and required royal registration of all papal decrees prior to enforcement.

The assault on Rome split Henry's advisors into two parties: a conservative group under Thomas More; and a reforming faction centred around Anne Boleyn and headed by Thomas Cromwell. By early 1533

Boleyn's supporters had won the day, and Cromwell fashioned a set of parliamentary statutes which severed legal ties to Rome. Thomas Cranmer became archbishop of Canterbury, and in May a special court of English churchmen annulled Henry's marriage to Catherine. Before the year's end, Henry's new wife Anne Boleyn had given birth to a daughter, Elizabeth. Henry imposed a loyalty oath to the new religious and political order and executed those who refused to swear allegiance, including Thomas More.

The breach with Rome established the Church of England under royal supremacy but did little to reform institutions, rites, or traditional practices. In 1536 Henry began dissolving hundreds of monasteries and convents and secularizing their properties and revenues. This was less ecclesiastical reform than state aggrandizement, for the confiscated revenues initially poured into royal coffers. Cranmer encouraged preaching from the Bible and shut down some pilgrimage centres, which triggered protests and a full-scale rebellion in 1536–7, known as the Pilgrimage of Grace, but Henry had no clear religious policy and even founded new monasteries while secularizing others. In early 1540 Cromwell's push for closer ties with German Protestants led to a disastrous marriage, Henry's fourth, with Anne of Cleves, and eventually to Cromwell's downfall. When Henry died in late January 1547, the Church of England still lacked a comprehensive doctrinal statement and retained its diocesan and parish structure along with most of its medieval rituals. The only clear difference lay in its legal relationship with the papal curia.

Henry's sickly successor, the young Edward VI (*1547–53), son of Henry's third wife, Jane Seymour, had grown up with his mother's family, who held strong Protestant sympathies. Under the regency of Edward Seymour, duke of Somerset, ecclesiastical reformers gradually inserted some English prayers into the Mass, offered the cup to the laity, and permitted clerical marriage; but there was little will to force these innovations on parish clergy, many of whom followed the old rites. Even Thomas Cranmer's new Prayer Book of 1549 was a cautious mix of traditional and new practices. Somerset's government fell that summer and was replaced by the duke of Northumberland's more aggressively Protestant regency. Before Edward's death in 1553, Northumberland's agents purged the Church of many of its surviving conservatives; and some bishops, such as Ridley in London, pushed aggressively for simplified vestments and ornaments. On Cranmer's invitation, Martin Bucer (1491–1551) spent his final years teaching theology at Oxford, advising the archbishop on ecclesiastical matters. The path to evangelical reform seemed clear, but everything came to a halt when the sixteen-year-old king died.

Northumberland attempted to preserve his power and the reform movement by staging a coup, but Mary (*1553–8), daughter of the divorced Catherine, was crowned as the legitimate heir with widespread popular support. Mary's political identity hinged on undoing her mother's annulment and restoring ties with Roman Catholicism. Though recognizing her legitimacy, Parliament feared reunion with Rome, for many members had acquired monastic properties in lieu of payment for loans to Henry and Edward. Mary also had to deal with animosity between her husband Philip II of Spain, and the papal curia. Compromise seemed possible when the Catholic reformer Reginald Pole was appointment in 1554 simultaneously as cardinal-legate to England and archbishop of Canterbury. Pope Julius III (*1550–5) offered to recognize the rights of those who held monastic lands, but his hard-line successor Paul IV (*1555–9) broke off negotiations and recalled Pole under accusations of heresy. Mary's religious restoration thus remained an English not a Roman Catholic revival. She restored traditional vestments and rituals and persecuted outspoken Protestants, sending nearly 300 dissenters to their deaths. Perhaps 800 others, primarily gentry, students, and ecclesiastical leaders, chose exile in Protestant towns in the Rhine valley and Geneva. The Marian exiles, who would form the backbone of the Protestant movement in early Elizabethan England, harboured a much deeper animosity toward Spain and the popes than the earlier generation of English reformers. The political marriage of Mary and Philip produced no heirs, and when Mary died in November of 1558, the only surviving child of Henry VIII was Anne Boleyn's daughter Elizabeth. The future trajectory of reform for the English Church was very much in doubt.

Catholic Continuities, Catholic Reforms, Catholic Counter-Reforms

Throughout the Middle Ages dissent and internal reform within the Church had operated in tandem, and this dynamic interplay persisted down to the 1550s. Historians of sixteenth-century Catholicism have characterized it within one of two frameworks: Catholic reform or counter-reform.[24] Studies of the Catholic reform focus on internal initiatives of renewal directed at the same problems the early Protestants found so troubling, while viewing at least early Catholic responses to Protestantism as sympathetic or ecumenical. Counter-reformation studies have focused on the Church's defensive posture and later aggression against "Protestant heretics". Both approaches had adherents among sixteenth-century Catholic churchmen and lay leaders, but by the 1550s the papacy would reassert its leadership, defending traditional faith and institutional practices, while its clerical and lay allies began an aggressive assault against Protestantism. In the century after 1550, counter-reform programmes would dominate Catholic ecclesiastical policies.

As we have seen, the late medieval Church had faced many critics, and calls from Catholics for institutional and moral reform continued into the 1540s. Within Italy itself, visionary moralists such as Girolamo Savonarola (1452–98), institutional reformers such as Giles of Viterbo (1469–1532), and political critics such as Francesco Guicciardini (1480–1540) and Niccolò Machiavelli (1469–1527), cried out against the papacy's involvement in courtly splendour and political intrigues. In the Empire, *gravamina* literature (grievance lists compiled for Imperial Diets) hammered on ecclesiastical abuses and, as would Luther, called on lay officials to spearhead religious renewal. Among the humanist treatises Erasmus's *Praise of Folly* parodied clerical vices, while Sebastian Brant's (1457–1521) *Ship of Fools* targeted the Church's trust in human wisdom rather than the true moral wisdom that came from God. Geiler von Kaysersberg's (1455–1510) sermons at Strasbourg were among the many popular calls for moral and spiritual regeneration among all Christians, and in France popular preachers luridly documented clerical immorality amid calls for renewal in Christian life.[25] In England clerical criticism could trace its roots to Wyclif, whose ideas infused texts such as *Piers Plowman* and Chaucer's *Canterbury Tales*. The English humanists Lord Chancellor Mellon of York and John Colet called on Henry VII and Henry VIII to end clerical ignorance and indifference. All of these calls for Catholic reform sought renewal within the established Church.

Unlike Luther and other Protestant reformers, who mocked traditional forms of piety, Catholic moralists understood religious renewal as coming not so much from God's power as from ethical religiosity. Individual private devotion through prayer, meditation, and acts of self-discipline would renew Christian faith, and this personal religiosity characterized the spiritual biographies of sixteenth-century Catholic saints such as Teresa of Ávila, John of the Cross, and Ignatius Loyola. All three experienced their faith as a pursuit of perfection in private meditational and sometimes mystical struggles, yet they responded to the impetus of their renewed faith by public expressions, as did institutional reformers among the Church's elite, such as Cardinal Francisco Ximénes de Cisneros, a pious Observant Franciscan who served in the world as Chancellor for Castile. Another devout ascetic, the English humanist layman Thomas More, critiqued ecclesiastical abuses and, as Lord Chancellor of England, persecuted Protestants and defended the Church to his death.

Collective manifestations of renewed Catholicism also flourished in the early sixteenth century. Lay prayer confraternities, known as oratorics, established hospitals and charitable foundations throughout Italy, and the Oratory of Divine Love at Rome attracted numerous devotees who later would direct Catholic renewal. New or reformed religious orders also sprang up in Italy in the 1520s, such as the Capuchins, who sought to return to the original rule of St Francis. In the 1530s and 1540s a group of Italian churchmen known as the *spirituali* accepted Luther's emphasis on salvation by faith and the importance of scripture alone as the basis of truth. They hoped to infuse their moderate Lutheran values into Roman Catholicism to find an ecumenical middle ground for reconciliation with the Protestants, but their particular vision of reformed Catholicism failed to take hold, and some abandoned the quest while others fled to Protestant churches.[26]

The career of Ignatius Loyola (1491–1556) bridged Catholic reform and counter-reform. Descended from a Basque noble family, Loyola trained to be a warrior and suffered severe leg wounds at the siege of Pamplona in 1521. Recognizing that his military career had ended, the crippled soldier came to the conviction that God wanted him to become a spiritual knight. He took up the ascetic life of a hermit at Manresa, near Barcelona, where he developed a discipline of prayer, self-mortification, and rigorous self-examination, which he eventually codified in a guide book entitled the *Spiritual Exercises*, shared in manuscript among his followers, and eventually published in 1548. The exercises were organized into four week-long stages of meditation designed to discipline and strengthen human will to serve God's will, moving from consideration of sin and its consequences, to reflections on the life and kingdom of Christ, Jesus's passion and death, and finally the Resurrection. The *Spiritual Exercises* recognized Christ's central role in human salvation. Like Calvin, Loyola understood the spiritual nature of both the internal struggle to faith and the external struggle for faith, but his process of coming to God began with individual effort to confront sin and to discipline the will.

Following his retreat and a pilgrimage to the Holy Land, Loyola decided to set up a school for boys at Jerusalem and so he prepared by attending the university at Alcalá, where he was examined by inquisitors and found orthodox. He then travelled to the Sorbonne, earning a Master of Arts degree and attracting a circle of followers who swore an oath to travel with him to the Holy Land and convert the Muslims through teaching. In 1537 the outbreak of war between Venice and the Turks prevented the planned mission, and the group detoured to Rome, where in 1540 Paul III sanctioned the rule of the tiny Society of Jesus. The Jesuits were monks without a monastery. The *Spiritual Exercises* created an interiorized monastery in each of them so that they could pursue their teaching and missionary work in the arena of the world. They swore the traditional monastic vows of poverty, chastity, and obedience, and a fourth vow of obedience to the pope, which would make them not only soldiers for Christ but soldiers for a revitalized papacy once the curia found the will to pursue reforms.

The late medieval conciliarist refrain to reform the Church "in head and members" still seasoned conversations within early sixteenth-century ecclesiastical circles, despite the failure of the council of Basel. Both Emperor Maximilian I and Charles V pressured popes to convene a council. Julius II had attempted to outmanoeuvre Maximilian by assembling a pliant council at the Lateran palace in Rome in 1512, which confirmed papal supremacy, condemned Conciliarism, and sought to curb the growing independence of regional Catholic churches. Luther himself initially invoked a council to resolve his case, but the curia's attention was fully focused on Italian affairs. A brief window of opportunity shut with the death of the Dutch pontiff Hadrian VI (*1522–3), who had close contacts with Erasmus and had tutored Charles V. Hadrian had also spent time in Ximénes de Cisneros's Spain and understood the scope of the Church's problems and the potential of reform. He was thwarted by the labyrinth of patronage and ambition which characterized papal administration.[27] He was succeeded by Clement VII (*1523–34), a Medici, who resumed the costly role of Italian prince, resulting in military defeat and the sack of Rome in 1527. By the end of Clement's disastrous pontificate, even the curia recognized the deteriorating situation, and his successor, Paul III (*1534–49), though cut from the same Renaissance cloth, formed a commission to explore avenues for ecclesiastical reform. Its report, *Counsel Concerning the Reform of the Church* (1537), identified numerous abuses and placed the blame squarely on the papal curia. Protestants cited this report in their own defence, but among Catholic churchmen it offered a blueprint for renewal. Political concerns, however, delayed the convening of a reform council until 1545. We will examine its decisions in the next chapter.

Imperial Politics and the Course of Reform

When Luther confronted Charles V at Worms, the young Emperor headed the Habsburg dynasty, which was the greatest power in Europe. Charles ruled over his Burgundian legacy in the Netherlands as well as the Spanish kingdoms of Castile and Aragon, with claims through these crowns to a colonial empire in the Americas and territories in southern Italy and along the Mediterranean coast of North Africa. His holdings were united only to his person, as noble estates in the various kingdoms zealously defended their traditional rights and liberties. His Imperial crown brought influence but neither territories nor real power, so he governed through his own substantial resources. The hereditary Habsburg lands extended across southern Germany from the Upper Rhine valley to the duchy of Austria, whose eastern and southern borders formed the Christian frontier with the Ottoman Turkish sultanate. The intermittent wars initiated by Süleyman I (*1520–66) would drain Habsburg dynastic resources and threaten the security of Central Europe. Moreover, Charles's possessions in Italy and Burgundy brought him prolonged and bitter conflict with the French Valois kings, who had claims to those territories and viewed the Habsburgs' composite holdings as a noose strangling France. Under the circumstances, the young Emperor's power was diffuse and threatened on numerous fronts. German Protestantism was one of many potential crises.

Having grown up in the Netherlands, Charles had little attachment to Austria, so in 1522 he and his younger brother Ferdinand split the dynastic legacy, with Ferdinand ruling the duchy of Austria. Four years later another stroke of dynastic luck saw Ferdinand elected as king in Bohemia, Moravia, and Hungary following their ruler's death at Mohács. Ferdinand's greatly enhanced possessions now stretched along the Ottoman frontier, and even though Charles felt no strong ties to Austria, his commitment to defend "Christendom" meant that his freedom of action within the Empire depended on peace with the "Turkish menace". Moreover, Francis I coordinated his offences in Italy to match vulnerable periods in Habsburg Imperial politics. The broader political circumstances favoured the Protestants, if they could sustain a united front.

Commitment to Lutheranism by any Imperial estate implied direct resistance to the Emperor's will as expressed in the Edict of Worms of 1521 and to the papal bull of excommunication. In late 1521, war between the Emperor and France along with the death of Pope Leo X gave Frederick the Wise and Luther's early political supporters some breathing room. Efforts by papal and Imperial officials at the Diets at Nuremberg (1522–3 and 1524), and later at Speyer in 1526, to coerce the growing number of evangelical estates to accept prohibitions against ecclesiastical innovations failed, and all that could be resolved was that each estate should govern its own affairs. In 1526 the Turkish victory at Mohács redirected the attentions of Ferdinand of Austria eastward, and the renewal of warfare in Italy, triggered by Clement VII's holy alliance with Milan, Venice, and France against Charles, ensured that the Catholic powers would not work in concert against the Lutheran estates for some time. In the hiatus the evangelical cities and principalities drafted their first Church ordinances. When the Imperial Diet next met, at Speyer in 1529, the evangelical estates felt secure enough to protest against a proposed "unanimous" Recess, which would have enforced the Edict of Worms against Luther.

As we have seen above, the Protestant party found religious and political harmony difficult to sustain as the colloquy at Marburg exposed bitter differences over the Lord's Supper, which were confirmed the following year with the formulation of three rival confessions. By late 1530 Charles, having emerged victorious in Italy, ordered the Protestant estates to submit within six months or face the consequences. With war looming, Philip of Hesse and the electoral duke John of Saxony (*1525–32) could only rally a handful of principalities and cities to the Schmalkaldic League because they insisted that members subscribe to the Augsburg Confession. In 1532 as the deadline neared, a new attack by Süleyman I forced Charles to delay the day of reckoning, so he signed a compromise religious peace at Nuremberg with only those Protestant estates that adhered to the Augsburg Confession, and promised not to proceed against them or any other estate that joined their confessional camp. These terms allowed the Schmalkaldic League to engineer Duke Ulrich's conversion and recovery of Württemberg in 1534 and inspired the Wittenberg accord, which brought Bucer and the South German Protestant cities into the Lutheran alliance by papering over differences between the Tetrapolitan and Augsburg confessions. In response to the consolidation of Protestant forces, the Catholic Imperial estates formed their own defensive alliances at Halle in 1533 and Nuremberg in 1538.

During the early 1540s efforts at reconciliation between the religious parties posed the potential for some sort of ecumenical settlement. Both sides held out hope that a general Church council might resolve differences, and moderate Catholics and Protestants approached Charles V to use his authority to pressure the pope. Martin Bucer and Philip Melanchthon worked assiduously with Catholic leaders such as Julius Pflug, Johann Gropper, and even Johann Eck to identify areas of compromise. The conciliar plan, however, stumbled through a series of false starts, because the Roman curia would not risk abrogating its power or its privileges to a council it couldn't control. No one knew what to expect. German Protestants would not submit to a council which would negate their reforms or declare them heretics. Everyone remembered Hus. Francis I continually meddled in the plan and was reluctant to have French bishops attend a council dominated by his enemy, Charles V. When a council with a clear anti-Protestant bias finally convened at Trent in 1545, German Protestants refused to attend, which triggered war.

Even before the "Schmalkaldic War" had begun, Protestant unity had suffered several setbacks. In 1540 Philip of Hesse had embarrassed himself as a bigamist whose clandestine second marriage had received the blessings of Luther, Melanchthon, and Bucer. Philip's Protestant allies abandoned him on this matter, and the Emperor used the landgrave's weakened position to extort concessions, including the re-Catholicization in 1541 of the duchy of Jülich-Cleves. The following year, Philip and the elector duke John-Frederick (*1532–54) of Saxony invaded Braunschweig-Wolfenbüttel ostensibly to defend its Protestant towns, but they afterwards established permanent garrisons, placing the towns under their protection. When it became clear that the council at Trent would not reconcile the confessional parties, the Emperor negotiated separate treaties with individual Catholic and Protestant princes and in 1546, the year of Luther's death, declared war on Philip, John-Frederick, and the remnants of their Schmalkaldic League. The short war ended in military disaster for the Protestants with Imperial forces capturing Wittenberg and other strongholds.

In 1548 the victorious Charles attempted to use the Imperial Diet at Augsburg as a forum to restore peace. Since he had previously signed treaties with the Protestant elector of Brandenburg and with John-Frederick's cousin Moritz (*1541–53), the Lutheran ruler of ducal Saxony, it would be impossible to demand a Catholic restoration. Even the Catholic estates were wary of granting the Emperor too much religious leverage for fear of the political gains he would acquire. In the end Charles issued an "Interim" (the Imperial Clarification of Religion) on his own authority. It prohibited further Protestant expansion, required the restoration of certain Catholic forms of worship, and sanctioned enclaves for Catholic religious services in Protestant cities, whose constitutions were revised to eliminate guild influence. Martin Bucer and other leading Protestant reformers went into exile, and John-Frederick lost his electoral office, which passed to the ambitious Moritz. Charles went so far as to forcibly re-Catholicize Constance and absorb it into Austria, but neither the Emperor nor other Catholic princes had the sustained will to enforce the Interim. Promises of French support sparked a new round of wars between Charles V and the Protestant princes, who saw the Interim as a direct religious and political threat. Finally, in 1555, the religious peace of Augsburg was signed by the Emperor and all Imperial estates. It legalized the Lutheran Confession of Augsburg and granted territorial rulers, though not explicitly civic magistrates, the right to determine the religion of their subjects. Zwinglian and Calvinist churches would be illegal, and Catholic ecclesiastical territories were to remain Catholic. The religious peace of Augsburg recognized the political success of the Protestant Reformation and the permanence of Luther's break with Rome. It also set the framework for a century of confessional tension and religious warfare.

Although political issues had not motivated most early evangelicals, the Reformation dramatically weakened the institutional Church even where Protestantism failed. Everywhere a new balance of power between Church and state evolved. In Germany, Switzerland, the Low Countries, and for a time in England reformers posited a communal model for all godly political relations. In South Germany the princes, aristocracy, and civic magistrates crushed or deflected radical social evangelism in 1525. The evangelical goal of fashioning a community of believers, however, did not require the end of hierarchical political relations, and many reformers eventually called on the princes and magistrates to bring godly order. In some regions the territorial church would become an important branch of government, while in others confessional tensions remained without undermining the established political order. Furthermore, Calvinist and Anabaptist ecclesiologies persisted in demonstrating that religious and social discipline did not require the traditional models of political relations. Luther's personal religious crisis had shattered the façade of Christian unity and exacerbated political tensions. Over the next century, ongoing Reformation would test the political stability of many kingdoms and fuel civil and dynastic wars.

4

REFORMATION AND RELIGIOUS
WAR, 1550–1650

After 1550 the European Reformation's central battlefields spread beyond the German-speaking regions, as communities of belief galvanized into confessional camps and the political cost of religious division became clear. Religious wars in France, the Netherlands, Central Europe, and England demonstrated the destructive potential of the new religious and political mix. Catholic, Lutheran, and Calvinist leaders drew up clear statements of "orthodox" beliefs referred to as "confessions", developed ecclesiastical systems to ensure discipline among the faithful, and forged alliances with political authorities to foster or force consensus. Confessional solidarity encouraged intolerance of religious minorities, but it also provided those minorities with the self-discipline necessary to resist pressures to conform. Within many states the ruler's power as head of the Church led to the integration of ecclesiastical institutions and personnel into government, broadening the state's bureaucratic base and increasing the scope of the ruler's patronage. Nevertheless, official churches also became sites for factional squabbling among elites, and provincial resistance to centralization.

The mix of the centripetal forces of Church-building and state-building with the centrifugal forces of regionalism and conflicting confessional identities stained the century after 1550 with religious bloodshed. Everywhere, the close association of faith and power raised the ante at each dramatic confrontation. Even in day-to-day affairs, officially sanctioned churches acted as the moral arm of the state through control of the pulpit, religious imagery, and the rote formulas of catechetical instruction. In fashioning men and women of conscience, ecclesiastical officials helped internalize the social discipline of modern citizens, but they also uncovered a complex and deeply embedded system of popular beliefs which stubbornly resisted "Christianization" along reformed guidelines. Every-where authoritative force inevitably generated resolved opposition, stiffened by economic misery and social anger.

The Price Revolution and Economic Crisis

From the outbreak of the "Luther affair" down to the end of the seventeenth century, perhaps 85 to 90 per cent of all Europeans lived in the countryside and engaged primarily in agricultural production. Their individual circumstances were extremely diverse due to differences in crops, land-holding systems, collective rights, and lordship, though as noted in Chapter 1, most peasants worked a plot of land, with the labouring resources provided by members of their household. The demographic crisis of the later fourteenth century had played out by 1450, at which point growth began anew and continued unabated until the end of the sixteenth century. In all, Europe's population rose from 52 million to 78 million. By the 1580s many regions had achieved population densities comparable to the decades before the Black Death, and food production could not keep up with the unrestrained growth. In the 1590s a series of murderous famines ushered in a century of plague, dearth, and warfare that would depopulate many communities and regions. By 1700 the continent's aggregate population stood at 83 million, an increase of only 5 million for the entire century. The prolonged misery made the seventeenth century a particularly stressful period for Europe's peasants and poor, though conditions varied from region to region. Central Europe's population stagnated, while the Mediterranean basin and Eastern Europe experienced decline. Only the British Isles, Scandinavia, France, and the Low Countries saw demographic growth.[1] These regions were predominantly though not entirely Protestant, and a distinct north-western European pattern of marriages, marked by younger couples and personal choice, may have fostered the population increase. Overall, however, variant factors of mortality, in particular war zones, along with traditional family structures, inheritance patterns, climate, and ecology affected population trends and distribution.[2]

Most European peasant communities were organized into households, normally under male heads. The house physically and metaphorically sheltered its residents. For example, the German legal principle of "house peace" (*Hausfrieden*) encompassed everyone within the dry space bounded by the drops that fell from the eaves during a rainstorm. Residents often hung protective herbs from those same eaves as a prophylactic against harmful witchcraft.[3] Domestic peace, however, was relative, for the male householder controlled the disposition of resources and claimed authority over wife, children, and servants, which he could secure by violence if necessary. Protestant and Catholic models of the godly household fortified male dominance.[4] Household membership determined a person's status through the household's collective rights to the land and its fruits. Peasant householders negotiated a tricky balance between providing for the personal security of their offspring and maintaining the family's land as a self-sufficient unit. In parts of England, western France, and south-western Germany tradition called for the division of economic rights among at least the male offspring. Elsewhere the head of the household, in some cases the widowed mother, dictated marriage and labour strategies for the children in order to sustain the household's economic viability, often measured in terms of its honour.

As the basic building blocks of rural society, households assembled into village communes that ranged from hamlets of five or six households to larger settlements of sixty or seventy units, bound together by the mortar of communal rights. Village assemblies, prominent in Spain, France, Switzerland, and southern Germany, recognized all householders with sufficient land to qualify for full rights. Participants deliberated over the use of communal resources, regulated collective work, and levied fines against those who violated custom. Unavoidable familiarity, life-long rivalries, and scarce resources meant that envy and violence were common features of daily life. Suspicious of outside adjudication, villagers practised their own form of collective discipline. The younger unmarried men sometimes assembled in "youth abbeys" to shame violators of marital and sexual norms in noisy public rituals called *charivari*. Women employed gossip and rumour to regulate deviant behaviour among themselves and the men. Catholic priests and Protestant pastors were householders within the villages, with economic rights to communal goods, yet they were also outsiders who represented the distant but real power of the Church and state. This dual status was the source of tremendous tensions and animosity, which often surfaced in religious contexts.[5]

The oppressive social weight of feudal lordship varied across the continent. In Eastern Europe where labourers were scarce, the nobles, with the support of the rulers, began to ratchet up demands on their peasants to the point where a newly instituted "second serfdom" bound the formerly free peasants to their villages and their lords.[6] To secure the new social order, seigneurial officials cooperated in returning run-aways and punishing resisters. In Western and Southern Europe, many of the visible vestiges of medieval feudalism had disappeared. Here the majority of peasants rented land from lords and could bequeath these contractual relationships as they wished. English peasants dispatched their obligations with the payment of their annual rent, while in southern France and Italy sharecropping predominated, where the lord gave the peasant a share of the seed and livestock and the peasant returned a comparable portion at the harvest. Elsewhere peasants paid rents along with a bundle of specific obligations such as fees for transferring property, or labour duties on the lord's land. Most transactions involved payments in kind rather than money. With enough land, reasonable harvests, and demographic luck, peasant households fared well enough. Unfortunately, cash-strapped lords sought to extract as much as possible from contracts with tenants and from their remaining seigneurial rights as the cost of "living nobly" skyrocketed. The fiscal demands of Church and state also grew continuously as tithing survived even in Protestant ter-ritories and states assessed new taxes in coin. Though formal serfdom had ended in much of Western Europe, the nobility, dressed in the robes of ecclesiastical or royal officers, still fed off the fruits of peasant labour as even "free" tenant farmers often realized only half of what they produced.[7]

The population growth in the sixteenth century increased demand on the agrarian economy's most valuable commodity, land. Everywhere hungry peasants ploughed marginal soils that had remained untilled for over two centuries. The crops produced from these poorer fields could not meet the growing demand; and grain, the staple of everyone's diet, became increasingly expensive. By the 1560s silver from the Americas inflated prices further. Scholars have traditionally associated the sixteenth-century "price revolution" with the influx of silver, but American bullion was one of many exacerbating factors.[8] Through the course of the century, beginning well before the increase in money supply, the price of grain rose by 400 per cent, doubling the increase in wages since demographic growth glutted the market with under-employed and hungry labourers. The rise in prices allowed some tenant farmers, through cunning, hard work, or luck, to become wealthy enough to form a peasant elite with large houses, full granaries, and servants. They assumed the local administrative offices associated with lordship and became part of the forces of oppression in the village.[9] In contrast to these richer householders, the majority of villagers fell into debt and dependence. Some held on to small plots of land which could not support them, offered their labour to wealthier neighbours, or took on supplemental work as spinners and weavers in the expanding rural cloth industry. Many others held no land at all and either migrated to the cities or struggled to survive in their cottages by pursuing an "economy of makeshifts", begging, borrowing, and working wherever or however they could.

Rural impoverishment accelerated in the early seventeenth century. In England the proportion of householders possessing only a garden rose from 11 per cent in 1560 to 40 per cent in 1640, while in south-western France the number of peasants unable to feed themselves without additional income doubled between the late fourteenth and the early seventeenth centuries.[10] The distance between the rich and poor expressed itself in many ways, both visibly in terms of housing, diet, and clothing and invisibly in terms of honour and status. The wealthier villagers would most closely and fully associate themselves with the new religious regime by internalizing and enforcing the values of good order, industry, and sobriety. They were more likely to be literate and thus more likely to be committed to the bible-based faith in Protestant areas; nevertheless, official churches rarely recruited their rural pastors from among the peasantry.

Demographic growth had also triggered a growth in the continent's market systems which affected both the great cities engaged in the urban trade network and the smaller central market towns.[11] Sixteenth-century townsfolk were generally more educated and literate than peasants, which made them prominent among the earliest supporters of Protestantism. Towns had greater social complexity and more economic resources than the countryside, yet the foundation of civic life also rested on productive households. At the peak of urban society, the merchant oligarchs were initially overshadowed by the arrival of ennobled officials for the burgeoning state, who now settled in towns that had become regional administrative centres. An expanding credit market for state and personal finance soon integrated noble and bourgeois elites.[12] Beneath the highest levels of urban society, most trades were organized into fraternities (guilds) of master craftsmen, who oversaw all aspects of production and communal craft life. Guilds protected their members by enforcing market monopolies, restricting the admission of new apprentices and masters, and defending corporate honour. Guildsmen tended to be conservative, and many were drawn to the Protestant message because it emphasized patriarchal domestic authority as an added ideological prop to the gender hierarchy of the traditional workshop. In addition to the craftsmen, agricultural labourers, gardeners, and vineyard workers played a significant economic role in even the largest towns and often banded together in their own "guilds". At the lowest levels of civic society, an impoverished and growing underclass comprising anywhere from 10 to 50 per cent of the residents, pursued their own "economy of makeshifts" built on religious charity and piecework.

The price revolution threatened the security of the guild economy and swelled the ranks of the urban poor and those reliant on wage labour. Some merchants grew rich in the new market, which polarized civic society even more dramatically than the countryside. Shifting patterns in long-distance trade and new commodities imported from overseas transformed some traditional centres of production into ghost towns. In some industries, such as silk-weaving in Antwerp and Lyons, independent weavers came to rely on the financial skills of entrepreneurs to market their products, and slid into dependence and poverty. Where guilds resisted the loss of control, buyers looked to neighbouring villages for cheaper labour. Some guilds prohibited new masters to preserve market share. With the possibility of becoming their own masters and heading a household being closed to them, journeymen developed their own associative culture, with a misogynist streak directed at widows and other women who sought to support themselves through collective work. Journeymen were also volatile sources of religious unrest. As conditions deteriorated, the urban poor became a central issue, and Protestant magistrates diverted traditional ecclesiastical revenues to poor relief. Both Catholic and Protestant communities centralized the collection of alms and supervised poor boxes. Officials also prohibited hoarding in times of dearth and distinguished between the indigenous poor, deserving charity, and vagrant or sturdy beggars, who were often whipped in public and sent to their home villages.[13]

Tridentine Catholicism and Counter-Reformation

As noted in Chapter 3, threads of reform and renewal laced the fabric of early sixteenth-century Catholicism, but as the century progressed, the struggle against Protestants came to dominate reforming sensibilities among Catholic leaders. Meanwhile Protestant reformers benefitted from the ongoing crisis in papal moral leadership along with the growing regionalization of religious and political loyalties among Catholic elites.

The struggle between the old faith and the new was waged town by town, duchy by duchy, kingdom by kingdom, and lay authorities normally had the final say over the confessional profile of established churches.

From the perspective of the papal curia, the spread of Protestantism appeared as a string of stunning setbacks. Beginning in 1517, down into the early 1530s, Luther's revolt seemed to sweep through the Empire, then into Scandinavia and the German-speaking communities of Eastern Europe. At roughly the same time, the Zwinglian movement spread from Zurich to other Swiss and South German towns. By the 1550s Zwinglianism had melded into Calvinism, which from its base in Geneva nourished enclaves in France, the Netherlands, Scotland, England, Hungary, and Poland. Papal relations with the English Church were as tenuous as the dynastic succession. Though hopes for reconciliation with German Protestants peaked at the colloquy at Regensburg in 1541, common ground proved too limited. The Italian popes also confronted the bitter rivalry between the Habsburgs and Valois, Europe's powerful Catholic dynasties, which made a united Catholic effort against the Protestants impossible. In this dynastic struggle Italy itself was a principal battlefield, and the popes often favoured political expediency over the crying need for religious reform, which had to begin at Rome.

In 1545 under pressure from Emperor Charles V, Pope Paul III finally convened a general Church council at Trent, a tiny ecclesiastical principality that bordered Austria and Italy. The Council of Trent would define doctrine and institutional practice for Roman Catholicism for the next four centuries, but none of its first delegates anticipated such a historical legacy. They looked backward to Constance and Luther rather than forward to the future of their faith. Charles V wanted the council to reform the Church in order to "shut the mouth of the Protestants", but Paul III favoured a doctrinal response to Luther's "heresy" with ecclesiastical reforms as a secondary concern.[14] The papal agenda won out. The vast majority of the inaugural delegates were Italians, and papal legates quickly secured approval for a vote by head, in reaction to the "national" voting blocks employed at Constance. The predominance of Italians at all the sessions, and the decision to push forward at each new session without revisiting earlier decrees, soon ensured that papal authority within the Church would not be challenged and that reform would only proceed as far as papal will deemed necessary.

At the first sessions, from 1545 to 1547, the delegates surveyed doctrine and delineated the boundaries between Protestant "heresy" and Tridentine Catholicism. Denying Protestant claims that justification

by faith through scripture was the sole vehicle to faith, the council recon-
firmed the importance of both scripture *and* tradition within the "true"
Church. The officials at Trent reaffirmed papal claims to sole authority
in interpreting scripture, based on "uninterrupted succession" from the
apostles. The council also upheld the doctrinal validity of the flawed
Vulgate Bible, which Catholic biblicists would eventually revise in 1592.
In opposition to Protestant beliefs on the fundamental corruption of
human nature and its total dependence on God's mercy, drawn from
Augustine of Hippo, Tridentine Catholicism reiterated the scholastic
view enshrined in the works of Thomas Aquinas that human nature
possesses the potential for good or evil and that individuals can choose
to work toward their own salvation. The delegates also validated all
seven sacraments, reasserting the sacerdotal power of the priesthood
and thus the clergy's special place as a distinct order in the institutional
Church.

Tensions between political agendas and needed ecclesiastical reforms
framed every session and decision at Trent. Following Charles V's
victory over the Lutheran Schmalkaldic League at Mühlberg in 1547,
Paul III recalled the council from Trent to Bologna in papal territories
to "protect" it from the Emperor's influence. The assembly at Bologna
was short-lived, and the delegates soon disbanded. When the council
reconvened at Trent in 1551, ecumenical advocates among the Protestants and Catholics were disappointed by Pope Julius III's (*1550–5)
unwillingness to revisit earlier decisions. The delegates pushed ahead,
confirming that the Holy Eucharist, transubstantiated during a Latin
Mass by a sacramentally anointed priest, was the means by which the
grace from Christ's sacrifice on the cross was transmitted to the faithful.
Commitment to transubstantiation eliminated any possibility of compromise with the Protestants, and reform-minded Catholic leaders
searching for a middle ground with the Protestants had to abjure or
submit. When political fortunes turned against Charles V in 1552, the
second period of conciliar sessions ended.

In 1561 the council gathered at Trent for a third time in a very different
political environment. Charles V had died, and the Habsburg territorial
legacy had been split between his son Philip II (*1556–98) of Spain and
his brother, Emperor Ferdinand I (*1556–64) of Austria. The peace of
Augsburg had granted legal recognition to Lutheranism within the
Empire. France was on the verge of religious civil war with a child king,
and Elizabeth I (*1558–1603) had restored the independence of the
English Church, which was assuming an increasingly Protestant posture.

Finally the reigning pope, Pius IV (*1559–65), was a zealous and auto-
cratic man who refused to allow the delegates to address any papal
reforms. The council outlawed the sale of indulgences but sanctioned
belief in Purgatory and the "treasury of merit" accumulated by good
deeds, which Christians could draw on through prayers for the souls of
the "faithfully departed". The council condemned absenteeism and
pluralism, though it turned a blind eye to officials in the Papal States
who were still paid from revenues of non-Italian bishoprics and abbacies
they never visited. Tridentine decrees encouraged resident bishops to
establish seminaries to raise the educational level of parish priests, who
were to remain celibate, and the bishops as "delegates of the Apostolic
see" were expected to conduct regular parish visitations throughout
their diocese.

When its work was completed, the Council of Trent had finalized the
separation between Catholicism and the Protestant "heretics" and
had confirmed longstanding traditions in Catholic faith and Church
governance.

The delegates at Trent had not tampered with the system of concordats,
so implementation of their decrees would require the sanction of
Europe's Catholic rulers. Philip II recognized the new order immediately
because none of it undermined his control over the Spanish Church.
The kings of Portugal and Poland soon followed, but the French
monarchs, faced with religious civil war, delayed formal recognition
indefinitely. Furthermore, the religious peace of Augsburg precluded
formal acceptance by the confessionally mixed Imperial Diet, while the
new Emperor, Maximilian II (*1564–76), was personally ambivalent.

Nevertheless, the hemorrhaging of Catholic principalities and kingdoms
to Protestantism had come to an end. In the ensuing decades the papacy
standardized the Latin liturgy for the Mass and other sacraments, composed a new Roman catechism, and called on all parish clergy to follow
the Protestant lead and maintain parish registers to identify Catholics by
recording their baptisms, marriages, and burials. The Roman curia
quickly established a seminary to serve as a model for other bishops; but
with the reinforcing of the bishops' authority within their dioceses, the
progress of Tridentine Catholicism in much of Europe would depend on
the pace of episcopal initiatives.[15] Cardinal-archbishop Carlo Borromeo
(*1564–84) of Milan devoted his energies to the practical application of
Tridentine Catholicism in his archdiocese and became a model and
saint. In France and Spain, however, where monarchs controlled diocesan
appointments, the success of reform programmes rested on the spiritual

sensitivities of royal patronage. Even where conditions were favourable it would take at least a generation to replace the existing episcopate, and longer to train the new parish clergy. Diocesan seminaries proved particularly difficult to realize, for their foundations required episcopal financial support. In France, for example, there were few seminaries before 1640. The late and often halting beginnings of Catholic parish registers were symptomatic of the delayed spread of Tridentine practices into the European parish system. With the medieval benefice system relatively untouched, the unequal distribution of income and inadequacy of pastoral training remained a problem long after Trent.[16]

Independent of the conciliar decrees, the papacy instituted two counter-reform instruments, the Papal Inquisition and the Index, to curb the dissemination of Protestant ideas. Papal inquisitions had fought individual medieval heresies but were not permanent fixtures. In 1478 Ferdinand and Isabella of Aragon and Castile had established the Spanish Inquisition with papal approval. Spain's inquisitors initially devoted their prosecutorial energies in an antisemitic assault on "new Christians" (*Conversos*), whose Jewish ancestors had undergone forced baptism in the late fourteenth century. The inquisitors suspected the *Conversos* of deceit, and these "unclean" (*marranos*) Christians suffered brutal persecution throughout the 1530s. The Spanish Inquisition also prosecuted Protestants, *Moriscos* (Muslims), homosexuals, and other "non-conformists", serving as the moral guardian of Hispanic Catholicism. When Philip II attempted to export the oppressive tribunal to his domains in Italy and the Netherlands, he met stiff resistance.[17] The revived Papal Inquisition became a permanent court, which operated in Italy investigating heretical beliefs, some Protestant but others unrelated to Protestantism, such as the *benedanti* who waged night battles to protect rural communities from witchcraft.[18] The roots of the Papal Index of 1559 lay in medieval compilations of censured writings, and Paul IV's Index of Prohibited Books included the works of Protestant reformers and Machiavelli's *The Prince*. Like other papal initiatives the Index was not recognized in all Catholic territories, but it clearly reflected the new attitude of constraint and repression cherished by the Counter-reform papacy.

Though the concordats and the central role of the bishops meant that Catholic renewal and counter-reform required the cooperation of regional political and religious authorities, one group sought to represent papal interests throughout Europe and the world: the Jesuits. They had served as papal advisors at Trent and would insist over the next two centuries on the papacy's centrality in Catholic life, which often put them at odds with lay authorities. Despite the fact that the first five Jesuit vicar-generals were Spanish subjects, Philip II found them too independent and pro-papal, though he tolerated their work in his territories and colonies. King Henry IV (*1589–1610) of France banned them from his domains between 1594 and 1603 following an assassination attempt, and officials at Venice expelled them in 1606 when Pope Paul V (*1605–21) placed the city under interdict.

The Jesuits' greatest contributions to Catholic renewal and counter-reform came from their commitment to higher education and their involvement in overseas missions. Beginning with the establishment of their first school, in Sicily in 1548, Jesuit colleges trained laymen for civil life, though some students later joined the order. By 1615 over 280 Jesuit colleges dotted the continent from Transylvania to the Azores, and many bishops relied on local colleges in place of costly seminaries to train parish clergy. Jesuit missionaries also spread Tridentine Catholicism from Peru to China.

As practitioners of Ignatius Loyola's *Spiritual Exercises*, Jesuits championed the human will's search for salvation, as opposed to Protestant views that emphasized the essential role of divine mercy through the gift of grace. In an attempt to reconcile human and divine will, the Jesuit Luis de Molina wrote the *Concordance of Free Will with the Gift of Grace* in 1588, which drew the awkward conclusion that God gives grace to those who He knows in advance will choose it. This "probabilist" view stimulated a counter-argument from a Flemish bishop and theologian, Cornelius Jansen (1585–1638), who like Luther and Calvin emphasized human unworthiness for salvation. Though flirting with Protestantism, the Jansenist movement remained Catholic due to elite patronage, particularly in France where it was centred at the Parisian convent of Port-Royal, whose nuns came from the kingdom's leading families. Jansenists imagined themselves members of a pure and elite spiritual church, for which they proved their worth through discipline and rigour. The papacy eventually condemned several Jansenist propositions in 1653, but well-placed lay guardians in France and in the duchy of Savoy continued to protect the movement. Throughout the seventeenth and eighteenth centuries, Jesuits and Jansenists would accuse one another of heresy. The coexistence of these strikingly different forms of Tridentine Catholicism reflected the political and religious tensions still at work within the Catholic Church. Divisiveness among Catholics could be problematic, but confessional divisions within a kingdom were normally deadly.

French Wars of Religion

In the mid-1540s, despite early stirring at Meaux and dramatic gestures such as the day of the Placards, Protestantism seemed moribund in France. Similar reform efforts in the Spanish kingdoms and Italy had dissolved or fallen into silence as a result of official opposition. The Concordat of Bologna (1516) granted Francis I rights of appointment over the kingdom's bishoprics and abbacies, making the Gallican Church a valuable reservoir for royal patronage. The king also received an annual gift (*don gratuit*) from the clergy in lieu of taxes. Moreover, he had no personal incentive to engineer a legal separation from Rome as had occurred in England. Beyond the frontiers Protestant printing houses at Anvers, Strasbourg, and Basel disseminated biblical translations and evangelical tracts, while occasional arrests in France produced dramatic martyrdoms. Calvin and others had fled the kingdom; and though Geneva had become an important refuge for French Protestants, Calvin's authority there was still very much in question until 1557. Following the death of Francis I in 1547, his son Henry II (*1547–59) escalated pressure against French Protestants by establishing a special tribunal (*chambre ardente*, or "burning chamber") within the Parlement of Paris, the kingdom's central court of appeals. Despite its reputation, enshrined in Protestant martyrologies, the "burning chamber" executed only thirty-seven individuals, roughly 7 per cent of those accused, and evidence from other courts demonstrates even greater tolerance.[19] Thus royal oppression was limited, and Henry's wars with Charles V encouraged this "most Catholic" king to negotiate alliances with German Lutherans.

In the 1550s pockets of Protestant believers, whom Catholics called Huguenot – a French transliteration of the Swiss "confederates" (*Eidgenossen*) – began to appear all over France, as worshippers gathered in houses, barns, and fields for preaching, scripture reading, and hymn singing. In his *Institutes* Calvin distinguished between a "seed church" of believers, with no resident minister (*église plantée*), and a "cultivated church" with a preaching pastor who dispensed sacraments, taught from a catechism, and exercised moral discipline (*église dressée*). To fill the growing need for pastors, Calvin dispatched over 200 from among the refugee community at Geneva along with thousands of books and hymnals, yet by 1560 over 1,200 Protestant communities existed in France, calling to worship perhaps 10 per cent of the population. This gap should caution generalizations about the degree of control over the Huguenots exercised by Calvin. Communities with Genevan-trained pastors remained the minority. The sudden growth of French Protestantism had instead fostered autonomy among individual communities, and the Huguenots built their organization church by church, from the bottom up. Pastors and elders of the local churches assembled in consistories to discuss discipline, and the consistories in turn sent representatives to provincial and national synods, the first of which convened at Paris in 1559. In 1571 the national synod at La Rochelle attracted Dutch and Genevan representatives and drew up a confession with forty articles that guides French Protestant communities to this day. Nevertheless, for a clandestine religious minority in opposition to the official Church, such public displays of solidarity were potentially dangerous, and the French "Reformed" Church, as they preferred to call themselves, operated as a set of localized cells held together by regular meetings of pastors, called presbyteries.

Scholars estimate that close to two million men and women had joined Huguenot churches by 1560, with communities concentrated in Normandy and in a broad south-western crescent from La Rochelle on the Atlantic to the Dauphiné.[20] Huguenots formed a majority in the urban centres of Montpelier, Nîmes, and La Rochelle, but elsewhere theirs was a minority church. It was also a French faith, with preaching, hymns, and scriptures in French, making it inaccessible for the rural and urban poor who spoke local patois. One could find Huguenots among princes of the blood, such as the Bourbons, and among noblemen, lawyers, merchants, and artisans, with support concentrated among small-town notables. Though the congregations depended heavily on elite protection, Protestantism attracted many adherents among middling urban householders. Women such as Jeanne D'Albret, mother of Henri de Bourbon, played critical roles in spreading Calvinist ideas among the nobility and probably elsewhere, but Church leadership remained exclusively male.

Early modern religion was a corporate experience informed by rituals. The decision to embrace this illegal faith separated Reformed believers from their Catholic neighbours and kin, and this alienation often expressed itself in acts of desecration. Huguenots would occasionally disrupt Mass, dramatically refuse to reverence statues or the Eucharist when these were displayed for Corpus Christi processions, and sometimes break into and desecrate churches with consecrated hosts as particular targets. Catholics responded by exacting immediate vigilante justice on individuals who threatened the delicate relationship between God and daily life. In a world in which the social order rested on secure relations with the spiritual, the insecurity generated by conflicting views on faith quickly escalated into violence.[21]

By 1560 the Huguenots had become too numerous to purge by persecution. A strong king might have negotiated a *modus vivendi* between the confessions, but the untimely death of Henry II from a jousting accident in 1559 elevated his young son, Francis II (*1559–60), to the throne. Francis had recently married Mary Queen of Scots, and was under the influence of her mother's ultra-Catholic French family, the Guises. Francis's death from illness fifteen months later left the throne to his ten-year-old brother Charles IX (*1560–74). Law required a regency to govern in the boy's name, headed by the first prince of the blood, the Huguenot Antoine de Bourbon, king of Navarre and duke of Béarn. Charles's mother Catherine de' Medici, however, sought to play off the bitter rivalry between the Catholic Guise and Calvinist Bourbon families to retain her influence. Seeking common religious ground, Catherine encouraged a colloquy at Poissy in 1561 between Catholic and Huguenot theologians, led by Calvin's successor at Geneva, Théodore de Bèze, which only succeeded in exposing the deep gulf between the faiths. Nonplussed, Catherine pushed through the Edict of St-Germain in January 1562, which permitted unarmed Huguenot assemblies to worship outside of walled towns and ordered both parties to avoid violence. In March, Duke François de Guise ambushed a Huguenot service at Vassy, killing seventy worshippers and precipitating the first of eight religious civil wars.

The French Wars of Religion saw few pitched battles but plenty of bloodshed. Though powerful noble clans headed both parties and pursued political agendas, scholars have recently re-emphasized the wars' religious animus, generated by two distinct world views about how one honoured God. Acts of violence generated vengeful retaliation as memories of past injustices sanctioned vicious murders and the ritual mutilation of men, women, and children, as holy acts. In the summer of 1572 Catherine de' Medici made a new attempt at reconciliation through an arranged marriage between the Huguenot Henri de Bourbon, Antoine's son and successor, and her daughter, Princess Marguerite. During the wedding celebration, there was a botched assassination attempt by the Guises against the Huguenot military leader Gaspard de Coligny. Fearing retaliation, the young king, Charles IX, authorized a religious riot, which led to the slaughter of perhaps 3,000 Huguenots gathered at Paris for the wedding, and thousands more elsewhere.[22] The St Bartholomew's day (24 August) massacres would haunt the king and his family, ending all hope of religious peace. The slaughter alienated moderate Catholics, who henceforth would be wary of Guise fanaticism, and brought home to the Huguenots that they could not win over the monarch and convert the kingdom. The massacres' brutality also generated numerous Protestant tracts advocating righteous resistance to unrighteous rulers. These resistance theories would be applied by other religious rebels in other contexts.

Following his wedding Henri de Bourbon, a virtual prisoner at the palace, "converted" to Catholicism. In 1574 Henry III (*1574–89), who had previously been elected king of Poland, succeeded his brother Charles, and returned to France. Two years later Henri de Bourbon fled to his own kingdom of Navarre and announced his return to Protestantism. As Huguenot forces rallied in Navarre, Henry III negotiated a new peace that granted toleration to Huguenots in areas where local authorities had already accepted them, except in Paris. By this time the wars had confessionally "cleansed" large sections of France, and the treaty confined the Huguenots to fortified zones in the south and west. Peace might have endured had Henry III produced a legitimate heir, but with the death of his last brother in 1584, the heir apparent became Henri de Bourbon. Fearing the religious power of a Huguenot king, Duke Henri de Guise and his supporters formed a Catholic League, signed a treaty with Spain, and pressured Henry III into declaring war against Henri de Bourbon. This "War of the Three Henris" engaged German and Swiss Protestants, Catholic Spain, and the French religious factions in a lengthy and debilitating struggle. Early victories by League forces brought Henri de Guise to Paris, where in 1588 a popular demonstration, the Day of the Barricades, proclaimed the Parisians' desire for the Catholic duke to succeed Henry III, who had fled the capital. The Guise family now controlled north-eastern France, but their ties with Spain troubled many potential allies among French Catholic elites. The Spanish Armada's surprising defeat that same year emboldened Henry III to have the duke and his brother, the cardinal of Lorraine, assassinated, triggering open rebellion among the Catholic Leaguers. The king's own assassination shortly afterwards did little to placate the rebels, for the Huguenot Henri de Bourbon declared himself king of France. It would take the new king, Henry IV (*1589–1610), nine years and a second conversion to Catholicism to pacify his kingdom and secure his throne.

In an edict delivered at Nantes in 1598, Henry IV granted full amnesty to the rebels and restoration of all Catholic property and worship. He reaffirmed the right of Huguenot nobles to private worship on their estates and conceded Protestant worship in localities where churches had existed in 1597. Finally, the settlement prohibited exclusion from education or office on grounds of religion. The Edict of Nantes created a confessionally divided state, with a Catholic king protecting Protestant churches. It also bolstered the privileges of France's Protestant nobility and notables, who had their own assemblies, fortresses, and ambassadors at court. Religious animosity did not disappear in the provinces because of royal decree. In Paris formal conversion to Catholicism often furthered Huguenot careers in royal service. Further down the social ladder conversions occurred in both directions.[23] The fragility of the Huguenots' position became evident in 1621, when Louis XIII's (*1610–43) decision to re-Catholicize the county of Béarn, where the edict did not apply, reignited a religious civil war that dragged on until 1628. Royal forces eventually suppressed Huguenot resistance centred on the fortified towns of La Rochelle, Nîmes, and Montauban, which were taken by siege. The Peace of Alès in 1629 stripped the Huguenot elite of their privileges and ended any dreams of a separate Huguenot state in south-western France. In the ensuing decades French Protestants became an increasingly isolated religious minority, whose legal survival depended on royal sufferance. The revocation of the Edict of Nantes was simply a matter of time.

Elizabethan Church Settlement and Civil War

In England the legacy of Mary Tudor's brief reign was to associate Catholic restoration with Spanish interests and to inspire a rich martyrology that nurtured collective Protestant identity. Her struggles with the pope, however, prevented full restoration of ties with the papal curia. Mary's 25-year-old successor, Elizabeth I (*1558–1603), the daughter of Anne Boleyn, ascended to a troubled throne confronted with political and religious threats, but would prove herself one of the most astute politicians of her age. She effectively used her marriageability to play off pressures from Catholic Spain and France, and as she aged she refashioned her virginity into a trope to secure her subjects' loyalty to a virgin queen. Though her own religious views were and are debated, her Church would become increasingly Protestant, and her reign saw the gradual Protestantization of English religious life.[24] The "Elizabethan Settlement", drawn up between 1559 and 1562, settled few of England's religious controversies but cleared enough space to allow further religious reforms. As had her predecessors, Elizabeth legalized the new order through Parliament, which first ratified the Act of Supremacy, repealing Mary's religious legislation and designating Elizabeth as "Supreme Governor of the Realm" in religious and temporal affairs.

As governor rather than head of the English Church, Elizabeth employed language less offensive to Catholics. All royal officials, both lay and ecclesiastical, had to swear an oath of loyalty under the statute. Shortly afterwards, the Act of Uniformity restored the liturgies of Edward's reign, including the Book of Common Prayer of 1552, though it was revised in 1559 with language that left the official stance on the Eucharist extremely vague. Images and clerical vestments remained in the churches, and a communion rail separated the sanctuary from the nave. Many of the Marian exiles who returned to England found the new religious order "popish", but they lacked the influence to push reforms further. Finally, in 1562, a deeply divided episcopate approved Thirty-Nine Articles which delineated the English Church's confessional identity, though they would not be ratified by Parliament until 1571.

The Elizabethan Settlement prevented the religious civil wars that plagued France but failed to end debate among England's leading churchmen or to placate Elizabeth's enemies. In 1570, Pope Pius V (*1566–72) excommunicated Elizabeth and released Catholics from their loyalty to her. Without heirs of her own, and with military threats from Philip II of Spain and the presence of a Catholic claimant with connections to the Guise faction in France, in the person of Mary Queen of Scots, Elizabeth and her advisors were pushed into closer alliances with Dutch, French, and German Protestants. Nevertheless, Elizabethan officials did not aggressively persecute English Catholics (known as "Recusants" for their choice to avoid mandatory Sunday services). The Recusants were mostly from poorer rural parishes in the north-west, or nobles who held private Masses in chapels on their estates. In the 1580s during the crisis caused by the threatened Spanish invasion, Recusant Catholicism assumed a more treasonous cast, and Elizabethan officials executed perhaps 200 Catholic clerics and laymen. Nevertheless, significant pockets of Catholicism would survive.

By far the most important domestic dissidents with regard to the Elizabethan Settlement were Protestants known as "Puritans", who sought to purify the Church of its "popish" residue. They did not form a self-conscious religious party, but most leaned to Calvinism and favoured a simplified religious experience based on scripture and preaching, with an emphasis on congregational worship. Some opposed the retention of bishoprics, endorsing instead consistorial religious discipline, in a Presbyterian model similar to Huguenot forms where local ministers and elders held sway. In the 1570s some bishops permitted Presbyterian experiments in their dioceses provided that the pastors recognized episcopal rights. By the 1580s, English Puritans had come to embrace a predestinarian Calvinism that assumed God had divided humankind into a small band of self-aware "elect" who would be saved, and a vast majority of reprobates who would be damned. Predestinarianism inspired sober collective religiosity among the chosen, whose pious dress and manners, along with their sometimes overbearing righteousness, alienated them from their less godly neighbours. Meanwhile within the official Church, older rituals were fading or transforming as religious experience became increasingly attached to words read from vernacular bibles and prayer books, or preached at regular sermons. The geographic distribution and social base of official English Protestantism, however, remained uneven into the seventeenth century. At Puritanism's "radical" fringe, non-conformist congregations gathered, often sustained by prophetic visions of apocalyptic change. These radicals threatened ecclesiastical order and at times attracted persecution. Elizabeth's Church was "big" enough to accommodate the beliefs of most of her subjects, and as two generations passed, Protestant forms of worship helped mould a "national" religious community comfortable with the status quo but anxious over the accession of her Scottish Stuart heir.

The late medieval Scottish Church had had its own shortcomings; but owing to the close alliance between the Scottish and French monarchies, little political support for religious reforms appeared prior to the 1540s. James IV (*1488–1513) invaded England as a French ally in 1513 only to suffer a crushing defeat at Flodden. His successor, James V (*1513–42), first married Francis I's daughter, and later Marie de Guise. Despite limited interest in religious reforms, James V left his mark on the Scottish Church. By 1500 monastic and episcopal patrons had appropriated over 85 per cent of parish tithe revenues, and local priests were poorly paid and poorly trained. In the 1530s James instituted a tax on Scotland's upper clergy that forced them to alienate their patronage rights and lands to lay creditors, in a system called "feuing". This policy created a new class of land-holding laymen enriched by tithe revenues, known as "lairds". Thus when James V died in 1542, his infant daughter Mary, and her mother, the regent Marie de Guise (*1543–60), inherited an unreformed Church that was politically and economically weak.

Marie de Guise sent her daughter to the French court to be educated, where she married Francis II in 1558. His early death in 1560, followed closely by that of her mother, brought Mary (*1561–7) back to Scotland to rule on her own. She found her country in open religious rebellion led by John Knox, a former Genevan refugee and committed Calvinist predestinarian. Knox justified his religious agenda with a misogynist diatribe against female rulers such as Marie de Guise, entitled *First Blast of the Trumpet against the Monstrous Regiment of Women*. Not all of Knox's supporters shared his convictions, but they did oppose Catholic institutions and forms of worship. Beyond Knox the young queen faced concerted opposition to her political will, reinforced by the anti-French and anti-papal sentiments of the lairds and urban magistrates. In 1561, Knox and his allies presented Mary with a Scottish *Book of Discipline*, a reform programme calling for the secularization of remaining ecclesiastical properties and revenues to provide income to staff parishes with competent Protestant ministers and teachers. The lairds, as tithe-holders, accepted Knox's plans so long as their revenues and patronage rights remained untouched. Thus the old church order survived in some districts, while the new Protestant "Kirk" emerged in others. The queen could not restore Catholicism, but Knox and his party could not expunge it fully. Mary's second husband, the pro-Catholic Henry Darnley, proved a political and personal disaster. Assassination plots, marital estrangement, and Darnley's eventual murder, in which the queen and her lover were impli-cated, forced Mary's abdication and flight to England in 1567. There she remained in protective custody until plots against Elizabeth necessitated Mary's execution, in 1586. In Scotland, Mary and Henry's young son, James VI (*1567–1624), ruled under a pro-Protestant regency, as evan-gelical leaders began the slow process of reforming Scottish religious life.

On Elizabeth's death in 1603, James VI succeeded her as James I of England (*1603–24). Since he had been tutored by Calvinists, his assumption of headship over the English Church fostered widespread expectation of a swing toward a "purer" and more Protestant stance. At a theological conference held at Hampton Court in 1604, however, James advocated continuity rather than change, and in particular, sanctioned the episcopacy, which frustrated Presbyterians. Under James, English bishops would tolerate pastors who favoured more purified ceremonies and preaching, so long as they did not openly challenge Church order. Popular religious alienation and elite factionalism plagued the early Stuart Church. Many common folk still believed in the efficacy of good works for salvation and preserved rites and sacramental objects of the old religion in domestic and communal rituals.[25] Meanwhile a schism among Calvinists had surfaced around the teachings of a Dutch scholar, Jacobus Arminius (1560–1609), who argued that God, though he knew some would deny him, offered salvation to all. For Arminian Calvinists human will and action became more central to salvation, and they endorsed tolerance and were less rigorous in employing Church courts for social discipline. Most Calvinist leaders, however, embraced the established view that from creation God had chosen a predestined elect. Under James, traditional predestinarianism held sway. His son and heir, Charles, however, espoused Arminian views.

The Stuart monarchs personally united the realms of Scotland, England, and Ireland, which should have made them European power-brokers. England's traditional enemy had been France, but Henry VIII's divorce from Catherine of Aragon and Elizabeth I's alienation from Roman Catholicism had elevated the Spanish Habsburgs as the monarchy's principal threat, culminating in the failed assault of the Spanish Armada in 1588. By 1600 relations with both of Europe's major Catholic powers were strained, and James I attempted to pacify the Habsburgs by withdrawing English military support for the Dutch Calvinist rebels in 1604, and seeking a Spanish bride for Prince Charles. For James the proposed Spanish alliance was simply a political union. He had married his favourite daughter to Frederick V, the Calvinist ruler of the Imperial Palatinate. Prior to 1603 James had effectively navigated through treacherous noble and religious factions in Scotland and was accustomed to ruling without parliamentary restrictions. Effective governance in England, however, required cooperation with local elites, known as gentry, who exercised their collective voice in Parliament. As king of England, James I could not raise new revenues without parliamentary consent, which necessitated hearing grievances and granting concessions. Rather than follow that course, he artfully employed existing royal prerogatives to raise funds, auctioning off monopoly rights to the production of soap and oil and later selling offices, peerages, and titles. In the 1620s the king's lengthy courtship with Spain collapsed, and James's son-in-law, the electoral count Palatine, rebelled against the Austrian Habsburgs, triggering the outbreak of the Thirty Years War. The cost of Stuart influence in European affairs quickly escalated, and artful dodging would no longer suffice.

Charles I (*1625–49) ultimately married a French Catholic princess, which combined with his Arminianism and affection for elaborate religious ceremonials deeply troubled English Puritans. Furthermore, Charles also disliked ruling with Parliament and disbanded the assembly in 1629 when members filed a Petition of Right against perceived religious and political injustices. The king would not recall the assembly for another eleven years. Charles, however, lacked the adroitness to rule alone and soon alienated religious and political leaders in his kingdoms. In 1633 Charles elevated William Laud, the conservative bishop of London, to be archbishop of Canterbury, and invited Laud and other Arminians to join his privy council. The ascendant Arminians revived some trad-itional ceremonies and vestments and began a troubling campaign to recover tithe revenues held by the gentry since the reign of Henry VIII. In 1637 royal efforts to consolidate the English and Scottish churches along Arminian lines, which included the restoration of Scottish bishoprics, caused the Scottish Presbyterians to rebel. Drawing from French Calvinist writings justifying resistance against an unrighteous ruler, the Scottish Kirk's leaders signed a "national covenant" to defend their religious liberties against Charles. Following military defeat at Newcastle and mutinies among his troops, the king needed more money than he could borrow or extort, and so he reluctantly summoned Parliament.

Eleven years of Charles's arbitrary rule had embittered the parlia-mentarians who assembled in April 1640. They immediately submitted a list of grievances, which Charles refused to sign, dissolving this "Short Parliament" after three weeks. Unfortunately his military situation continued to deteriorate during the summer, and the beleaguered king had to reconvene Parliament in November 1640. This new "Long Parlia-ment" would sit continuously for thirteen years. Parliamentary officials first moved to impeach the leading royal advisors including Archbishop Laud. Following a year of continued political turmoil punctuated by a bloody rebellion of Catholic peasants in Ireland, the Protestant Parlia-ment passed the Grand Remonstrance in November 1641, which spelled out reforms to purify church services. In January 1642 the king attempted to arrest his leading opponents in Parliament, and when he failed, civil war ensued, which eventually embroiled all of the kingdoms under Charles's rule, as ingrained local feuds combined with anger over forced religious innovations among Irish Catholics and Scottish Presby-terians to escalate the violence. Within England itself, Recusant nobles found themselves allied with the king for religious and social reasons, while Puritan ministers rallied the parliamentary gentry to protect rule by consent of the elect. Everywhere religious choice became politically significant and new voices with new visions of the religious "community of the realm" emerged.

Riding these tides of religious unrest, the parliamentary and royal camps attempted to rule independently. Parliamentary districts adopted a Puritan Directory of Public Worship in 1645; abolished bishoprics, replacing them with a Presbyterian system organized into regional consistories known as "classes"; and passed the Blasphemy Act in 1648, which authorized the death penalty for those denying the basic tenets of Christianity, and imprisonment for critics of the new Presbyterian order. The ascendant Puritan officials suppressed village festivals, church ales, and ball games, and supervised the destruction of stained glass windows and other residue of "popery" in local churches. The new parliamentary Church order was unpopular in the countryside and soon lost favour in the parliamentary camp itself as Presbyterian influence waned before the rising power of Oliver Cromwell, the leading general of Parliament's New Model Army after 1645. Cromwell headed the Independent movement, which advocated a decentralized church system of congregations with elected pastors. Though unquestionably Protestant and personally puritanical, the Independents, as a minority religious group, favoured a pluralistic tolerance that encompassed most Christians. Cromwell's New Model Army routed the royalists in June 1645, and by 1647 Charles, who had surrendered to the Scottish forces, was in the custody of Parliament. When the king escaped to the Isle of Wight in November 1647 a mixture of royalist supporters along with some conservative Presbyterians rallied to Charles to renew the war. Their quick defeat soon led to the purging of Presbyterians from Parliament, the declaration of a republic, and the trial and execution of the king. Protestant England had entered unchartered political and religious waters.

Revolt and Reformation in the Netherlands

The Reformation in the Netherlands was an international religious and political event. The Habsburgs had acquired the seventeen provinces of the Low Countries in 1477 through marriage, but the region was pockmarked with independent lordships and linguistically divided between German-speaking Dutch in the north-east and French-speaking Walloons in the south-west and lacked administrative coherency.[26] Emperor Charles V treated this wealthy and highly urbanized region as the administrative centre of his European domains, but effective government in the provinces themselves depended on the cooperation of merchant and noble elites, who regularly assembled in local estates and sometimes collectively in the "States General". Charles V coordinated his administration by appointing provincial governors (*Stadholder*), who supervised affairs within individual provinces and reported to various bureaus of the Council of State at Charles's court in Brussels. Despite the centralized shell, particularism and the familial interests of the region's leading nobles informed politics throughout the Reformation era.

The fifteenth-century Netherlands had nurtured Christian humanists and reform groups such as the Brethren of the Common Life. By 1520 Luther's writings had reached a wide audience among the German-speaking Dutch in the region, and the Inquisition executed Europe's first "Lutheran martyrs" at Brussels in 1523. The early Reformation movement in the Netherlands percolated from below and faced withering persecution except where protected by sympathetic elites. Private support for the evangelical cause was substantially broader and deeper than public witness, which required an unflagging commitment evidenced primarily among radical Anabaptist groups, such as the followers of Jan Matthijs at Münster and later the Batenburgers, who burned churches and monasteries and were themselves burned. By the 1550s most Anabaptists in the Netherlands had retreated into pacifism and private devotion under Menno Simons' leadership, though these "Mennonites" still faced persecution if caught. Between 1523 and 1566 the Inquisition executed around 1,300 "heretics" in the provinces, nearly all of whom were Anabaptists.

In the 1550s, the first Calvinist impulses reached the French-speaking southern Netherlands from France and Geneva. At the time, attendance at Sunday Mass remained mandatory, while marriages not contracted in church were unrecognized, and unblessed burials were suspect. Fearing torture and punishment, most individuals with Reformed convictions participated in Catholic services to allay suspicion, but Calvin condemned this "nicodemite" behaviour because he argued no true Christian should take part in any "popish superstition". To placate Calvin and avoid persecution, "Reformed" Dutch- and French-speakers fled the provinces to refugee churches in the neighbouring Imperial city of Emden in East Friesland or to London. In the southern Netherlands, those who couldn't flee formed "churches under the cross", with clandestine services held in private homes. The great port city of Antwerp with its international commercial community offered the safest conditions for Protestant worship and soon became the principal centre for Calvinism in the Netherlands.[27] In 1561, representatives of the refugee and clandestine churches met at Emden to craft the *Confessio Belgica* and an order of discipline that tied Protestants in the Netherlands more firmly to Geneva. Nevertheless, enforcing Church discipline was only possible among the refugee communities where a stern and dedicated cadre of leaders predominated. By their secret nature clandestine communities had to accept divergent personal views on baptism, communion, predestination, and proper ecclesiastical governance.

Despite the spread of Calvinist communities, there was nothing inevitable about the religious and political revolt that was to split the Netherlands into two separate religious states. The initial impetus came from political tensions between Charles's successor, Philip II of Spain, and the States General. In 1559 after four years of direct rule, Philip left the Netherlands for Spain and appointed his half-sister Margaret, the duchess of Parma, as governor-general of the provinces. Rather than ruling through the Council of State, Margaret was assigned three privy councillors, led by the high-handed Cardinal Antoine Perronet de Granvelle. Granvelle and Philip had earlier devised a plan for ecclesiastical reform that would partition the region's four great bishoprics into eighteen smaller sees. Philip's intent was to combat heresy, but the new episcopal posts required learned incumbents, to the exclusion of the great noble families who normally claimed these offices. An opposition party quickly jelled under William, the prince of Orange, Stadholder in Holland, Zealand, and Utrecht, and the count of Egmont, Stadholder in Flanders. In 1565 with Margaret's support, the nobles petitioned Philip to convoke the States General, to disband the Inquisition, and to restore the nobility to its rightful place in governance. Philip flatly refused, and rebellion followed.

Noble resistance initially dismantled Habsburg institutions of religious oversight and repression, triggering widespread iconoclasm in Flanders and elsewhere, much of it quietly and systematically carried out under the supervision of local officials. The disgruntled Council of State refused to restore order unless Margaret permitted Protestant sermons and field conventicles. When she acquiesced, Calvinist communities sprang up everywhere. In 1567 Philip responded by sending the duke of Alba as Margaret's replacement. Alba restored order by force, instituting a special "Council of Troubles" at Brussels, which condemned thousands for heresy and treason between 1567 and 1573 with a particular focus on the rebellious nobility, including Egmont. Conviction for both heresy and treason resulted in the loss of life *and* property, a punishment that affected not only the heretics but their surviving kin. William of Orange resigned his posts and fled to his brother's Imperial territory of

Nassau-Dillenburg. Thousands of others chose exile in Elizabethan England, Emden, and other havens in the Empire. To sustain his campaign, Alba levied new taxes to pay his troops, alienating even those who favoured Catholicism and Spanish rule. Alba further steeled the rebels in their resolve after his troops murdered the populations at the towns of Mechelen and Naarden who had resisted him.

By 1573 the disparate rebel forces were united in opposition to Alva and his "Council of Blood". A group of disinherited nobles organized a flotilla of raiders, known as "sea beggars", who terrorized Spanish shipping from secure bases on the islands and in isolated villages along the coast. William of Orange formed his own army among allies in Holland and Zealand, while even the Mennonites compromised their pacifism by financing Protestant militia. Thus social pride and provincial loyalty united the religiously diverse rebels. As the cost of suppression escalated, Philip recalled Alva in 1573 and had difficulty finding a capable successor. In the interim, unpaid Spanish troops mutinied and brutally sacked Antwerp. In response the seventeen provinces assembled their own States General and assumed governing responsibilities. Finally, in 1578, a new Spanish governor-general, the duke of Parma, divided the rebels by restoring the Council of State and granting amnesty to the leading noble families, except for the house of Orange-Nassau. Most nobles reaffirmed their Catholic faith and became allies of the new regime. Parma then disbanded the States General and provided Protestants a grace period to abjure, or sell their possessions and leave those areas now firmly under Spanish control.

In January 1579 three breakaway northern provinces, Holland, Zealand, and Utrecht, signed the Union of Utrecht as the "United Provinces of the Dutch Republic". By 1590 four other northern provinces had joined them. A war of sieges and bold acts of piracy on the high seas ensued as two states gradually took shape in the Netherlands, the ten Catholic southern provinces under Spain, and the seven northern United Provinces, with a privileged Calvinist Church but a religiously mixed population. By 1620 the confessional and political boundary between the Spanish Netherlands and the Dutch Republic had solidified. The Spanish domains remained a multilingual political conglomeration of prince-bishoprics and lordships where Catholicism predominated under Spanish tutelage. The Dutch Republic was a political anomaly governed by an assembly of estates, themselves representing smaller assemblies in towns and manors. At first glance the Dutch system seems modern or at least representative, but Dutch politics was oligarchic and corporate, reflecting older medieval political values. Spain's stubborn efforts to crush the Republic would drive and frustrate its foreign policies down to 1648.

The out-migration from the southern provinces, along with the return of refugee communities from abroad, brought a significant number of militant Calvinists into the Dutch Republic, and many residents feared that such militancy would foster Calvinist "popery", with the consistories becoming Genevan inquisitions. Efforts to construct a Dutch "Reformed" Church had produced an order of discipline, composed at Emden in 1571, which advocated governance by Presbyterian synods, with moral discipline in the hands of a consistory of pastors and elders. Nevertheless, the Union of Utrecht granted freedom of conscience, and the Dutch Republic never became a Calvinist state. For example, in Holland – the most powerful province – the magistracy and Church failed to reach a working agreement, so consistorial discipline was limited to Calvinist transgressions. Dutch Calvinists themselves remained divided over fundamental issues of faith. In the early seventeenth century, debate over the doctrine of predestination coalesced around two theologians from the university at Leiden, Jacobus Arminius and Franciscus Gomarus. Arminius opposed the predestinarian belief that God had determined the saved and the damned before the fall of Adam, which he argued detracted from God's glory and from human responsibility. Gomarus, on the other hand, championed the unyielding model of predestination at creation, which denied the efficacy of human will. For those who had suffered through persecution and the threat of martyrdom, Gomarus's righteous view of the elect resonated strongly. In 1618–19 the synod of Dordrecht drew Calvinist delegates from the Palatinate, Geneva, England, Emden, and other German Calvinist areas. The participants condemned Arminianism, and the Dutch national synod dismissed 200 pastors. Nevertheless, the movement endured.

Recent historiography has shown that levels of cooperation between Church and state differed widely from province to province and city to city. The Dutch Reformed Church enjoyed the protection of lay officials, but Calvinists comprised a privileged minority, never attracting more than 20 per cent of the population. In Haarlem in 1620, for example, only half the population had definitively committed to a particular church: 20% Reformed, 12.5% Catholic, 14% Anabaptist, 1% Lutheran, and 1% Walloon.[28] As late as 1647 the rights of presentation to many parish incumbencies in the Dutch Republic remained in the hands of Catholics and Mennonites. The Dutch Reformed Church assumed a loose-fitting "official" mantle, though it was never the state Church; it could not enforce religious conformity, only provide access to official privileges. In theory, holders of public office should be Calvinists, but in practice others, including Catholics, were tolerated to secure broad support for the political order. In the late seventeenth century, the Dutch Republic would offer a haven of religious toleration for Anabaptists, Jews, Catholics, and free thinkers. In time, Dutch tolerance would extend to "heretic" Arminians, who would form the Remonstrant Church.

The Struggle for Religious Peace in the Holy Roman Empire

After 1555 the Holy Roman Empire's administrative complexities thickened as confessional tensions striated Imperial politics. The peace of Augsburg had made the individual rulers responsible for their subjects' religious welfare. In practice this meant that rulers determined the confessional affiliation of their territorial church and expected their subjects' religious compliance. Among the seven Imperial electors, three were now Protestants, the margrave of Brandenburg, the count Palatine, and the duke of Saxony. Catholic electors included the Habsburg king of Bohemia and the electoral archbishops of Trier, Mainz, and Cologne. Within the Imperial Diet, nearly all of the larger lay principalities had adopted the Augsburg Confession, with the exception of Bavaria, Jülich-Cleves, Baden-Baden, and the Habsburg Austrian lands. Many prince-bishoprics, particularly in the north-east, had also espoused Lutheranism. Unlike princes, civic magistrates were not free to demand confessional conformity from their fellow citizens, and several cities including Augsburg were confessionally mixed, with legal guarantees securing the religious minority's rights.[29] Confessional differences often divided the Diet and undermined the effectiveness of the Imperial Chamber Court (*Reichskammergericht*). Religious debates could quickly grind Imperial business to a halt. The Habsburg emperors relied increasingly on their personal court, the Imperial Aulic Council (*Reichshofrat*), as the site for adjudicating disputes among Imperial estates. In that setting, Protestants rarely received "justice".

Few realized it but Lutheranism's advances had nearly come to an end. Martin Luther's effort to de-politicize his church limited Lutheran clergy to preaching and administering the sacraments under the protection of lay authorities, and left room for princes and magistrates to intervene in religious life, but the Lutheran clergy did not accept lay supervision quietly. Conflicts over church administration and social discipline pitted outspoken ministers against regimes. In Strasbourg the magistrates, ministers, and citizens formed three competing groups who haggled over the direction of the city's ongoing reformation from the treatment of religious minorities to forms of worship.[30] Among Lutheran theologians, a major division emerged between Philippists – followers of the humanist Philip Melanchthon – and the self-styled "true" or Gnesio-Lutherans, over Melanchthon's willingness to accommodate changes in worship associated with the Interim as "matters of indifference" (*adiaphora*). Deeper than this issue was the question of Christian ethics. The Philippists argued that those justified by faith could ensure their repentance and acceptance of God's mercy by good works. The Gnesio-Lutherans, led by Matthias Flacius Illyricus (1520–75), argued that any justification through works questioned the omnipotence of God and diverged from Luther's theology. The issues may seem narrow, but given the legal status of the Augsburg Confession, accusations of innovative theology opened the target and his lay protectors to legal censure. Along with the debate over justification, the theologians continued to wrestle with Luther's belief in consubstantiation. Melanchthon and many of his supporters had doubts, and their view bordered on the sacramentarian belief in the "spiritual presence". Gnesio-Lutherans were quick to label the Philippists as "crypto-Calvinists", a claim that carried real bite as illegal Calvinist churches appeared in the Empire in the 1560s.

The political threat of internal divisiveness was not lost on the Lutheran princes, and many called on their leading theologians to compile territorial confessions. From 1567 onward, the duchy of Württemberg played an increasingly significant role in German Lutheranism due to its well-organized Church and excellent university at Tübingen guided by its leading theologian, Jacob Andreae (1529–90). In 1577 Andreae and the Gnesio-Lutherans drew up a Formula of Concord and called on Lutheran princes and magistrates to defend the formula in the interest of their subjects' souls. The authors attempted to find a balance, but the document, though intended as mediation, muted most of the Philippist arguments, while condemning Calvinist beliefs regarding predestination and Anabaptist tenets. Within the principalities and estates that adopted the Formula of Concord, all religious and administrative officials were required to subscribe, as conformity of conscience became a fundamental component of a career in the Lutheran ministry. The Philippist camp, centred in electoral Saxony, gradually fell out of political favour and dissolved. In 1580 when the Book of Concord, which included all of the critical confessional documents of Orthodox Lutheranism, was published, the era of vigorous Lutheran expansion had ended. Counter-reform Catholicism and Calvinism became the dynamic confessions in Imperial affairs.

Despite challengers and contested elections, Habsburgs had served as emperors since 1438. Ferdinand I (*1555–64) and his son Maximilian II (*1564–76) ruled effectively by honouring compromise in the name of religious peace. Maximilian's son Rudolf II (*1576–1612), however, was personally indifferent to religious questions and during his tenure the confessional initiative swung to the Imperial estates, heightening tensions and triggering confrontations. By the 1580s three issues in Imperial politics had emerged that would cause instability for the next several decades. First, several princes, most significantly the electoral count Palatine, along with a handful of civic regimes, embraced Calvinism and established illegal Calvinist churches. Secondly, ecclesiastical princes, such as the bishop of Magdeburg, abjured Catholicism and sought to secularize their territories, which was constitutionally questionable. Finally, the powerful Wittelsbach dukes of Bavaria implemented the Counter-Reformation within their territories and began to rally a strong Catholic party independent of the Emperor.

Calvinism was neither recognized nor protected by the religious peace, yet the movement achieved its greatest success in the Empire between 1560 and 1620. Initiated by English, Dutch, and French exiles at Emden, Aachen, and in other Rhenish towns, the movement formally entered the Imperial confessional arena when the electoral count Palatine Frederick III (*1559–76) converted in 1563 and proclaimed the Calvinist Heidelberg Confession. Heinz Schilling has called the movement Germany's "second Reformation".[31] Within German Protestantism the movement was "Puritan", for Calvinists sought to eradicate the visible remnants of "popery" in the Lutheran church: vestments, altars, and images. The Calvinists also saw themselves as completing the German Reformation and they assaulted Lutheran sacraments, which had preserved some Catholic residue. Calvinists replaced the unleavened Lutheran wafer with bread for communion and purged the baptismal ritual of references to exorcism. Imperial Calvinism was a prince's religion, and its survival depended on the active support of rulers and magistrates. This distinguished it from other Calvinist and Puritan movements where the ministry operated independently of lay power. The failure of the Emperor or the Diet to halt the illegal spread of Calvinism demonstrated the weakness of the religious settlement of 1555.

The fate of ecclesiastical principalities posed the second threat to peace. In 1582, Gebhard Truchsess von Waldburg, the electoral archbishop of Cologne, announced his conversion to Calvinism and initiated steps to secularize his state, threatening the confessional stability of the Lower Rhine valley and the Catholic majority among electors. Rudolf II was typically slow to act. Pope Gregory XIII (*1572–85), however, quickly deposed the archbishop, and Spanish troops from the Netherlands joined Bavarian forces to drive Gebhard from his lands. The new archbishop was Ernst, a member of the Bavarian ducal Wittelsbach family, who already held the sees of Liège, Friesing, Hildesheim, and Münster. Wittelsbach archbishops would rule in Cologne until 1761, as episcopal pluralism, despite its condemnation at Trent, served to secure Catholicism in Imperial ecclesiastical principalities. In this case it also secured Wittelsbach predominance in Imperial affairs. The "Cologne War" put an end to the secularization of ecclesiastical principalities and Church properties. As cooperation among Bavaria, Spain, and the papacy became a dynamic factor in Imperial politics, Catholic officials identified 1552 as the legal end point for secularization, which necessitated re-Catholicization in several territories including the bishopric of Magdeburg. As tensions mounted in the 1590s, Rudolf II retreated from Imperial affairs. Meanwhile Catholic princes ratcheted up pressure against Calvinist Imperial cities. In 1598 the Imperial Aulic Council authorized the re-Catholicization of Aachen, again carried out by Spanish troops, and in 1607 came the seizure of the confessionally mixed Donauwörth by Maximilian I of Bavaria, who expelled its Lutherans and annexed the city.

By the early 1600s the Palatinate and its university at Heidelberg had become the centre for Calvinist activities within the Empire. With the threat of counter-reformation, supported by Spanish and Bavarian armies, confronting the Protestant Imperial estates, the electoral count Palatine, Frederick IV (*1583–1610), formed a Protestant Union in 1609 with Lutheran Hesse-Cassel and Württemberg and a number of smaller Calvinist principalities. Saxony and most Lutheran states, however, gave the alliance a chilly response. Meanwhile, Maximilian of Bavaria organized a Catholic League, which he headed without the Emperor's involvement.

The first test of the confessional parties' political resolve came in 1609 when the duke of Jülich-Cleves died without a direct male heir, leaving

rival Lutheran claimants. In a breach of normal practice, they offered to
rule jointly until a panel of Lutheran princes could adjudicate their
claims. The Emperor opposed Lutheran rule in Jülich because the
majority of its population was Catholic, and placed his cousin Leopold as
protector over the territory. Moreover, Jülich offered an excellent staging
point for assaults on the Dutch Republic, so the dispute threatened the
recently signed twelve-year truce between Spain and the Dutch along
with the uneasy peace between Spain and France. Forces from the
Protestant Union, joined by French and Dutch troops, recaptured the
great fortress at Jülich, but the assassination of the French king, Henry
IV, and the Dutch and Spanish commitment to their truce, prevented
further escalation. The Jülich-Cleves crisis reopened in 1613–14 when
one claimant, Johann-Sigismund, the elector margrave of Brandenburg,
converted to Calvinism and the other, Wolfgang Wilhelm of Neuburg,
became Catholic and married Maximilian of Bavaria's sister. Johann-
Sigismund quickly joined the Protestant Union, but Dutch and Spanish
forces again occupied key fortresses within the territories before either
the Protestant Union or the Catholic League could act. The Treaty of
Xanten in 1614 awarded Cleves to the Calvinist elector and Jülich to the
Catholic duke of Neuburg. Despite the settlement the Dutch and Spanish
garrisons remained. The Jülich-Cleves crisis had demonstrated the
weakness of confessional federations within the Empire and the potential
for Imperial disputes to escalate into much broader wars.

Protestantism in Northern and Eastern Europe

In Northern and Eastern Europe the trajectory of further reformation,
both Protestant and Catholic, depended on political factors: either the
will of the king in Denmark and Sweden or the independence of the
nobility in Poland-Lithuania and Hungary. By 1550 the Baltic and
North Sea basins were essentially Protestant with the Churches in
Denmark and Sweden more or less affiliated with Lutheranism, but
these kingdoms were locked in an intractable struggle for control of the
Danish Sound, a narrow strip of water through which funnelled the
grain from the great feudal estates of the Eastern European plain to
ports in the Netherlands and beyond. In 1550 Denmark held sway in the
Baltic, only to be eclipsed by Sweden during the Thirty Years War. The
need to marshal their kingdoms' resources to wage war would eventually
force the Scandinavian monarchs to compromise with ecclesiastical leaders

to secure political unity. In the sprawling kingdoms of Poland-Lithuania and Hungary the monarchs' weakness placed the religious initiative in the hands of the nobility from the outset, which resulted in religious pluralism and tacit toleration, at least into the mid-seventeenth century.

In Denmark, Frederick I (*1523–33) and Christian III (*1534–59) had secularized ecclesiastical property and under the Church ordinance of 1537 established Lutheran forms of worship within their territories, which included Schleswig-Holstein, Denmark, Norway, the Faeroe Islands, and Iceland. Superintendents replaced bishops, though the episcopal structure remained, and the clergy attended provincial and national synods.[32] At the parish level, ecclesiastical and lay officials conducted periodic visitations to examine pastors, schools, and lay behaviour. Building Lutheran communities, however, took time as resident Catholic priests kept their benefices, and parish churches preserved their high altars, chantries, and religious imagery. Despite Denmark's Lutheran credentials, no document specifically identified the Church with the Augsburg Confession, even though all parties operated under the assumption of compliance. To obtain clarity, Frederick II (*1559–88) called for a new Church ordinance in 1561; but he never authorized it, for the document seemed to push Danish Lutheranism further towards Gnesio-Lutheran orthodoxy than the king wished to go. The ambiguity of Denmark's Lutheran identity embroiled its ecclesiastical elite in debates between Philippists and the Gnesio ("Orthodox") factions, while division at the top discouraged further reform at the parish level. Initially the balance of power favoured the Philippists under the leadership of Niels Hemmingson, but by 1575 pressure from victorious Orthodox Lutherans in the Empire led to Hemmingson's deposition from the university of Copenhagen's theological faculty. Frederick, however, would not sanction the Orthodox victory by accepting the Formula of Concord (1577) and later burned the copies of the Book of Concord sent to him.

Frederick's son Christian IV (*1588–1648) devoted less attention to religious matters, pursuing military ambitions instead. Drawing on the revenues from the tolls levied in the Sound, he ruled without the estates (*Riksdag*) or Council (*Rigsrådet*). In foreign policy his campaigns against Sweden and his disastrous involvement in the Thirty Years War ruined any hope of Danish hegemony in the Baltic. Christian took little interest in the Danish Church, and during his reign Danish Lutheranism swung firmly into the Orthodox camp under the leadership of Hans Poulsen Resen, who composed the official Danish Bible in 1607 and became bishop/superintendent of Zealand in 1615. Resen institutionally centralized and doctrinally homogenized Danish Lutheranism as the common folk began to internalize the new religious values. In 1621 new statutes for the university at Copenhagen required all professors to swear allegiance to the Augsburg Confession. All pastors and Latin schoolteachers had to complete two years of university education and pass an exam before clerical appointment. At the local level, Church officials emphasized catechizing children and indoctrinating an educated Lutheran elite through a system of secondary Latin schools which served as feeders to the university.

Orthodox Lutheranism honoured secular authority and assigned to the lay ruler responsibility for preserving the collective spiritual welfare of his subjects. It also implied that the subjects' spiritual health, if properly internalized, would sustain the kingdom from calamities associated with divine wrath. Christian's political defeats led to an examination of national conscience, and the losses were blamed on insufficient piety rather than poor leadership. Church leaders set aside Fridays for public penance in the towns, while among the peasants a monthly day of penance sufficed. Ecclesiastical officials further enshrined collective piety in the penitential ordinance of 1629, which created a committee of elders to assist the parish clergy in supervising not so much the outward forms of worship, such as regular church attendance, but the inner spirit of parishioners. Punishment escalated from private admonition to banishment for impious recalcitrants. Ironically, by the 1650s political defeat had helped build an official and oppressive religious culture in Denmark's state-controlled Church.

In Sweden, the Protestant Church remained a political foundation without a clear doctrinal stand until the death of Gustav Vasa in 1560.[33] In his confessionally ambiguous coronation oath, Gustav's heir, Erik XIV (*1560–9), promised to preserve the pure word of God and to protect the Church and its ministers. He clearly opposed Roman Catholicism and sheltered Dutch and Huguenot refugees. When their Calvinist proselytizing generated negative reactions among Swedish churchmen, Erik refused to banish the Calvinists or force their conscience. Eventually Erik's mental instability, combined with a string of defeats against Denmark, forced his deposition and the elevation of his younger brother John III (*1569–92), ending Sweden's flirtation with Calvinism.

In 1571 John authorized Sweden's first Protestant Church ordinance, which was loosely modelled on Lutheran structures though vague on doctrinal questions. The ordinance emphasized preaching from scripture alone, while retaining many traditional ceremonies that were banned in other Protestant lands. It made no reference to the Augsburg Confession. John married a Catholic Polish princess and her personal entourage became a conduit for Jesuit missionaries who infiltrated the Swedish Church in the 1570s. This clandestine counter-reform movement surfaced in 1577 when the king introduced a new and more Catholic liturgy, known as the Red Book, triggering anti-papal riots that led to the exile of the Jesuits and other Catholic leaders. The queen's death in 1583 effectively ended Sweden's counter-reformation, but the ongoing fear of a royal religious coup shadowed John's reign and would cost his Catholic son, Sigismund I (*1592–1600), his throne. Sigismund already held the elective kingship of Poland when elevated to Sweden's throne. He chose to remain in Poland while his uncle Charles served as regent in Sweden. Charles exploited religious anxieties about the Catholic Sigismund to attract the Protestant ecclesiastical elite to Uppsala in 1593 where they signed a document challenging the constitutionality of Sigismund serving as defender of the Protestant Swedish Church. Charles then distributed the Uppsala Resolution among the nobility, garnering over 2,000 signatures. Finally, in 1600, the Swedish parliament renounced its loyalty to Sigismund but balked at accepting Charles IX (*1604–11) as king until four years later.

Though the Uppsala Assembly had championed Protestant religious unity, the doctrinal foundation of that unity remained vague as the signers merely denounced the Red Book and affirmed the Augsburg Confession rather than the Book of Concord as Sweden's religious template. Nevertheless, the Uppsala Resolution gave Swedish ecclesiastical officials greater control over their Church's religious future, and they struggled long and hard with Charles to have him recognize the binding nature of the document on his own religious agenda. Charles's successors, beginning with Gustavus Adolphus (*1611–32), swore at their coronations to preserve the Augsburg Confession and Uppsala Resolution. Nevertheless, throughout the early modern era, the Swedish Lutheran Church followed its own path, epitomized by the decision to celebrate the Reformation's centennial in 1621, the year of Gustav Vasa's rebellion, rather than 1617 as elsewhere. With its episcopal structure and hybrid ceremonies, Swedish Lutheranism possessed a distinct confessional identity.

The composite kingdom of Poland-Lithuania comprised a third power in the Baltic basin although its only outlet to the sea was a strip of coastland surrounding the great port of Gdansk (Danzig). In 1569 the Union of Lublin would join Poland and Lithuania into an immense ethnically and religiously mixed state, twice the size of France, that sheltered large minorities of Jews, Muslim Tartars, and Orthodox Ruthenians. In the early sixteenth century the Polish gentry had extracted concessions from the rulers to make the monarchy elective and to place decisions of war, mobilization, and taxation in the hands of the Diet (*Sejm*), where the nobles predominated. By the 1550s Poland seemed ripe for turning Protestant, but within Polish history the Reformation would be an episode.[34] The Reformation had spread early and rapidly among the German communities in the towns of ducal Prussia, Silesia, and Poland itself. Commitment to Lutheranism helped forge German ethnic solidarity, but few Lutheran writings were translated into Polish and other Slavic languages. In 1559, King Sigismund II Augustus (*1548–72) granted the Lutherans in Gdansk and other Prussian towns freedom of worship. In 1563 he also acknowledged the rights of the noble gentry (*szlachta*) to choose whether or not to honour verdicts of ecclesiastical courts against heretics. The fate of Poland's Reformation would rest in the hands of its nobles.

The gentry's freedom of religious choice nurtured Poland's reputation as a haven for splinter groups, such as the circle of intellectuals associated with an Italian anti-Trinitarian named Faustus Socinius who denied both the divinity of Jesus and the Holy Spirit's existence. Most Polish Protestants, however, were Calvinists, and Polish Calvinism owed much to the work of Jan Łaski (1499–1560), who travelled throughout Europe before returning to Poland in 1556 with the goal of uniting Polish Protestants behind a Calvinist confession and Church ordinance. By 1572 perhaps 650 Calvinist congregations were scattered across Poland-Lithuania with around a sixth of the nobility professing Protestantism. The following year the Confederation of Warsaw guaranteed freedom of worship for the gentry in what had become a "commonwealth of nobles". Though noble religious privileges held until 1795, the age of Protestant expansion had ended.

Delineating outlines of confessional identity in Poland is impossible; Catholic gentry would welcome and shelter Mennonites escaping the Netherlands or Protestants driven from Bohemia and Moravia by the Austrian counter-reformation during the Thirty Years War, granting them rights to build churches and schools, on account of the economic benefit offered by these new settlements. These same gentry would persecute native heretics, allowing the desecration of Protestant churches and cemeteries that were not specifically protected. Though the Confederation of Warsaw gave Protestant nobles a free hand to spread their faith, they made little effort to convert their serfs. Among the peasantry, the religious views of their lords carried little weight, and the initial religious indifference of Catholic and Protestant elites to peasant beliefs resulted in Polish witch-hunting being an eighteenth-century phenomenon associated with the belated Catholic counter-reform.

Under King Stefan Bátory (*1576–86), Polish forces captured the secularized crusading state formerly governed by the Grand Order of the Livonian Knights. To defend Livonia and its Baltic ports, Stefan and future Polish kings fought sporadic wars with Sweden and Muscovy. Conflict with Sweden intensified when Stefan's successor, the Catholic Vasa prince Sigismund III (*1587–1632), had his Swedish throne usurped by his uncle in 1600. The Jesuits had established their first colleges in Poland in the 1560s, and they had recruited a cohort of young noblemen for training in Rome between 1565 and 1586 who later became leaders in the *Sejm*. Poland's Vasa rulers developed close ties with the Jesuits, and the last Vasa king, John Casimir II (*1648–68), resigned from the order with papal blessing to assume his crown. Nevertheless, Poland's Catholic monarchs could never force religious policies within the kingdom and relied on royal patronage to re-convert most nobles, who realized that access to positions of influence required Catholic commitment. In the century after 1650, Catholicism slowly came to dominate as Protestantism withered without noble support.

Despite fears of Turkish expansion deep into Christian Europe, the Ottoman forces had reached a practical limit with their conquest of southern Hungary in 1526. Wars continued until 1541 when a truce divided Hungary into three regions: royal Hungary in the north-west with its Habsburg king, Ferdinand I of Austria; the principality of Transylvania in the north-east, an Ottoman tributary state with a Christian prince, Johan Sigismund Zápolyai (*1540–71); and the Ottoman-controlled south, centred around Buda. The Habsburgs would attempt to annex Transylvania on several occasions, but their staunch opposition to Protestantism, as opposed to the relative indifference of the Ottomans, encouraged Transylvania's elite to favour Ottoman tutelage. The Habsburg kings themselves owed annual tribute to Istanbul.[35] Following the death of Süleyman I in 1566, the sultanate went through a period of relative military quiescence due to a succession of weaker rulers and a prolonged crisis along its Persian frontier. When provoked by Habsburg aggression in Hungary, however, the Turkish forces could react effectively, as they did in the Thirteen Years War from 1593 to 1606. Meanwhile, Transylvania remained the linchpin for regional political stability while its laws guaranteed freedom of religious conscience, which made its ruler a champion for Hungarian Protestants. This support aided Bethlen Gábor (*1613–29), who for a time threatened to replace the Habsburgs as ruler in both Christian sections of Hungary.

Protestantism spread widely through the three Hungaries in the 1540s as Márton Kálmancsehi Sánta and István Szegedi Kis carried the faith from noble estate to noble estate. Hungarian Protestantism was disseminated almost entirely through preaching as so few could read Magyar.[36] Lutheranism had found adherents among the German-speaking communities in Hungarian towns, but as in Poland, Hungarian Lutheranism was a Germanic faith. Among the Magyar-speaking elites who welcomed the Reformed message offered in their native tongue, Protestants favoured ties with Heinrich Bullinger at Zurich and adopted a Swiss model of ecclesiastical governance and liturgy, in the Hungarian Church ordinance of 1559. Hungarian Protestantism remained local and cellular, and efforts by Anna Bátory and others to consolidate ecclesiastical governance around "national" synods failed.

The Habsburg rulers opposed Protestantism, but Austrian control over this frontier region was too limited to hinder Protestant growth. By 1590 only 10 per cent of the non-Muslim population in the three Hungaries remained Catholic with over 80 per cent identified as Protestants, along with small Jewish and Orthodox minorities. With the absence of a centralized authority, freedom of conscience thrived for a time. Socinian anti-Trinitarian believers found refuge in Transylvania until the arrest of their most prominent leader, Ferenc Dávid, in 1579 drove them underground. Meanwhile Catholic bishops preserved all of their institutional resources, their seats in the diet, and their revenues, but this cumbersome hierarchy watched over souls in only 300 parishes. Given the centripetal forces in Hungarian politics, Protestantism remained a hybrid compilation of non-Roman Catholicism. Hymnals, such as The Songs in Three Orders, compiled by a Lutheran minister, included Catholic psalms along with Calvinist and anti-Trinitarian hymns. The publication of a Hungarian vernacular Bible at Vizsoly in 1590 reflected how late and limited the evangelical movement was. The absence of a clear dogmatic centre, the dependence on support from the local nobility, the oral nature of faith, and the limited efforts to proselytize among the non-Magyar-speaking enserfed peasantry would expose the Hungarian reformation to concerted counter-reform assaults in the late seventeenth century.

The Thirty Years War

The chief business of an early modern prince was to wage war for dynastic interest, and wars or the threat of wars permeated the century after 1550, culminating in devastating violence between 1618 and 1648. The great power struggle between the Habsburgs and French monarchs, combined with the unresolved revolt in the Netherlands, the contest between Denmark and Sweden for hegemony in the Baltic, and the Imperial constitutional crisis, resulted in a deadly vortex that would exhaust all of the participants and leave much of Central Europe and Italy a wasteland. The wars had religious overtones, and many of the worst atrocities derived from religious hatreds and bigotry. Nevertheless, political ambition fuelled the conflicts and prolonged them. The cluster of wars known to historians collectively as the Thirty Years War had their origin in a religious and constitutional struggle between the Habsburg king and the Bohemian estates.

Bohemia's religious freedoms originated with the Hussites and depended on the autonomy of its estates, dominated by the towns and rural nobility. The Bohemian estates secured their power in a formal capitulation offered by the king prior to his election. Since 1526 the Habsburg dukes of Austria had held the Bohemian crown, and Rudolf II did little to disturb the political status quo during his long residence at Prague after 1583. Rudolf was also king of Hungary and Moravia, as well as Emperor. The heir apparent was his brother Matthias, whom Rudolf personally despised. Between 1606 and 1608 the impatient Matthias offered further legal and religious concessions to the estates of Hungary, Moravia, and ducal Austria, all of which were heavily seasoned with Protestants, for their support in his bid to wrest these lands from the mentally unstable Rudolf. Matthias then approached the Bohemian estates with a similar offer, and they elected him king several months before Rudolf's death in January 1612. Shortly afterwards the Imperial electors presented Matthias (*1612–19) with the final prize of his ambition, but the new Emperor had squandered his regalian rights undermining Rudolf and, lacking *Hausmacht*, could only play a peripheral role in Imperial affairs. Frustrated with the deterioration of Imperial authority, Matthias's Habsburg cousin, Philip III (*1598–1621) of Spain, turned to the Bavarian Wittelsbach dukes; and as we have seen, their alliance worked effectively during the Jülich-Cleves crisis. The ageing Matthias lacked direct heirs and had relied on his younger cousin and heir apparent, Archduke Ferdinand of Styria, as an ally against Rudolf. Ferdinand now persuaded Matthias to appoint him king-designate of Bohemia, Moravia, and Hungary, to ensure a smooth transition of authority. The Bohemian estates accepted the proposal provided Ferdinand promise to observe their traditional religious privileges including the recent concessions from Matthias. Though educated by the Jesuits and an effective steward of counter-reformation in Styria, Ferdinand apparently agreed.[37]

In 1617, though Matthias still ruled in name, Ferdinand began to behave as king in Bohemia, setting up his personal court in Vienna and appointing Catholic regents to govern in his name in Prague. Under Ferdinand's orders the regents systematically excluded Protestant nobles from appointments to vacant governmental posts and then forcibly re-Catholicized the towns of Broumov and Hroby, whose Protestant churches were not protected under the capitulation. On 23 May 1618 the indignant noble *defensores* of the Bohemian Utraquist Church reprised the act that had ignited the Hussite rebellion by defenestrating three Catholic regents from the royal castle at Prague. With Mathias dying, Ferdinand (*1619–37) restrained his response until he could negotiate his Imperial election. Having ritually deposed Ferdinand, the Bohemian rebels shopped their crown to various Protestant princes until the Calvinist electoral count Palatine, Frederick V, accepted. The new Bohemian king would prove a poor choice, for he had limited personal resources, no military experience, and as a Calvinist, few significant confessional allies in the Empire. The Bohemian estates also negotiated a military alliance with Bethlen Gábor, the ruler of Transylvania, who invaded royal Hungary with the goal of overthrowing Ferdinand and stirred up simultaneous Protestant rebellions in Moravia, Silesia, and Austria.

By early 1620 Ferdinand's position in Bohemia and Hungary had deteriorated, but he had gained critical allies. In October 1619 the Emperor surrendered command of military affairs in Bohemia to Maximilian of Bavaria, promising him territory and the rebellious count Palatine's electoral seat in the Imperial Diet. In March 1620 Ferdinand negotiated an alliance with the Lutheran electoral duke of Saxony, John George, who would attack the Bohemian district of Lusatia. Finally, in May, fearing the growth of Calvinist influence in the Rhineland, Philip III authorized a Spanish military campaign in the Palatinate. On 8 November 1620 the joint Imperial–Bavarian army crushed Bohemian forces at the battle of White Mountain (Bílá Hora), and the revolt quickly collapsed. The defeat ended Bohemian autonomy as Ferdinand outlawed Protestantism, executed the ring-leaders, and confiscated their estates.

Henceforth, Bohemia would be a Catholic state, and Czech would no longer serve as a language of public discourse.

Frederick V escaped Bohemia, but his lands in the Empire offered no haven. Maximilian of Bavaria soon invaded the Upper Palatinate, which bordered his duchy, and there routed Frederick's mercenaries. Meanwhile Spanish forces occupied much of the Lower Palatinate, and Frederick fled into exile in Amsterdam. To pay off his allies, the Emperor bestowed Lusatia to John George of Saxony, permitted Spanish forces to retain several key fortresses in the Rhineland as staging areas for assaults on the Dutch, and ceded the Upper Palatinate to Maximilian of Bavaria along with the electoral title. This last act troubled Imperial princes, both Protestant and Catholic, for Ferdinand had altered the Empire's constitutional structure without assembling the diet. Other territories, particularly eight secularized bishoprics in northern Germany, were open for conquest and forced re-Catholicization, as Ferdinand saw the potential of counter-reformation by force. Meanwhile, the French watched the expansion of Spanish power in the Rhineland with dismay, as did the Dutch, who renewed their war with Spain when the twelve-year truce ended in 1621.

No Imperial Protestant power existed that could thwart Ferdinand and the Catholic forces. In France, Louis XIII was engaged in a second round of religious wars against the Huguenots, which made an open alliance with the Empire's Protestants unthinkable. The Dutch were willing, but focused on their war with Spain. The defeated and deposed Frederick's father-in-law, James I of England, could offer financial assistance but few troops. At this point the ambitious Lutheran king of Denmark, Christian IV, stepped into the breach, for as duke of Holstein he was an Imperial prince with a personal interest in the archbishopric of Bremen, now targeted by Imperial forces for a Catholic restoration. In December 1625, Denmark, England, and the Dutch Republic formed a new Protestant Union along with several Imperial states and Bethlen Gábor, who continued his campaigns in Austria. The Emperor's army in northern Germany totalled 112,000 men, under the command of Albrecht von Waldstein, better known as Wallenstein, a military entrepreneur and a convert who had amassed a fortune in confiscated Bohemian lands while in Ferdinand's service. By the spring of 1628, Wallenstein and forces from the Bavarian-led Catholic League had crushed the Danish coalition and occupied the North German bishoprics along with the duchies of Mecklenburg and Pomerania on the Baltic coast. In May 1629 the humiliated Danish king withdrew from the war, and the Emperor and his allies were unchallenged masters in Imperial affairs.

Two months earlier Ferdinand had arbitrarily announced a religious settlement for the Empire, known as the Edict of Restitution, which realized the long-held counter-reform goal of re-Catholicizing the five bishoprics secularized since 1552, along with properties in numerous other Imperial estates. The edict also reaffirmed that the religious peace of 1555 only applied to Protestants adhering to the Augsburg Confession, which resulted in the expulsion of Calvinist clergy and adherents in several Imperial cities. The edict destroyed any semblance of political or confessional balance in the Empire, equating counter-reformation with undisputed Habsburg power. Even the Catholic leaders who supported and benefitted from the religious changes feared Ferdinand's unconstitutional acts. In mid-August 1630, they successfully convinced the Emperor that he should dismiss Wallenstein, hoping to restore the constitutional balance.

Five weeks earlier at the height of Catholic power, the Lutheran king of Sweden, Gustavus Adolphus, had invaded Pomerania with 14,000 veterans of wars against Denmark and Poland. From this modest entry, the Swedish forces, employing new tactics, defeated several Catholic armies over the next two years and occupied the Bavarian capital at Munich, while their ally the elector of Saxony captured Prague. Gustavus's stunning victories swung the confessional balance completely, and in the heady rush of events some Protestant leaders called for the secularization of all Imperial ecclesiastical properties. None the less, relations between the Swedish king and his leading Protestant allies within the Empire, Saxony and Brandenburg, were stormy; and no one wanted to negotiate for peace when the Swedes held such a strong hand. In March 1632, when the Swedes invaded Bavaria, Maximilian, who had been one of Wallenstein's bitterest enemies, persuaded the Emperor to recommission the mercenary general. In November the Imperial and Swedish armies fought a bloody but indecisive battle at Lützen. Among the dead on the field was Gustavus Adolphus, leaving his three-year-old daughter Christina (*1632–54) as successor and throwing Sweden's war aims into disarray. Gustavus's able Chancellor, Axel Oxenstierna, attempted to rally the Protestant cause and preserve Swedish interests through the League of Heilbronn in 1633, but Brandenburg and Saxony refused to support him. In September 1634, Swedish forces suffered a second blow with the crushing defeat at Nördlingen, and they withdrew into northern Germany. Wallenstein did not live to see the fruits of his ultimate triumph, having been assassinated with the Emperor's complicity in February.

With the religious and political balance restored, Ferdinand successfully negotiated a treaty with John George of Saxony and many of the leading Lutheran powers, at Prague in 1635. It revoked the Edict of Restitution and designated 1624 as the normative year for confessional rights within Imperial territories. It denied these rights, however, to Calvinists. The Swedes had not participated in the negotiations, and found themselves isolated as the Imperial allies sued for peace. The collapse of Sweden's Heilbronn League and the Peace of Prague forced Catholic France to enter the war as an ally of the Swedes and Imperial Calvinist princes, because Cardinal Richelieu and Louis XIII could not allow the Austrian and Spanish Habsburgs to dominate Central Europe. For thirteen more years, armies campaigned, besieged fortresses, foraged, and laid waste the open countryside in the Netherlands, Central Europe, and Italy.

Formal negotiations for a general peace began in 1643, as Catholic plenipotentiaries assembled in the Westphalian town of Münster, and Protestant officials at neighbouring Osnabrück. The treaty was not realized until October 1648. The Thirty Years War involved a bundle of conflicts, and the Peace of Westphalia addressed most of them. At Westphalia the Dutch gained perpetual peace with Spain and recognition as a free and sovereign republic, in exchange for withdrawal from their alliance with France and a promise not to harass Spanish colonial shipping. The new Emperor, Ferdinand III (*1637–57), had his absolute sovereignty over Austria and Bohemia recognized, which secured his father's counter-reform polices there. In Habsburg Silesia and Hungary, however, both the Protestants and the noble estates who protected them retained some rights.

What the Austrian Habsburgs gained in their hereditary lands, they lost in the Empire. The Peace of Westphalia extended legal recognition to Calvinists, and the power of princes to demand confessional conformity among their subjects was restrained to the point that religious minorities, except Anabaptists, could gather for private worship. What the princes sacrificed in religious power they gained in secular authority as the treaty accorded them territorial superiority (*Landeshoheit*) in political matters, including the right to form alliances, provided these were not directed against the Emperor. The post-Westphalian Imperial order would rest on the will of the princes embodied in the Imperial Diet and other bodies, such as the Imperial Chamber Court, where Protestant estates, including the Calvinists, had a voice. Most territorial boundaries reverted to their pre-1618 configuration, but Saxony retained Lusatia, Bavaria held the Upper Palatinate with its electoral title, and Brandenburg acquired the secularized bishoprics of Halberstadt, Minden, and Magdeburg. The eldest son of the former electoral count Palatine, Karl Ludwig, returned to the Lower Palatinate with a newly created eighth electoral title.

The victors of the Peace were France and Sweden. The young French king, Louis XIV (*1643–1715), gained recognition of his sovereignty over the bishoprics of Metz, Toul, and Verdun along with Austria's territories and rights in Alsace, and with it access to Imperial politics. Austria also pledged neutrality in the ongoing war between France and Spain, which dragged on until 1659. Sweden received western Pomerania with its strategic port of Stettin, the secularized bishoprics of Bremen and Verden, and ports in Mecklenburg, which together made Sweden a German and Baltic power. Finally Sweden received five million *riksdalers* as "satisfaction" for its troops, who were paid off and demilitarized. Even with such a comprehensive treaty, wars continued for another dozen years in the Baltic between Sweden and its enemies, and between France and Spain on a number of fronts.

The age of religious wars had ended. In the late sixteenth century the influence of the Habsburgs had spread from the kingdom of Hungary to the Atlantic coast. The political and cultural heartland of Europe lay in Italy and the Empire, while France was torn apart by religious civil war. The Habsburgs had sought to combine active support for Catholic counter-reform with the concentration of power within their holdings and its expansion into Protestant territories. The strategy led to devastating wars in the Netherlands, Italy, and the Empire, which ruined and depopulated these regions and led to the dissipation of Habsburg might, everywhere except in the hereditary lands of Austria. France too had suffered, but the Catholic kingdom had the demographic, economic, and political resources to rebound within a generation. The devastation wrought on the battlegrounds of these great struggles would take longer to heal. In the British Isles, religious civil war had cost a king his life and had settled little regarding faith. After 1650 religion would play less and less of a role in international and domestic politics. New models of political allegiance would reduce the urgency for religious conformity among subjects. Economic and political concerns would encourage many lay authorities to welcome enclaves of religious refugees who might enrich

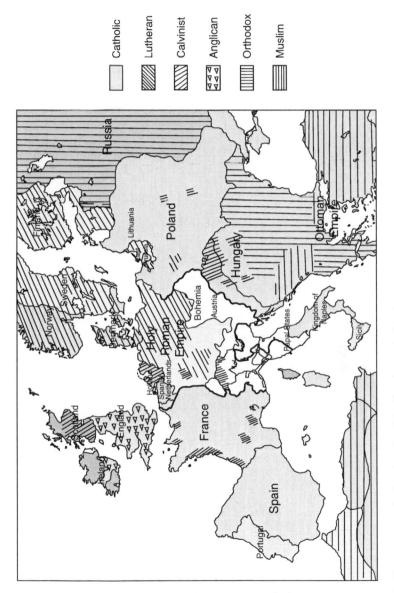

Map 2 European confessional and political landscape in 1650
Note: Heavier line marks the boundary of the Holy Roman Empire.

the emerging market economies. In the following century, movements calling for further reform would spring up within each confession, while the firmly institutionalized territorial churches began to bring the message of Reformed Christianities to common parishioners in town and countryside. These trends would produce the settlements of Europe's long Reformation.

Part II
THE WEFT: MAKING SENSE OF THE LONG EUROPEAN REFORMATION

5

SETTLEMENTS, 1600–1750: CHURCH BUILDING, STATE BUILDING, AND SOCIAL DISCIPLINE

The Peace of Westphalia appeared to mark the end of religious warfare between states, though confessional tensions continued within territories. During the century after Westphalia the political and religious pressures that had driven the European Reformation dissipated. In 1695, the historian Veit Ludwig von Seckendorff first characterized the Reformation as an era in Church history, an era that had passed.[1] In the eighteenth century the drive for further reforms would resolve itself in a series of settlements that recognized the plurality of legitimate churches and the right of dissent within confessional communities. Official intolerance against religious minorities sometimes victimized groups on a large scale such as the French Huguenots in the 1680s and Protestants in the archdiocese of Salzburg in the 1730s, yet refugees from religious persecution could readily find safe havens in confessionally-mixed cities and states, such as Brandenburg-Prussia, where mercantile needs overrode religious intolerance.

New forms of piety emerged. Jansenist Catholicism, Pietist Lutheranism, Arminian Calvinism, and English Non-conformism were often inspired by the "better sort" within communities, but the movements also drew support from among commoners. All over Europe there was a new outpouring of popular confessionalized piety, from the erection of personal roadside shrines in Catholic lands to the composition of emotionally charged Methodist hymns. More and more ecclesiastical authorities responded with tolerance to divergent religious enthusiasm.

Toleration reflected both the secure position of territorial churches and the gradual depreciation of religious conformity for increasingly secularized segments of the political and social elite, for whom "enlightened reason" supplanted faith in understanding the world and intimated the possibility for a more ecumenical and peaceful continent. By 1750 the original evangelical goal of religious renewal could be documented all over Europe. Reformed Christianity, however, had become pluralistic rather than unitary, and popularly inspired as much as officially determined.

Society in Post-Westphalian Europe

At the beginning of the eighteenth century, Europe's population totalled some 95 million, but the demographic crisis of the early seventeenth century left its mark on the distribution of that population. The Thirty Years War had laid waste to extensive areas in Central Europe and Italy. The wars of the late seventeenth and early eighteenth century would extend the demographic misery to eastern Central Europe, the Baltic basin, and the Balkan peninsula. Bubonic plague disappeared from Europe after its last outbreak at Marseilles in 1721, though other infectious diseases remained endemic in the continent's crowded cities. Wealthier Europeans lived in spacious housing, consumed more food and more protein, and grew taller than their poorer neighbours, but life expectancy remained short at all levels of society, especially among the dispossessed and destitute. Poor harvests resulted in periods of hunger, and a combination of war and bad weather could trigger devastating famines such as those of the 1690s and 1709. Furthermore, accidents and illnesses such as smallpox left the survivors disfigured. Everyone bore the touch of some malady. Throughout Europe ecclesiastical institutions met the demands of modern social service organizations. Local churches and pious individuals offered charitable relief for countless orphans as well as the crippled and dangerously ill. On the surface, little had changed since the Black Death, but in the early eighteenth century mortality rates began to decline, and by 1750 Europe was moving into a new demographic regime marked by unprecedented growth.

The mechanization of cloth production which ushered in the Industrial Revolution would not begin until late in the century, and the rhythm of work still followed late medieval patterns. Rural children began their working lives as early as the age of six, collecting manure, tending livestock, and supervising younger brothers and sisters. By the age of fourteen most children had left home either to begin their apprenticeship, enter domestic service, or join the agricultural labour force. Adults shared tasks, particularly in agriculture where men and women worked together during the critical planting and harvesting seasons. The household, whether godly or ungodly, remained the centre of human life where people shared food, wisdom, comforts, and hardships under a common roof. Solitary life was normally a sign of abject poverty. As had been the case in 1350, more people worked in agriculture producing food, fodder, and textile crops than at any other task, but some patterns had changed. In the century after the Peace of Westphalia, the European breadbasket became the southern Baltic lowlands of Prussia, Poland, and the Ukraine, whose grain was shipped through Amsterdam in the seventeenth century, and then directly to urban centres of north-western Europe in the eighteenth. Bread was the principal dietary staple, and an adult male needed two to three pounds of bread per day to survive. Wheat and rye were the most important grain crops. When granted a wish, the heroes and heroines of fairy tales often chose to have a loaf of fine wheat bread that replenished itself.[2]

In many parts of Europe, improvements in agricultural techniques and transportation began to have a positive effect on crop yields. In England and the Low Countries they rose to fourteen to one, which is around one-third of the modern yield. Eastern European yields, however, remained around three or four to one, the same as they were in ancient times. Poor harvests and crop failures were common, but the developing infrastructure of trade ensured that grain would find markets where dearth offered profits. New technologies in drainage allowed the cultivation of some boggy soils, for example the crop lands in Prussia increased by nearly 15 per cent; yet the real take-off in agricultural production came from new crop rotations, in particular the development of fodder crops such as alfalfa in late seventeenth-century Flanders. Fodder crops feed cattle. Prior to this time, cattle had grazed on fallow fields, which meant that as much as half the land was not being worked. By alternating fodder crops with grain, farmers provided more feed for cattle, which fattened individual animals, enlarged the herds, and increased the supply of manure, which helps the soil hold water. In addition, planting turnips and clover, crops that restored nitrogen – essential for grain production – to the soil, increased yields by preventing the exhaustion of the land's productive capacity. Flemish farmers had developed these techniques before 1650, and the practice would spread slowly, appearing in England, Scotland, and parts of France, Sweden, Germany, Spain, and Italy by 1750. Along with crop rotation, new exotic crops, especially maize and potatoes from the Americas, offered more calories per acre than traditional grains. In the eighteenth century exotic colonial products, such as cane sugar, chocolate, coffee, tea, and tobacco, also began to penetrate European markets. Prices were high, and the rituals of consumption associated with the new products were limited to the rich.

Despite all of this, it would be misleading to think of early eighteenth-century Europe as undergoing an agricultural revolution. Most peasant farmers followed traditional methods and clung to familiar crops on land that they essentially share-cropped. Peasants also had to meet tax responsibilities, including the ecclesiastical tithe, which kept most of them in debt. A family of four could feed itself by growing wheat on one hectare (two to three acres) of good land, but in fact they needed to farm much more land to meet their rent and tax obligations.[3] The hopes and fears of Europe's rural majority had changed little since the fourteenth century, and the seasonal rituals, talismans, and prayers that were a spiritual tool-kit used to protect the fruits of endless labour remained vital personal resources in a threatening and unpredictable world. The local clergy could rail against the superstitions harboured by their parishioners or find ways to accommodate them, but the persistence of "folk ways" demonstrates how the new forms of learned religiosity advocated by the reformers did not address all the religious needs of the common people.[4]

Europe's economic growth had favoured its towns, where wages and profits were higher. By 1700 Amsterdam, Lisbon, London, Madrid, Milan, Palermo, Paris, Naples, Rome, and Venice sheltered more than 100,000 people, and finding adequate supplies of food and water taxed the efforts of urban officials and drained the productive capacity of thousands of square miles of hinterland. Of these great urban centres, only London and Amsterdam were Protestant cities. A large city boasted 10,000 residents, and by 1700 perhaps 13 per cent of the population in north-western Europe lived in such centres. The dynamic towns of the early eighteenth century were those associated with the expanding royal governments, and the once proud independent urban centres such as Augsburg and Florence had become economic backwaters.

By the early eighteenth century, urban artisan households had more disposable income and used it to purchase non-perishable goods. Even perishable items, such as tobacco and coffee, had paraphernalia, pipes and cups, associated with their consumption. The acquisition of household artefacts including religious books and objects, which could be pawned at a pinch, was a form of savings, and less likely to be stolen or squandered. With accumulation came a new attitude towards objects, which we might call materialistic, an attitude that challenged core assumptions about proper Christian living. The new consumer revolution began first in the larger cities, only spreading to smaller urban centres and the countryside in the decades after our survey. Materialism formed a significant facet of a general secularization of attitudes and behaviour in the eighteenth century that denigrated the purer forms of religiosity and asceticism associated with the second Reformation among Calvinists and Catholics, at least in Europe's political centres. The new attitude was one of the factors that took the steam out of official drives to bring the Reformation to the commoners at a time when piety in the countryside was on the rise.

Europe's Post-Westphalian Political Order

The dynastic rivalry between the Catholic Habsburgs, rulers of Spain and Austria, and the Catholic French kings, which had framed European power relations since the 1490s, was resolved for the most part by the Peace of Westphalia for France and Austria and the Peace of the Pyrenees in 1659 for France and Spain. Though Austria and France would remain rivals until the 1750s, Spain ceased to be a force in power politics. In France, Louis XIV (*1643–1715) ruled over 20 million subjects in the richest kingdom in Europe, which allowed him to pursue personal glory on the battlefield more aggressively than any of his rivals. Given his own mechanisms for self-aggrandizement, it is easy to read political history in the century after Westphalia from a French bias. Other rulers, from petty German princes to Peter the Great (*1689–1725), tsar of Russia, mimicked French administration as well as the court culture of Louis's monumental palace at Versailles. French replaced Latin and Italian as the language of diplomacy, and by 1750 nearly all significant cultural conversations were conducted in French, the language of *les lumières* (the enlightened). Nevertheless, the most significant political shift in the century after Westphalia was the emergence of new European powers, the Great Britain, Russia, and Prussia, who joined France and Austria in a balance that would frame international affairs in Europe into the twentieth century.

170

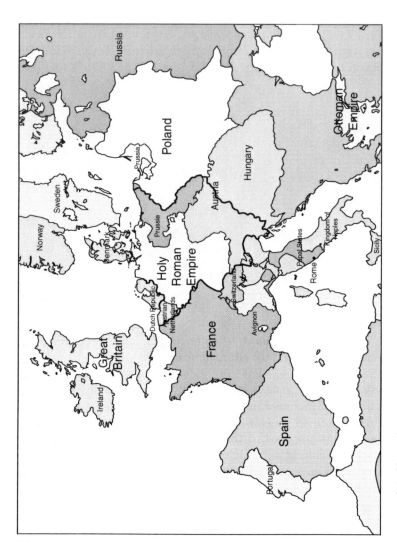

Map 3 European political boundaries in 1750
Note: Heavier line marks the boundary of the Holy Roman Empire.

A half-century of wars between 1672 and 1721, with three separate theatres of operation, would be the anvil on which Europe's new power structure was forged.[5] In the Balkans, the Austrian Habsburgs fought the last Crusade, formally declared by Pope Innocent XII (*1691–1700), against the Ottoman Turks with the frontier kingdom of Hungary as the prize. The support of Hungary's Protestant nobility would be crucial to the Habsburgs' success. The Ottomans had initiated the struggle when they besieged Vienna in 1683, only to be driven off. The Austrian counter-offensive secured Hungary and Transylvania in 1699 and penetrated into northern Serbia by 1718. Though wars between Muslim and Christian powers would continue in the Balkans into the twentieth century, the Ottoman threat to Central Europe that had overshadowed the entire Reformation era was over. Hungary now formed a significant buffer state for Austria, and Vienna experienced a dramatic rebuilding high-lighted by baroque churches and noble palaces, which sprang up in the now secure suburbs around the old city. Vienna's population more than doubled to 175,000, and a vibrant and wealthy court established Austria as the cultural centre for baroque Catholicism.

The second great conflict revolved around Louis XIV's ambition to secure his kingdom's "natural frontier" on the Rhine river. Lurking behind French aggression was the question of who would succeed the sickly and childless Charles II (*1665–1700) of Spain. Louis asserted his rights through his wife, Charles's sister, while the Spanish monarch's Habsburg cousins in Austria also advanced a legitimate claim. The wars had little to do with religion, though French campaigns in the Netherlands and Louis's bitter rivalry with the Calvinist Dutch Stadholder, William III, prince of Orange (*1672–1702), may have inspired the expulsion of the Calvinist Huguenots from France in 1685. For his part William of Orange used the spectre of French hegemony over Western Europe to crib together an alliance against France that included the Dutch, German Protestant princes, Catholic Austria, and England, whose crown the Stadholder usurped by coup in 1688 from his unpopular Catholic father-in-law James II (*1685–8). William's coalition held through two long wars from 1689 to 1714, with the second fought over succession to the Spanish legacy. The Peace of Utrecht ended the bloodshed, awarding the Spanish crown and its overseas dominions to Louis's great-grandson Philip V (*1700–46), and ceding Spain's European holdings in Italy and the Netherlands to the Austrian Habsburgs. The treaty left Austria as the dominant Catholic power in Germany, increasing Habsburg leverage and *Hausmacht* in Imperial affairs. The real beneficiary was Great Britain, officially the United Kingdom of England, Ireland, and, after 1707, Scotland. In the eighteenth century the British navy and small but well-trained army would be a pivotal force in European warfare and the sinew that held together a sprawling empire.

The third zone of conflict was the Baltic basin, where Lutheran Sweden had emerged as a major power during the Thirty Years War. The Swedes continued to dominate their traditional enemies, Lutheran Denmark and Catholic Poland-Lithuania, only to succumb to Peter the Great's Russian armies. Sweden ceded significant lands at the Peace of Nystad in 1721, which granted Russia a Baltic port to foster trade and cultural exchanges with Western Europe. Orthodox Russia became the dominant power in the Baltic basin and a new force in European affairs. In the eighteenth century, Swedish and Danish political influence rapidly declined, while the composite state of Brandenburg-Prussia rose to become the dominant Protestant power in Germany. In 1701 the Polish monarch recognized Brandenburg-Prussia's ruler, Frederick, as king of Prussia (formerly a Polish duchy). This highly militarized state soon became a significant European power. In the long run the great loser in the northern wars was Poland-Lithuania, which drifted into dependence on Russia and Prussia, opening the way for its dismemberment during the French revolutionary wars.

Although non-monarchical states such as Venice, the Dutch Republic, and the Swiss Confederacy survived, the model for political authority during the era was "absolute" monarchy, under which rulers claimed full sovereignty over all their subjects and personally directed the work of government. The stimulus for "absolutist" administrative centralization and the concomitant expanding scope of governance in the daily lives of subjects derived from pressures for military modernization. In the late seventeenth century, shifts in organization and financing, along with new technologies, concentrated military power in the hands of a few great states. The use of artillery made the cost of fortifications prohibitive, ending the independence of most urban republics. Gradual improvements in musketry and the development of the bayonet demanded a collective battlefield discipline inculcated by regular close-order drill, which professionalized military life, first in the form of mercenary units and later in conscript standing armies drawn from the kingdom's dependent peasantry and poor. Standing armies remained in active service during peacetime and required year-round housing in barracks in place of the older practice of temporarily quartering troops in private homes. An effective organization and chain of command allowed armies to mushroom in size, particularly in the late seventeenth and eighteenth centuries. Most national armies exceeded 100,000 men, and by 1710 perhaps a million European men were under arms.[6] It was often the case that four-fifths of state expenditures went to the army or to debts accrued in wars. Finance ministers carefully nurtured bond markets for investment in government debt and concocted innovative means of extracting tax revenues from royal subjects, particularly the peasantry.

Absolute monarchs faced two significant obstacles in their push for centralized and personal control. First, European kingdoms remained essentially composite states, assembled over centuries by dynastic unions and conquest, with each territorial component normally entitled to "ancient" rights and privileges, which its elite jealously guarded against royal incursions.[7] The Austrian Habsburgs faced linguistic and religious barriers in ruling a dynastic empire that included Italian-, Flemish-, and Hungarian-speaking subjects, and relied on Latin as the common legal language. The German-speaking ruler of the United Kingdom, George I (*1715–27), governed Scotland and Ireland by negotiating with "national" parliaments at Edinburgh and Dublin. Even Louis XIV had to appeal to provincial estates to authorize new taxes and to register laws. He also recognized independent foreign enclaves, such as the duchy of Lorraine and the papal county of Venaissin surrounding Avignon, within his kingdom's "natural frontiers". In addition, bishops, clerical corporate groups such as Cathedral chapters and universities, along with towns and noble estates, tenaciously held on to corporate rights and privileges that exempted them from taxation or the purview of new laws. Both in Protestant and Catholic states, the one institution which could penetrate into every village of the kingdom was the Church, whose pastors, when effective, provided the ruler with a mouthpiece to reach nearly all of his or her subjects.

Even when and where the monarch's sovereignty was realized, governing operated through factionalized networks of patrons and clients. Much of the administration was comprised of venal office-holders, individuals who had purchased their posts and were reluctant to accept any reform that might threaten their personal investment. Furthermore, despite a spate of reforms that had created new governmental bureaus staffed by professional administrators with a growing awareness of public duty, the elaborate and ritualized culture of royal courts remained essential in decision-making. Handling the monarch's daily schedule gave tremendous informal power to a privy councillor, while official or unofficial mistresses could exercise significant influence over policies. The royal household was the centre of a web of households, private offices, salons, and coffee houses where schemes and contracts were negotiated. Access to financial capital, marriage ties, and inside information allowed individuals to emerge as power-brokers who could secure royal favour for a project or override resistance to a new governmental policy at the provincial level.[8] In all, government officials comprised less than 1 per cent of the population, and effective rule required negotiation, accommodation, and largesse. In such a setting political insiders, nearly always drawn from the nobility, were essential. The early eighteenth century was an age of networking and cronyism that permeated all aspects of government including ecclesiastical affairs.

Religion in the Century after Westphalia

Since the age of the apostles, Christians have advocated two models for the Church: one favoured a broader visible Church open to all; the other a smaller spiritual Church of true believers. In the late seventeenth century, advocates for the smaller spiritual Church emerged in all four leading Christian communities: Catholic, Lutheran, Calvinist, and English Protestant. Moreover, frustration with the religiosity of the masses affected even the supporters of the more open Church. On a second front, religious developments after 1650 owed much to the incomplete resolution of the inter- and intra-confessional crises in the early decades of the seventeenth century. With the end of the Thirty Years War, the possibility of any established Church securing its cause by force grew remote. With the complete cooperation of secular authorities, it remained possible to purge visible non-conformists within the boundaries of a territorial state, as had occurred for the most part in Spain, but even here much of the population continued to understand and practise their faith in diverse and localized ways.[9] Even the great expulsion of Protestants from the archdiocese of Salzburg in 1732 owed much to political forces within the Empire and the social alienation between the Protestant upland communities and their lowland Catholic neighbours.[10] Though religious wars had ended, leaders within official Churches steeled themselves for a long and bitter struggle to preserve their gains and to undermine their opponents wherever possible.

By 1650 established Churches had developed educational infrastructures of secondary Latin schools and universities to train the parish clergy, their ecclesiastical supervisors, and the lay officials who occupied the new bureaus of the expanding states. Education entailed religious indoctrination, and at this social and intellectual level the sixteenth-century reformers had succeeded in their goals of renewing the faith, as is evidenced by the detailed spiritual diaries kept by educated seventeenth-century Christians.[11] The continued spectre of the plague, the devastating effects of famine and warfare, and the ever-present tragedy of childhood death under the old demographic regime encouraged reflection on mortality. Introspection and self-examination could trigger crises of conscience when the believer was overwhelmed by a sense of personal inadequacy and doubted his or her salvation. Christians, in all confessions, came to see themselves as tragic actors seeking personal salvation from a jealous and punitive God in a world full of spiritual portents, challenges, and ordeals; and they sought guarantees or assurances that they were among God's chosen.

With the successful inculcation of confessional identity among elites, enthusiastic advocates of further reform sought to turn passive Christians into active ones, who not only attended ritual activities stage-managed by others but also internalized faith as a moral code and way of living. Unfortunately the expectation of a personal, born-again conversion, which would transform an individual, raised the standards of church membership to levels that only a devout minority could hope to attain, creating an elite cadre of true believers and relegating the multitudes to a questionable religious status. The clash of the religious expectations of those who had fully internalized the reformers' message with the reality of conditions at the parish level disillusioned the devout. In many ways the new emphasis on personal religious experience and the mushrooming of gathered communities of true believers reflected a recognition among the elite of the failure to realize the broader goals of "priesthood" for all believers.

"Renewed" Catholicism

Within Catholicism the Council of Trent had confirmed traditional religious practices and ecclesiastical institutions and had placed responsibility for further reform in the hands of the pope and the bishops. The pace and scope of Catholic renewal thus hinged on concerted efforts to reform papal administration, which were only partially realized, and changes in episcopal recruitment – also complicated by the late medieval system of concordats, which left appointments in the hands of secular authorities.

During the seventeenth and eighteenth centuries the papacy essentially became a regional monarchy deeply embedded in Italian politics, at the expense of its role as spiritual leader for Catholics.[12] Between 1540 and 1758, all twenty-seven popes were Italians, primarily drawn from elite families in northern Italy and the Papal States. As elective rather than hereditary monarchs, new popes had spent long and successful careers manoeuvring through the patronage networks of the Roman curia.[13] As the ultimate patron, the pope lavished ecclesiastical offices on family members, headed by the "cardinal-nephew", a kinsman who served as vice-regent. Despite condemnation of the practice at Trent, nearly all leading papal officials were pluralists, though the scope of their plunder was restricted primarily to the Italian Church. Furthermore, the reforms of the College of Cardinals secured at the council of Constance had fallen into disfavour. The number of cardinals, originally capped at thirty, expanded steadily to seventy in 1586 when Sixtus V (*1585–90) set this as the official limit. The Consistory of Cardinals, moreover, lost its role as an institutional check on papal autocracy and devolved instead into a reservoir for papal bureaucrats. Papal reforms were rare and often driven by non-spiritual forces. Pope Innocent XII (*1691–1700) finally abolished official nepotism in the wake of a fiscal crisis in 1692. Political agendas consistently relegated spiritual concerns to secondary status. Thus the failure, once again, to reform the "head" left the initiative for Catholic renewal to the episcopal "members".

The decrees ratified at Trent called for regular provincial synods, diocesan seminaries, and parish visitations, all of which enhanced episcopal pastoral responsibilities.[14] Though bishops were to be central agents for spiritual reform, no effort was made to redraw diocesan boundaries or to reform the benefice system, which would have required too many sacrifices among vested interests. Philip II's diocesan restructuring, which had triggered the Dutch revolt, survived in the Southern Netherlands where Spanish power secured the new system. Elsewhere little changed. In 1650 there were around 620 Catholic dioceses in Europe with more than half of them in Italy. Sprawling sees, such as Toledo, Seville, Paris, Strasbourg, and Cracow, commanded rich endowments, and their bishops dispensed significant ecclesiastical patronage. At the other extreme papal officials required a portfolio of impoverished Italian dioceses to generate a significant income.

Throughout Catholic Europe, episcopal efforts at reform proceeded at a pace acceptable to lay elites. In France, where the king appointed all bishops, reform moved steadily forward. By the 1630s pluralism had ended, and all episcopal candidates had received holy orders. In counterpoint, pluralism and non-priestly bishops persisted in the Empire where the great princely dynasties, such as the Bavarian Wittelsbachs, treated episcopal posts as family legacies. Despite the bishops' new spiritual duties, royal patrons saw their appointees primarily as diocesan governors and selected candidates from noble families "naturally endowed" with administrative competence. Increasingly, however, rulers expected their bishops to cultivate their natural talent with higher education, at least in the Jesuit colleges. In France, Louis XIV preferred candidates with theological degrees, but elsewhere bishops normally pursued studies in canon and civil law. By 1700 nearly all bishops had degrees, except for the Imperial prince-bishops, of whom less than 15 per cent had attended university. Overall, the effectiveness of episcopal religious leadership varied from region to region and, within a given diocese, from bishop to bishop; but Catholic renewal had ensured that in most cases the eighteenth-century episcopate was better educated and more engaged in diocesan affairs than their fifteenth-century counterparts. Nevertheless, one thing had not changed. A social chasm, which often generated misunderstandings, separated bishops from their parish clergy.

The parish remained the centre of religious life for all Catholics, and building a cadre of educated parish clergy to foster reform and renewal at the parish level was a slow and expensive process. Bishops were reluctant to found seminaries, which had to be financed in part from episcopal resources. Down into the eighteenth century, many dioceses had no seminary. Jesuit colleges filled the void, but clerical education was expensive and scholarships rare. As a result, urban families of middling wealth, who could pay for schooling and the personal stipend necessary to support a newly-ordained secular priest until he received a beneficed living, formed the social reservoir for parish clergy in both town and countryside in what remained a career rather than a vocation.[15] The survival of the benefice system meant that bishops continued to hold appointment rights over only a fraction of their dioceses' parishes, and in some cases Catholic parishioners relied on the good graces of Protestant patrons. Beneficed endowments varied, and priests jealously competed for the more lucrative livings. Despite the residue of traditional structures and habits, it became the case that shared educational backgrounds, careful examinations of potential priests on their knowledge of

Catholic doctrine, networks of rural deaneries where parish priests met regularly with their colleagues, and periodic visitations provided episcopal officials with the means to censure ineffective or unruly priests and helped foster *esprit de corps* among the pastorate. By the early eighteenth century, in dioceses like Speyer and Grenoble a renewed pastorate fostered and supported new forms of Catholic religious expression among their parishioners.[16]

The Protestant Reformation had been particularly hard on monastic communities, which were suppressed in those territories embracing the new faith. Even in Catholic territories many traditional orders, such as the Benedictines, Dominicans, and Franciscans, were in decline, except where the fifteenth-century Observant movements had succeeded in revitalizing individual houses. It would be new religious orders, in particular the Capuchins and Jesuits, rather than long-established communities, which would be the dynamic force in the seventeenth- and early eighteenth-century Catholic Church. Significantly these orders operated across diocesan and territorial boundaries.[17]

The Capuchins were Italian Franciscans who had broken from the Observant movement in the 1520s to pursue the earliest rule of St Francis more closely as hermits. Supported by reform-minded noble patrons, the movement grew to several thousand members by the early seventeenth century. In Central and Eastern Europe the wandering preachers sought converts within Protestant lands. In Italy they assumed responsibility for social services, creating food banks and ministering to victims of plague. In Catholic regions in Germany and elsewhere, they conducted rural missions, preaching in plain language and organizing penitential communities.[18] Their commitment to preaching, communal acts of lay piety, and social service, inspired dozens of other smaller religious communities and lay confraternities, marking one arena where elite religiosity and popular faith effectively combined.

The Jesuits were the pre-eminent religious order of Catholic renewal and counter-reform. The Jesuits operated "in the world" and had no monasteries. Each member of the Society of Jesus was a self-disciplined religious foot soldier who reinvigorated his commitment at personal "retreats" marked by private meditation on Ignatius Loyola's *Spiritual Exercises*. The Jesuits had sworn to obey the pope, which made them key agents of papal religious "foreign" policy, while a "general" headed the Society from offices in Rome. Jesuits sought to convert non-Christians in missionary work in Asia, Africa, and the Americas, where efforts to translate Catholic belief into local idioms made them Europe's first ethnographers. They served as shock troops for the Counter-reformation in Central, Northern, and Eastern Europe, suffering martyrdom in England, expulsion in Sweden, and success in Poland. Their greatest contribution to their Church came from the network of colleges, seminaries, and universities that they established throughout Europe and around the globe. By 1749, Ignatius Loyola's initial company of ten had grown to over 22,000. The Jesuits participated in every religious controversy that challenged early modern Catholicism, accumulating religious and political enemies. As a result between 1759 and 1771, they would be expelled from much of Catholic Europe in what might be seen as the final step in securing "national" Catholic churches.

Given the absence of centralizing forces, the post-Tridentine Church never represented a united front, either institutionally or religiously. Devout Catholics bitterly feuded over the nature of piety, the role of the lay believer, and the degree to which individual human will helped realize salvation. The roots of the debates lay in the tense decades of the early seventeenth century, but the dialogues continued with increasing vehemence deep into the eighteenth. Within French-speaking Catholicism, the followers of Cornelius Jansen (1585–1638) advocated a view of salvation that belittled human free will and the efficacy of good works. The Jansenists discouraged participatory piety, especially the reception of communion, and leaned towards the belief in God's predestination of a chosen few. They emphasized stoic personal faith, reinforced by reading and meditation on the Scriptures and demonstrated by scrupulous attention to morality. The movement drew its strength from the nobility, and in particular noble women involved with the convent of Port-Royal.[19] Jansenists and Jesuits engaged in a long-running debate over the proper beliefs of orthodox Catholicism, which resulted in condemnation of Jansenist beliefs in the papal bull *Unigenitus* in 1713. The movement endured among the nuns in several noble convents and in clandestine meetings held in noble households. None the less, as it had in the later Middle Ages, outward piety, manifested by participation in religious services, particularly the Mass, remained the official path to Catholic salvation.

Lutheranism between Orthodoxy and Pietism

In 1617 Lutheran communities throughout the Empire marked the centennial of the Reformation with poems, plays, and public celebrations that often juxtaposed the pious and saintly Martin Luther against the papal Antichrist. Luther would have cringed at the personal hagiography and the accounts of miraculous happenings associated with his images.[20] This was the first in a long series of commemorative anniversaries of key dates in Luther's life and the formation of the Lutheran Church: 1483, 1517, 1530, 1546, 1555, and 1580. Set free from medieval Christian traditions, this plotting of Lutheran history in collective confessional memory created the base for a Lutheran culture, informed by the Book of Concord. The sanctioned Gnesio-Lutheran Orthodoxy required an independent and authoritative clergy, whose ritual activities played a critical role in fostering faith. A second dissenting stream of Lutheranism, with its source in "crypto-Calvinist" Philippist traditions, resurfaced in late seventeenth-century Pietism. Pietists re-emphasized the centrality of scriptural reading and personal meditation over clergy-led services, and championed the spiritual power of prayer. Here again was a potent call for a priesthood of all believers.

Orthodox Lutheran churches retained the division between clergy and laity as well as the traditional notion of three orders or estates within society. According to the Augsburg Confession, the clergy's prime task was preaching the Word of God as a vehicle of faith essential for salvation. The mediating role of a privileged clergy had reappeared. Given Luther's insistence on consubstantiation, moreover, sacramental rituals, including baptism, communion, and absolution in penitential services, as forms of the visible Word, made ministers "the essential link between the laity and the supernatural".[21] By 1600 most Lutheran states followed a model for clerical preparation, formalized in the duchy of Württemberg, that required university education in theology but little training in pastoral care. More often than not, pastors were sons of other pastors or the duchy's lay officials, and they stood apart from the laity, particularly in the countryside.[22]

The concept of justification by faith, as embodied in Orthodox Lutheranism, provided little moral incentive for believers beyond conventional observation of formal religious obligations such as attending services. In juxtaposition to the parishioners' passive witness, Lutheran ministers were constantly busy with liturgical responsibilities and preaching. Much of the finer points of Lutheran faith rested on subtle theological arguments mastered at the university, which the ministers appreciated but the laity found mystifying. As moral watchdogs in the community, often in conjunction with state authority, pastors and their families inevitably fell into conflict with their neighbours.[23] Orthodox Lutheranism, then, became a new and highly demanding form of clericalism, whose rigid doctrines and intense moralism were ill-suited to win general lay support. The Danish Church ordinance of 1645 required lay elders to patrol the pews with sticks, poking those who dozed off during hour-long sermons.[24] For the common believers, their role as sheep offered little incentive to internalize their faith, thus thwarting efforts to bring the Reformation to the people.

In the wake of the Thirty Years War, Pietism swept through Lutheran Germany like a revivalist movement. The Pietists saw the war as God's just punishment for German sins. Despite the fact that they drew on the literature and practice of Dutch Reformed piety and English Puritanism and that Orthodox opponents quickly tagged the new movement as "crypto-Calvinist", Pietism must be understood within a Lutheran context. Pietists felt that Orthodox Lutheran leaders had devoted too much energy to reforming the Church and too little energy in determining how the Church might reform the world, which the Pietists argued could only be realized through the shared effort of clergy and laity. Pietist practices activated the laity to nurture personal faith, particularly through prayer. Philipp Jakob Spener (1635–1705), the most prominent of the early Pietists, argued that the unbound or inward power of the Holy Spirit was accessible to the believer without clergy, and he called for clandestine conventicles of lay men and women for bible reading, repetition and discussion of sermons, and collective prayer.

The crucial issue that divided Orthodox from Pietist was the penitential rite. Luther had not considered confession of sins a sacrament, but the expectation remained that prior to the communion service the faithful would engage in a private, self-reflective examination of conscience and admission of faults to God, followed by public absolution administered by the pastor for the community. By the late seventeenth century, this religiously and psychologically charged experience had devolved into a mechanical recitation of memorized responses to pastoral questions, followed by a perfunctory exposition of Christian doctrine by the minister, and culminating in collective absolution. Even in this form, the pastor could in his choice of topics embarrass his parishioners, and when necessary humble enemies among his neighbours.[25] Pietists found this practice too formulaic to sustain inner conversion of the heart, and they doubted that pastoral absolution conferred grace. Religious introspection, confession of sin, and trust in God's mercy were personal acts of faith for Pietists and not the first step in a ritualized affirmation of Lutheran "priestcraft".[26] Pietists also attacked the pastors' power to excommunicate parishioners; and where the movement was successful, consistories dominated by lay officials assumed that role. In short, Pietism offered a model of Lutheranism which undermined clerical privilege. In response, Orthodox ministers vilified pietistic practices in defence of their threatened authority. The dispute deeply divided eighteenth-century Lutheranism, and political authorities were left to settle the matter.

From the beginning the spread of Lutheranism had depended on the protection of rulers and magistrates, which resulted in dozens of essentially independently administered Lutheran state churches. In Denmark the royal status as supreme head of the Church resulted in confessional allegiance to the Augsburg Confession but not the Book of Concord. This foundation created a hybrid Lutheran Church in which the episcopal structure survived along with elements of medieval Catholicism, including iconography and high altars. Danish peasants demanded ritual blessings of their fields at Eastertide, and their ministers obliged them. The royal ordinance of 1665 recognized the clergy as a distinct estate under the titular leadership of the archbishop of Zealand, but the king ruled unchallenged in religious matters and personally welcomed Huguenot refugees in 1685 over the protests of Orthodox leaders. In Denmark, Pietist communities were one among many groups that operated under the wide umbrella of royal protection and tolerance.[27]

In the duchy of Württemberg, the powerful and well-entrenched Orthodox territorial church also had to submit to the tolerant policies of Duke Eberhard Ludwig (*1677–1733), who repopulated his devastated lands with Huguenot and Waldensian refugees. The duke supported Pietism as a counter-force to the Orthodox establishment, though the movement, consisting of small cells of quiet and bookish believers, made little headway in the official Church. In contrast, Pietism in Brandenburg-Prussia was politically significant. Spener, who moved to Berlin in 1691, had planted the seed, but it was August Hermann Francke (1663–1727), an exile of conscience from Saxony, who set the tone as a pastor near Halle. Francke called for active piety, for the human being was not a vessel for faith but a tool of faith. He founded a series of pietistic institutions (*Stiftungen*) from orphanages to missionary organizations to publishing houses. Though Calvinists themselves, the elector margrave Frederick III (*1688–1713), who declared himself King Frederick I of Prussia in 1701, and his successor Frederick William I (*1713–40), supported Prussian Pietism. In turn the movement's leaders enhanced royal power through an ideology of service and self-discipline that helped unify the monarchy's diverse and scattered territories. Grateful for royal patronage the Pietists stifled their social criticism of courtly decadence and focused on public service in social projects. By the 1730s a Pietist education and a personal profession of Pietism, however cynical, were essential prerequisites for state service in the emerging Prussian bureaucracy.[28]

As with Catholicism, eighteenth-century Lutheranism was a divided confession with practitioners spread across the devotional landscape. Some Lutherans honoured practices that Luther had railed against in his own sermons. The majority accepted Orthodox traditions where parishioners followed the lead of a proud, educated, and at times self-righteous ministry. Others embraced various forms of internalized piety drawn from a rich tradition of lay religiosity with Lutheran and non-Lutheran antecedents. Though the earliest Lutheran churches had relied on lay authorities to defend their reforms, nearly everywhere the relationship between Church and state in Lutheran territories was becoming increasingly ambivalent.

Calvinisms

Jean Calvin was a refugee of conscience, ministering to an illegal underground church from exile in a city where he had powerful enemies as well as supporters, and serving as a beacon for a European-wide confederation of like-minded "Reformed" Christians. His life became a template for his religious movement: personal commitment, flight, clandestine services, often problematical relationships with political authorities, and an "international" network of support. Though Calvinist leaders made sincere efforts to coordinate their scattered churches and to delineate a clear confessional stand, the decentralized nature of Church governance and ongoing dissent against the prevailing predestinarian orthodoxy meant that being "Calvinist" implied different things in different times and places. The most traumatic event for early modern Calvinism, the outlawing of a million French Huguenots in France in 1685, brought all of these aspects of the early modern Calvinist experience to the fore.

By 1600, "Reformed" religious communities that looked to Geneva for models of ecclesiastical organization and forms of worship could be found in France, the British Isles, the Netherlands, Switzerland, the Holy Roman Empire, Poland, Hungary, and Transylvania. The movement was self-consciously international, quickly generating a network of support to finance the military defence of La Rochelle in 1572 and Geneva decades later.[29] Religious repression periodically drove believers into exile, and sympathetic lay officials in London, Emden, Heidelberg and elsewhere offered safe havens for refugee congregations. Calvinists shared a common disgust for much of the ritual and paraphernalia associated with late medieval Catholicism and still evidenced in Lutheran churches, but most Reformed churches, such as the Scottish, French, and Belgian, had their own "national" confessions and catechisms. Calvinist ecclesiology recognized the practical autonomy of each community, led by its pastor and consistory, who governed nearly all aspects of the congregation's religious and moral life. Though Calvinist religious and lay leaders pushed for greater institutional cohesion through regional synods and sought to define a Calvinist orthodoxy applicable to all, their efforts to control belief required a willing cooperation from local churches that was not always forthcoming.

The core principle of seventeenth-century Calvinist orthodoxy was the concept of double predestination – the belief that God knew and had determined those who would be saved and those who would be damned, before creating the world. Théodore de Bèze, Calvin's successor at Geneva, had developed this principle as a logical extension of the reformer's view of divine election. Under Bèze's guidance various confessional statements drawn up by Reformed Churches from the 1550s onwards emphasized this predestination of souls to salvation or damnation, along with the assurance provided to the "saved" that they could never fall from grace. As God's chosen saints they were expected to fulfil the divine purpose by individually and collectively doing God's will on earth. The spiritual imperative behind such assurance made believers moral activists who sought to re-form society into a "godly commonwealth", which entailed implementing corrective measures against those damned before all time, the "reprobates". Their sometimes haughty moral righteousness directed against festivals, dancing, alcohol, and manifestations of lewdness, often set Calvinists at odds with their less committed neighbours.

Bèze's model was not universally embraced. In the early seventeenth century, the Dutch theologian Jacobus Arminius directly countered this extreme predestinarian theology by claiming that God in his mercy willed all men and women to be saved but foresaw that some would resist this saving grace. Knowing who would be saved did not mean willing it to happen. Furthermore, salvation was not assured. Though faith in God's mercy was the essential first step, according to Arminius, the "saved" must actively persist in holiness and obedience to God's will. For those Calvinists "assured" of sanctification, Arminius's views raised doubts of conscience and questioned the elect's moral superiority. He and his followers, who came to be known as "Remonstrants", a name based on the title of their confessional statement drawn up in 1610, were condemned by the predestinarian majority at a synod held at Dordrecht in the United Provinces in 1618–19. The protocols of Dordrecht, along with the Swiss Consensus of 1675, defined Calvinism for the vast majority of its adherents. Nevertheless, Arminianism retained significant support in England and the Netherlands, for lay authorities were unwilling to persecute dissenters, who simply formed their own congregations. In resisting efforts to enforce a particular type of discipline, Reformed religion at the local level remained vital and diverse, as was seen most obviously among Calvinists in England in the wake of the Civil War, as dissent and non-conformity opened up a dynamic array of new religious expressions. In time, Dutch and English Calvinists of all stripes were forced to abandon their heady pursuit of a "godly nation" based on a single religious communion and to fall back on another conception of civil society, which guaranteed certain rights and liberties for all, even if personal religious discrimination continued to operate.

In France, where the principle of "one king, one faith, one law" (*un roi, une foi, une loi*) was a commonplace in political discourse, tolerance of religious dissent was in the long run impossible. The Edict of Nantes, which had temporarily ended the French Wars of Religion in 1598, allowed public profession of the "so-called Reformed religion" (*Religion prétendue réformée*) as defined by the Calvinist Gallican Confession of 1559. The Edict, however, also restored France as a Catholic kingdom in which what the Calvinists called the "Reformed churches of France" (*Églises réformés de France*) lacked the legal footing of the Catholic Church.[30] Catholic parish boundaries officially blanketed the country, even in Huguenot regions, and Protestants had to pay tithes to "their" parish priests and observe Catholic feast days by avoiding work. The wars had religiously "cleansed" much of the kingdom, and the vast majority of Huguenots lived in enclaves protected by royal grace, in western and southern France. Henry IV, a convert from Calvinism, had promised to pay the regional synods to compensate for tithing, but his son Louis XIII (*1610–43) and grandson Louis XIV seldom honoured this obligation. Following Protestant defeat in a second round of religious civil war in the 1620s, Huguenot nobles began to abjure, and the French Calvinist churches gradually lost their political guardians and leverage. It was now only a question of time before the protections granted at Nantes were revoked.

Being Protestant in France after 1630 meant choosing to remain one, and this fostered an obstinate particularism. Consistories governed increasingly isolated congregations. Officials continued to meet in regional colloquies and annual provincial synods, but the national assemblies became less frequent after 1626 and ceased in 1659. Over time, financially strapped congregations found it more and more difficult to meet their ministers' salaries, which totalled a paltry 400 to 500 *livres*, well below the local priest's income. Ministers, lacking personal resources and denied official support, often had to threaten parishioners with excommunication to collect congregational dues. Lacking the status of law courts, the consistories, too, soon found themselves unable to enforce compliance, and the congregation's leaders grew increasingly reluctant to serve as elders.[31]

In 1670 Louis XIV began undermining the Edict of Nantes's legal guarantees, closing many churches and offering tempting tax exemptions to converts. When revocation finally came in 1685, it was an anti-climax. Of the one million Huguenots in France, roughly 5 per cent of the kingdom's population, perhaps 200,000 emigrated over the next two generations, settling in Holland, Switzerland, Brandenburg and other German states, Denmark, Sweden, England, Ireland, North America, and South Africa. The bulk of those who fled were merchants and skilled craftsmen, whose wealth and labour were not tied to land. The refugees found havens even in regions where their church had no roots but where political authorities saw the economic benefit of tolerating an industrious and prosperous community. The vast majority of Huguenots lacked such mobility and became "newly converted" or "new Catholics", whose religious commitment remained ambivalent deep into the eighteenth century.[32]

Was there such a thing as Calvinist identity in the early eighteenth century? The image of a somberly dressed man full of moral rectitude and informed by a sense of vocation that made him self-disciplined, driven to succeed, and often insensitive to failings in others, certainly defined many Reformed elders. Yet that imagery comes in part from the brushes of Dutch Calvinist artists, whose interiors and landscapes are alive with human spirit.[33] More than any other religious group, early modern Calvinists have been associated with the modern values embodied in liberalism and capitalism, but a simplified label for Calvinists obscures the diversity of worship, faith, communal organization, and social ethics that characterized the movement. This becomes most obvious when exploring the fate of Calvinism in the British Isles.

The Church of England from revolution to toleration

From its inception, the course of the English Reformation depended on the political will of the monarch in cooperation with the Parliament and to some degree the ecclesiastical elites. The Elizabethan Settlement had hoped to create a Church open enough to accommodate most shades of Protestant belief, but it faced outside opposition from Recusant Catholics and disgruntled Calvinist Puritans. By the early seventeenth century, English Church leaders embraced predestinarian Calvinist Protestantism, and James I's delegates ratified the anti-Arminian decisions reached at Dordrecht. Charles I, however, favoured Arminian views; and when he attempted to steer his Church in a new direction without parliamentary support, his religious programme helped precipitate civil war. Ironically, Parliament's victory and the king's execution left the English Church rudderless because without the king it lacked a visible head. Parliamentary and Puritan leaders advocated a new religious polity modelled after Calvin's theocratic republic at Geneva, but this "godly commonwealth" proved impossible to realize in a country as large and diverse as England. In the century after the revolution, the restored kings with Parliament's cooperation re-established the English Church on its Elizabethan foundations and learned to tolerate most forms of dissent and religious separatism.

During the Civil War the Long Parliament attempted to restructure the Church along predestinarian Calvinist lines. Parliamentary statutes purged Archbishop Laud's "popish" innovations, such as altars and communion rails, and abolished the episcopacy and the Elizabethan prayer book. In 1645 the Westminister Assembly of Divines, comprised of parliamentary representatives, Scottish Presbyterians, and Puritan churchmen, published a new Directory of Public Worship with a shortened version of the former prayer book, purified of offensive ceremonies. The Directory dispensed with godparents and the rites of exorcism for infant baptisms, prohibited the purifying ritual of "churching" for women forty days following a birth, and, as amended in 1653, ended church weddings. In place of the former diocesan system, parliament reorganized local ecclesiastical government into Presbyterian consistories known as "classes", through which pastors and local lay elites managed

ecclesiastical administration and regulated moral discipline. Predestinarian Calvinism, under the direction of these "assured" saints, was fully
ascendant. To protect the "godly" commonwealth the Blasphemy Act of
1648 threatened those convicted of denying the central tenets of
Christianity with death, and those dissenting from Calvinist orthodoxy
with imprisonment.

The Parliamentary effort to enforce consensus failed miserably. In
the countryside few English parishes welcomed the new liturgy with
enthusiasm, and many pastors continued to read the services from the
Elizabethan Book of Common Prayer. Among English Calvinists, the
Arminian dissenters split into a conservative faction that fondly recalled
the episcopacy and Laudian forms of worship, and a radical branch with
little interest in bishops or Presbyterian classes but with a profound
belief that all who sought grace could find salvation. These left-wing
Arminians refused to conform to the new official Church or its Directory
of Worship, gathering in separate independent congregations. For
example, "General" Baptists believed in God's gift of salvation for all,
while "Particular" Baptists called for a second adult baptism for true
believers. Due to freedoms of the press introduced during the Civil War,
non-conformist groups like the Baptists could advocate their views in
print, and for a time women, such as Katherine Chidley in her *Justification
of the Independent Churches of Christ* (1641), openly expressed their views
on religion and politics. These independent churches represented
perhaps 7 per cent of the population, and the Blasphemy Act sought to
silence them.

The political tide turned quickly against Parliament and its Church.
In late 1648 the parliamentary New Model Army, well seasoned with
religious independents, drove the Presbyterians from power and ended
compulsory attendance at Sunday services. In 1650 under the guidance
of the army's commander Oliver Cromwell, the remaining "Rump"
members of the Long Parliament repealed the Blasphemy Act of 1648
and instituted new laws that limited persecution to fringe groups such as
the Ranters, whose self-proclaimed amoral behaviour shocked all parties.
Though everyone was legally required to attend Sunday worship, most
individuals, except for Catholics and Episcopalians, could choose the site
and form of that worship. This new ecclesiastical regime legitimized
non-conformist congregations, and local officials often turned a blind
eye to private Catholic and Episcopalian gatherings if they were discrete.
Tolerance of diverse forms of worship, however, assumed godliness, and
Cromwell and his officials considered improving the morality of the

English people as one of their chief priorities. They closed brothels and gambling houses, enforced prohibition against labour and drinking on Sundays, and outlawed the popular and sometimes unruly festivities associated with traditional holidays such as Christmas and May Day.[34]

Within this tolerant atmosphere a new dynamic non-conformist movement, known as the Quakers or Society of Friends, emerged in the 1650s in north-western England under the leadership of George Fox. As radical Arminians the Quakers rejected the predestinarian clericalism of the Presbyterian Order to the extent that they eliminated the ministry altogether. They preached a liberating theology which argued that an inner light of faith existed in all God's children, and that all one needed to do was to recognize the power of the spirit within oneself. Quakers held unstructured meetings in houses, where periods of silence were punctuated by men and women bearing witness to God when the spirit moved them. The spiritual and practical egalitarianism of the early Quaker movement attracted many women, who were active among the society's leadership. By 1660 there were perhaps 30,000 Quakers.

When Charles II (*1660–85) returned to England in 1660 following Cromwell's death, he re-instituted the compulsory state Church, with Laudian rituals, and ended the freedoms of the 1650s. The Act of Uniformity of 1662 required all churchmen to accept the Elizabethan Thirty-Nine Articles and the liturgically conservative Prayer Book of 1662. The bishops returned, while nearly 1,000 pastors, unwilling to accept the new order, abandoned their livings. The restored ecclesiastical leaders recognized the Church's dependence on the monarchy and worked tirelessly to shore up royal institutions. A set of statutes passed between 1661 and 1665, inspired by the earl of Clarendon and known as the Clarendon Codes, required that all government officials attend the king's church and that religious "dissenters" must register their sites of worship with state authorities. Secret "conventicles" held in violation of the codes were widespread, and recalcitrant dissenters, in particular Quakers, often faced time in jail.

Official oppression began to soften in the 1670s as some leading churchmen and parliamentary officials came to advocate religious tolerance, and Charles II relented in hopes of fostering political support for his pro-French Catholic brother, James II (*1685–8). The strategy initially succeeded, but James's open legalization of Catholicism combined with the birth of a Catholic heir the following year appeared to ensure an eventual return to Rome. To defend English Protestantism, parliamentary and Church officials conspired with the Calvinist Dutch Stadholder

William III (*1688–1702) of Orange, the king's son-in-law, in a successful and relatively bloodless coup known as the Glorious Revolution.

The Glorious Revolution secured a Protestant monarchy for England, and confirmed Parliament's increasing political and religious power in the Bill of Rights passed in 1689. The Bill established the rule of law as a constraint to "arbitrary" governance. In the ecclesiastical context this secured the future of English Protestantism, now grounded on a century and a half of parliamentary statutes. The Bill also granted freedom of worship to dissenters, except Catholics, though religious dissent continued to bar an individual from government service. During the reign of William and Mary, "parties" within the established Church of England split along lines that matched factions within Parliament. The "low church" party was sympathetic to non-conformists and cooperative with Whig leaders in Parliament who had conspired against James II and opposed "arbitrary" royal governance in political or religious affairs. "High church" advocates supported the parliamentary Tory faction, which favoured royal prerogatives and the claims of the deposed Stuarts. Around 500 "high church" clergy had resigned in protest against the parliamentary coup that produced the Glorious Revolution. Under the new regime the remaining "high church" leaders pushed to have the English Church governed by regular "convocations" of bishops and leading theologians, hoping to make the Church a more independent institution. It would be the Whigs, however, who dominated eighteenth-century parliamentary and religious life. The episcopal convocation of 1717 would be the last to meet for 125 years. The emerging "Anglican" Church (the term was first used in 1830) operated under the monarchy but with real authority in Parliament. Through the eighteenth century, Whig loyalties were essential for appointment to episcopal sees and other lucrative livings.

The eighteenth-century "Anglican" Church was central to the kingdom's emerging aristocratic order, providing the spiritual underpinning for the political and social hierarchy.[35] The ministers preached of a beneficial God of providence, who ordered and sustained the world reasonably for the social good of humankind. Religious teachers taught duty and deference; poorer children learned to read the Bible in preparation for service; and parishes tended to the poor and chastised the indigent. Ecclesiastical charity served the oligarchy by alleviating the pain of social ills generated by the unequal distribution of income, while pastoral ministry became a career that connected the incumbent to the "better sort" in local society. Meanwhile, "high church" sympathizers formed a "shadow church" with its own smaller patronage network and designated colleges at Oxford. John Wesley was nurtured in the high church tradition as the son of a Tory parson. His frustrations as a missionary in colonial Georgia and his contact with Moravian Brethren there led to a conversion experience in 1738, which reoriented him and brought him to a new mission in life. Wesley's Methodist movement demonstrated the dynamic energies within English Protestantism, but the full effect of his religious vision would not be felt until the rapidly modernizing social and political context of the later eighteenth century.

Confessionalization and Social Discipline

In recent decades scholarship on the Reformation and its religious legacies has undergone dramatic transformation. Narratives, informed by denominational perspectives and highlighting the lives and works of the leading reformers, have given way to studies contrasting Protestant or Catholic dogmas with the beliefs and practices of Protestants and Catholics. The realization that the belief systems articulated by religious reformers only gradually resonated among the common folk initially encouraged historians to dichotomize elite and popular cultures, with popular culture read as pagan, alien, and disorderly through the discourse embedded in the evidence produced by contemporary religious authorities.[36] More recently scholars have emphasized the interpenetration of beliefs, values, and ideas at all levels of early modern society, and the common folk have emerged as self-conscious participants in the political and social dynamics within village communities, and as practitioners of complex, functional, if "unorthodox", religions.[37] The question remains open, however, as to whether the impetus for early modern religious reforms came from elite officials ("from above") or from the common folk within their parish communities ("from below"). German-language scholarship has proposed a general pattern of religious change, identified as "confessionalization" (*Konfessionalisierung*), under which modern religious identity was imposed "from above" on the common people subject to each of the three German "Confessions", Lutheran, Reformed, and Catholic.[38] Confessionalization has generated a great deal of scholarly analysis and debate.

A confession is an acknowledgement of faith, in word or deed. As we have seen, in the decades following Luther's break with Rome, religious leaders drafted a series of Confessions, such as the Augsburg and Helvetic

Confessions, which listed and codified beliefs for official adherents –
primarily the parish ministry and territorial magistrates – to acknowledge
by oath and signature. By the 1540s many territorial lords and civic
magistrates within the Empire had personally embraced a confession
and then sought to bring their chosen faith to their subjects through the
gradual and sometimes forced integration of local ecclesiastical institutions
into the civic regime or territorial state. Lutheran rulers confiscated
Church properties, established institutions to recruit and train ministers,
regulated their appointments to ecclesiastical holdings, monitored
them, and sought to use the pulpit and the village school to mould
obedient subjects.[39] Catholic princes such as the Habsburgs and the
dukes of Bavaria, though recognizing the Church's corporate autonomy,
also took an active role in reforming ecclesiastical institutions and
in supporting the efforts of Jesuit and Capuchin missionaries to bring
Tridentine Catholicism to their subjects.[40]

The religious peace of Augsburg in 1555 had not sanctioned Calvinism,
and Calvin had fashioned a Church designed to function, if necessary,
independently of political authorities. None the less, despite Calvinism's
illegal status, in those Imperial states where it became the official faith,
such as the Palatinate and the county of Lippe, political authorities built
a territorial Calvinist church and demanded religious obedience from
their subjects. In Lippe, Lutheranism rather than Calvinism became the
confession of resistance.[41] For the principal proponents of this historical
model, Wolfgang Reinhard and Heinz Schilling, the consolidation of
official religion among the elite opened the door for a second phase of
confessionalization, initiated in the early seventeenth century and
revived following the Thirty Years War.[42] Through preaching, catechism
classes, parish visitations, consistorial courts, and even religious theatre,
elites of all confessional parties sought to transform the complex and
diffuse local religious beliefs into regulated, distinct, and homogenized
patterns of behaviour and to internalize among their parishioners new
religiously grounded values of social discipline which, Reinhard and
Schilling argue, helped mould a modern citizenry for a modern state.

Despite the combined weight of Church and state, however, recent
scholarship has demonstrated the permeability of confessional borders,
the variability of practices within confessional churches, and the deter-
mination of the common folk to define "from below" what would be
acceptable religious practice. Monographic studies at the territorial,
diocesan, and even parish level have exposed the complexities of the
process of early modern religious change, which involved negotiations

between the parish ministry, as ecclesiastical agents of the central government, and village and town leaders. In the diocese of Speyer, Bishop Damien Hugo von Schönborn could bemoan the failure to implement Tridentine Catholicism in 1724, though a pious, communal, and renewed Catholic identity had been forged at the parish level despite episcopal shortcomings.[43] In south-western Germany, where Catholic territories were politically weak, the common folk integrated older forms of piety, such as pilgrimages, with newer religious expressions, such as confraternities, into a new community-based Catholic religiosity.[44] Capuchin and Jesuit priests might complain that the religious enthusiasm generated by their missions to rural parishes soon faded, yet new devotions took root and older practices were gradually uprooted or desacralized, transforming rural Catholicism into expressions acceptable to ecclesiastical authorities and the local believers alike.[45] In Protestant Imperial states the patterns were similar, with residual Catholic practices, such as honouring saints' days, "Lutheranized" by long-established habit.[46] In the confessionally-mixed towns of Augsburg and Oppenheim, hybrid forms of ritual defined unique localized confessional churches.[47]

The limitations of confessionalization as an explanatory model become more evident when moving beyond the Empire. In Eastern Europe the absence of a centralizing state structure, low literacy rates, linguistic fragmentation, and vestigial ecclesiastical structures resulted in multivalent confessional forms which were internalized in very individualistic ways. Thus István Szilvássy, a forty-year-old Hungarian villager who had converted from Lutheranism to Catholicism at the age of twenty and could read, was entrusted with religious books by the local priest, from which he preached "Calvinism" to his neighbours.[48] In Protestant Scandinavia new manifestations of traditional religiosity, most famously pilgrimages to the holy spring at Kippinge in Denmark, continued to emerge into the eighteenth century.[49] In Catholic southern Italy, episcopal officials could initiate local religious reforms only after intensive negotiations with parish lay leaders.[50] In the French diocese of Grenoble, leading families within rural parishes used the new religious confraternities to consolidate their status and power within their villages.[51] These examples could be repeated for Iberia and the British Isles.

Throughout Europe new forms of faith developed through negotiations between reformers "from above" and reformers "from below". Official confessions established certain critical areas of faith that had to be observed, and accepted local variations in areas seen as less central to orthodoxy. Local believers defended aspects of traditional faith that seemed essential to their needs and appropriated devotions from the Reformed official faith that furthered communal interests. The thrust of confessionalization was designed both to unleash new forms of spirituality and to keep the lower orders in line, yet conflicts over holy days, holy sites, and patterns of personal behaviour fostered resistance, disorder, and eventually negotiation. Official pressure might have put an end to some popular practices, but ultimately the will to convert the masses was lacking. In the internalized forms of Catholicism, Lutheranism, and Calvinism that spread among the elite in the seventeenth century, ignorance, superstition, and ungodliness among the masses had their place and confirmed the righteousness of the godly cadre. These parochial realities justified rule by the few and reassured the true believers of their election, as the insistence on proper knowledge as a sign of faith, and of full membership in the Church, favoured the educated and acted as a social filter. Developments in the area of science, and the spread of reason through enlightenment, would complete the social and cultural separation of the educated and uneducated, relegating religious faith for secularized "enlightened" thinkers to a pacifying insulator against the social anger of the poor and dispossessed.

Science, Natural Philosophy, and Religion

We tend to contrast religion and science, and too often histories of science present the "revolution" in early modern European theoretical and applied sciences as unfolding in opposition to clerical suppression. Early modern thinkers referred to science as "natural philosophy", and did not view it as distinct from or in conflict with theology. Knowledge about the natural world was also knowledge about the divine purpose, and contributors to the scientific revolution did so in a distinctly religious spirit and with clerical support. In many ways, religion and science moved in parallel tracks, supporting rather than hindering one another.[52]

I will focus on the discoveries associated with Copernicus, Kepler, Galileo, and Newton that helped explain the motion of heavenly and earthly bodies, but significant developments in physiology, biology, and eventually chemistry occurred simultaneously with this "revolution" in physics. Ancient and medieval theorists had separated the forces at work in the heavens – supra-lunar space, or the visible sky beyond the moon – from the sub-lunar world. Supra-lunar objects moved in perfect circles because the heavens themselves had to be perfect. Sub-lunar motion took on all sorts of chaotic, irregular patterns determined by underlining affinities of objects with the four forms of visible nature: earth, wind, water, and fire. The discoveries of early modern science occurred within these belief systems until very late in the process, when the weight of new data overwhelmed the traditional explanatory models for some, but not all, natural philosophers.

The acceptance of a new understanding about motion required early modern scientists to internalize a paradigm shift; that is, a whole new way of perceiving how the world operated.[53] For most people such a shift is a discomforting experience and occurs only if the old ideas have proved unsuccessful or problematic in numerous instances. Confronted with more and more unsolved problems (known as "anomalies"), scientists will begin systematically to grope for some new model that can explain both the observations that "worked" under the old system and the unsolved anomalies. Once an individual discovers a new theory, then she must disseminate it to others. Eventually the theory is embraced by the community of scholars and becomes the new paradigm. The early modern paradigm shift in the natural philosophy of motion involved an accumulation of observed anomalies that weakened the attraction of the old paradigm; individual pursuit of a new workable paradigm; and then the discovery, dissemination, and modification of the new theory until it was generally accepted as "reasonable" by the increasingly self-conscious community of scholars.

In astronomy, the study of heavenly motion, the ancient writings of Ptolemy offered a complex model of the universe which allowed one to plot the movements of celestial bodies from the perspective of a central and fixed Earth. This geocentric system imagined the heavens as a set of concentric spheres, with the stars fixed to the outermost sphere and the visible planets, including the sun, moving in their individual spheres against the background of the fixed stars. The main problem in the model was that the planets appeared to "back up" (taking on a retrograde motion) at certain irregular points in their "normal" path through the stars. Natural philosophers first attempted to refine the Ptolemaic system and explain these anomalies by imagining planets turning on smaller spheres, attached like bubbles on the great planetary spheres. The model was cumbersome but normally effective and is still used in navigation. In the 1530s Nicolaus Copernicus (1473–1543), a Polish priest and astronomer, began to experiment with alternative ancient models that assumed a sun-centred, or heliocentric, universe. His system relocated the planets in their actual sequence from the sun, with the moon revolving around the earth. Copernican heavenly objects still moved in "perfect" circles, but he could calculate the apparent irregularities more simply. Copernicus shared his discoveries with colleagues at the papal curia, and his book, published in Latin in 1543, was not placed on the Papal Index until much later.

Early modern natural philosophers operated in an intellectual environment in which scientific study mixed freely with occult research. They were one and the same. In the 1590s, the careful observations of a Ptolemaic Catholic astronomer, Tycho Brahe (1546–1601), who served as court astrologer for Emperor Rudolph II, provided the database for the mathematical insights of his Copernican and Lutheran colleague Johann Kepler (1571–1630). Kepler himself was a practising yet sceptical astrologer who was fascinated by the "music" of the celestial spheres. In his search for harmony Kepler modified the Copernican model by imagining elliptical planetary orbits around the sun. His insight required far fewer calculations and was published in Latin as *A New Astronomy* in 1609.

Despite its simplicity Kepler's model was not widely accepted until the 1660s. Galileo Galilei (1564–1642), for one, continued to insist on circular orbits. His own telescopic observations, however, suggested that the heavens were much more complex and irregular than previously imagined, and he found an immediate and much wider audience because he published in Italian with illustrations. As a natural philosopher, Galileo's real contribution involved his study of falling objects on earth, where he recognized that the dragging effect of friction distorted measurements of what should be a mathematically constant descent. What appeared as irregular motion was in fact uniform, and from that premise Galileo suggested in his *Dialogue of Two World Systems*, in 1632, that celestial and terrestrial motion probably conformed to the same laws. Of all the early modern scientists, Galileo is most often presented as the victim of religious ignorance and repression, yet it was his thirst for public recognition that led to him mocking ideas associated with Pope Urban VIII (*1623–44) in the *Dialogue*. The pope's response was the moderate censure of house arrest and the more pointed punishment of silence.

The French philosopher René Descartes (1596–1650) had more to fear from religious authorities than Galileo, and settled in the tolerant Dutch Republic to pursue his studies. Descartes extended the premise that the universe operated according to a handful of mathematical formulas, from physical motion to other areas of study including humankind. If the motion of earthly objects did not entail their affinities to the four underlying essences, Descartes argued that all objects, including the human body, must be subject to the same measurable physical forces. By extension he posited that physical human nature was not unique in God's created universe: rather, human uniqueness derived from our minds, which were immaterial. None the less, he separated human consciousness from the divine mind. Christian philosophers and theologians believed that human thought resonated, more or less clearly, concepts housed in the mind of God. In Descartes' view, ideas were a product of individual human intellects, and they could be modified or discarded if in conflict with observable reality. Descartes believed that God had created the world, but since knowledge of God was beyond reason, scientific study should take place without reference to God. The world could then be studied like a machine, to determine how it operated rather than why. Descartes's works were banned in his native France and elsewhere; and as was the case with Copernicus and Kepler, Cartesian philosophy was not immediately embraced by the scientific community. Newton's gravitational theory, for example, assumed that bodies attracted each other at great distances through a void, and ran counter to Descartes's belief in a field of forces.[54]

Newton's work benefitted from the late seventeenth-century development of a network of agencies created to foster the interchange of scientific theories and technological applications. By the 1660s the Royal Academy in London and the French Royal Academy of Sciences formed the apogee of numerous societies, academies, and scientific journals that brought scholars together to share their work, or published new findings for distribution to subscribers scattered across Europe. In retrospect, the publication of Newton's Latin treatise, *Principia* (1687), which presented a model of gravitational force that applied to the heavens and the earth, appeared to be the culmination of the "scientific revolution", in establishing a new paradigm that would hold until the late nineteenth century. At the time, however, this highly technical treatise had a limited impact on European thought, and it took forty years for Newtonian physics to find real support in enlightened France. Later writers lumped Newton's ideas with those of Descartes, claiming that the new science offered an image of God as the great clock-maker who stood back from creation once it was completed, but the Newtonian cosmos, though subject to mathematical laws, was not purely mechanistic. It had come into being by God's will and required considerable divine intervention to correct irregularities and to supply energy. Even in this defining work of early modern science, religious assumptions filled in mathematical gaps.

"Enlightenment", Rational Christianity, and Tolerance

Debate over the meaning of the Enlightenment began in the eighteenth century and continues among scholars to this day. For Immanuel Kant, Enlightenment was "'man's release from his self-incurred immaturity', by the use of his own reason undistorted by prejudice and without the guidance of others". Inspired by advances in natural philosophy, enlightened thinkers wanted humankind to follow "reason" rather than faith, superstition, or revelation, because human reason could improve society and liberate individuals from the constraints of custom and arbitrary authority. Modern intellectual historians such as Peter Gay have equated these constraints with organized religion, but Jürgen Habermas defined them more broadly as any narrow ethnic, class, gender, or religious bias against which enlightened thinkers championed universal values such as freedom, justice, and objectivity.[55] For Habermas Enlightenment offered and offers, because the process is ongoing, a complete secular arsenal of human values whose internalization would end the moral and cultural hegemony of Reformed Christianity.

In the eighteenth century, according to Habermas, the European "middle class" organized the flow of cultural materials in an expanding world economy in which they were the principal consumers. Enlightened ideas were among these cultural materials and were transmitted and exchanged in an emerging "public sphere", a cultural space where public opinion could challenge the privileged authorities, such as official churches.[56] Habermas argued that, in the public sphere, individuals could escape from their status as subjects and gain intellectual autonomy as established religions became one of many competing perspectives on life. In fact the emerging influence of enlightened values in the public sphere convinced political authorities to relax their demands for religious conformity as the association of faith with power faded. Habermas's model has formed the backdrop for recent studies on eighteenth-century European political culture and enlightenment.

Scholars have identified specific social and cultural sites where new ideas circulated, from smoke-filled coffee houses to private salons. The settings encouraged sociability as men and women gathered together and consumed the new colonial products, such as coffee, tea, sugar and tobacco, purchased journals, and discussed the latest plays or essays. The intellectual environment was urbane, which ensured that ambitious writers flocked to Europe's capitals, especially Paris, where concentrations of wealth and sophistication promised patronage. Despite critiques against privilege and cultural constraints, the social world of the Enlightenment was no "Republic of Letters" but rather a socially strained mix of literary lions, such as Voltaire, and hack novelists, playwrights, and scandalmongers, who occupied a literary underworld Robert Darnton has characterized as "Grub Street".[57] In the provinces, philosophical societies and academies sprang up, with entrance fees that limited membership to elites, though the most famous of these lodges, the Freemasons, welcomed a broader social spectrum. Originally established as centres advocating the moral regeneration of society and individuals without reference to established religions, Masonic lodges soon developed their own rituals and secrets. Despite Masonic egalitarianism the Enlightenment must be appreciated as an urban and elite phenomenon, which in its first impact softened the drive for religious conformity from above by causing many elites to question the foundations of their own religiosity.

Scholars have long associated the Enlightenment with secular values and irreligiosity, and certainly key figures such as Voltaire and Diderot sharply criticized the Church and questioned the core tenets of Christianity. Nevertheless, for most adherents enlightened values did not necessarily challenge God. Many believed simply that human intelligence, by observation and deduction, could understand the natural world that divine wisdom and benevolence had instituted for human happiness. Enlightened Christians believed that the study of God's laws operating through nature, including human nature, did not involve a direct challenge to the biblical commandments. In "enlightened" theology the jealous and exclusive God gave way to a beneficent Creator who had designed the universe for human benefit in this world, not as a proving ground for an elite force training for the next life.[58]

The Enlightenment's chief effect on organized religion was to foster further toleration.[59] In the seventeenth century individuals had begun advocating toleration in reaction to the viciousness of persecution; yet given the close association of established religion with the state, proposals for religious toleration raised questions about the "divine right" of monarchs and, given the role of oaths in political life, about how a subject could honour a faith different from his or her ruler and still be loyal. In England the monarch was the supreme head of the Church, and in Europe the king of Prussia was the "supreme bishop" of the territorial Lutheran Church. For enlightened thinkers, state-sanctioned religious toleration suited a new model of an impersonal state in which religious faith could be separated from political obedience. With the Toleration Act of 1689, British politics had begun to embrace this model. In the

1740s the Calvinist Frederick II of Prussia (*1740–86) sanctioned religious tolerance in his Lutheran lands, even allocating state funds towards the construction of a Catholic cathedral in Berlin. In 1750 Frederick granted Prussian Jews the right to be judged by their own laws and to possess their own schools, cemeteries, and synagogues. Not all rulers embraced toleration. Closet Huguenots in France faced new rounds of persecution in the 1730s, as did Protestant peasants in Bohemia and, most dramatically, in the archdiocese of Salzburg. Yet these religious refugees quickly found homes in other parts of Europe. After two centuries of trying to force religious opponents to abjure, most political and religious leaders turned to more reasonable forms of persuasion.

The search for reasonable Christianity, however, exposed the unreasonable assumptions behind biblical revelation. Religious believers and enlightened thinkers held fundamentally different views on human nature. Enlightened writers believed in the natural goodness and perfectibility of man, while the Christian view on salvation was predicated on the basic sinfulness of human nature. Biblical miracles required the suspension of the laws of nature, and "rational" deists such as David Hume, who believed in a Newtonian God but not a divine Jesus, challenged the "authoritative testimony" of the Gospels as sufficient cause to accept the stories of divine intervention as true. Arguing that the flawed Bible offered poor guidelines for moral human action, enlightened ethicists suggested that God had fashioned human nature so that pursuit of self-fulfilment served the common good. God's "invisible hand" imparted moral goodness to profit-seeking in market relations, for individual effort brought material improvement to humanity. Through "enlightened" self-interest, individuals would naturally identify personal advantage with the good of the community at least in the long run. From this perspective, the source of evil was ignorance. For enlightened men, religious faith and fear of damnation remained useful means for keeping the ignorant, among whom they included their social inferiors and women, in line.

For those Christian intellectuals at odds with the rationalists, the revival movements of the eighteenth century offered a return to faith in revelation and a call to personal witness and evangelizing. The zealous spirituality of movements such as Lutheran Pietism, English Methodism, or the Great Awakening in the British colonies may be seen in part as reactions to the religious indifference of an increasingly secularized elite culture. Among the "ignorant", the emotional and ethical comfort provided by new forms of spirituality offered a "counter-culture" to the prevailing faith in market relations and materialism, as religion became for some a form of social criticism.

We traditionally associate the eighteenth century with the application of reason to all aspects of European life. Reason desacralized politics and social relations, yet Church and state remained wedded throughout Europe. The Enlightenment encouraged free thinking and anthropologized religious behaviour as a form of human cultural expression. The disassociation of established churches with the true revelation of God's plan for humankind may have fostered religious tolerance, yet laws prohibited the public exercise of Catholicism in England and Calvinism in France, the two most "enlightened" countries in Europe. Furthermore, even in this "age of reason" the religious dynamism experienced within official churches and among dissenters confirmed the continual pull of the "irrational".

6

REREADING THE REFORMATION THROUGH GENDER ANALYSIS

Through the 1960s, Reformation scholarship was predominantly a male endeavour, and as a result, accounts of the Reformation have emphasized the role of men as theological innovators, religious activists, and victims of persecution. Beginning in the 1960s, feminist scholarship, initially conducted almost entirely by women, has revisited the collected writings of the reformers and religious enthusiasts, looking at pamphlet literature, parish visitation protocols, and court records to explore the Reformation's impact on women's lives and the effect of women on the Reformation.[1] Their findings have challenged established interpretative models. One may not be able to claim, as Joan Kelly has, so pointedly, for the Renaissance, that women had no Reformation;[2] but by rereading the Reformation's legacies from the perspective of women's historical experiences, it is possible to see that in fact, despite early promises, religious reform, both Catholic and Protestant, stifled much of late medieval female spirituality.

Building on these initial studies, in the 1980s some feminist scholars broadened their research from women's history to historical analyses of gender, exploring how past societies fashioned and inculcated norms of what it meant to be male and female. Gender analysis stresses that gender, though grounded in biological differences, is culturally constructed. Thus how we learn to be "male" and "female" varies from culture to culture and over time. Women's history was and is important in uncovering the historical experience of half of humankind and in historicizing the way in which women are identified in the contemporary world. Gender analysis extends those insights to men and women, as masculinity is as much a cultural construction as femininity. More importantly, Joan Wallach Scott has emphasized that "gender is a primary way of signifying relationships of power".[3] In reweaving the early modern social fabric along godly lines, male religious reformers and their lay collaborators reinforced patriarchal power in the household, the parish, and the political arena. Women and some men did argue for spiritual equality and women's fuller participation in public worship and discourse, but from the perspective of gender relations the general thrust of the Reformation increased the authority and power of men at the expense of women. The stresses caused by this shift emerged perhaps most clearly during the European witch-hunts of the late sixteenth and early seventeenth centuries, as gender-bias, social pressures, and religious bigotry combined in a deadly mix. This brief chapter will reread the European Reformation through the lens of gender analysis.

Spiritual Equality, Religious Inequality

Prior to 1350 the vast majority of religious writers saw women as inferior to men, and intellectuals could draw on Judeo-Christian traditions and classical models to demonstrate women's negative qualities. The Bible presents two accounts of creation: one in which men and women were created together as equals, and the other in which God (Yahweh), who is himself conceptualized as masculine, decided that Adam needed a helpmate and created Eve from his rib. This latter account was and is the most familiar to Christians. Furthermore, Eve's "responsibility" for the temptation of Adam in the Garden of Eden and the "fall" of humankind from our original state of grace defined women as the source of sin since creation. All women were potential Eves, and their sinfulness was encapsulated in their sexuality, as male insecurity resulted in the projection of sexual appetite on woman as temptress.[4] Furthermore, anxiety over determining fatherhood resulted in monogamous marriages in which the virginity of the bride was essential and wifely adultery punishable by death. Property passed from father to son, and ensuring paternity required strict control over potentially "dangerous" female sexuality.

As presented in the Gospels, Jesus's ministry was gender-balanced. He preached that men and women could both attain salvation equally and that they should not allow domestic responsibilities to interfere with their higher spiritual calling, a more radical call for women than for men in the contemporary social context. Women played significant roles among his followers and were the first to discover the empty tomb following the Resurrection. Paul's epistles, which were the product of several writers, presented mixed messages. He too saw no difference between men and women in the spirit, but elsewhere he commanded that women should be silent in church. Feminist scholarship on the history of the early Church notes that the religious role for women deteriorated as the Church grew, and following Christianity's legal recognition by Constantine, males came to monopolize clerical functions. Of the early Church "fathers", Augustine of Hippo had the profoundest effect on gender relations in later Christianity. Augustine argued that Adam and Eve's sin ended free will for all time, for sexual desire proved that men could not control their sexual organs by will alone. For Augustine this was the "original sin", and he believed that sexual relations, even within marriage, were sinful.[5] That argument was the seed for the medieval Church's association of true spirituality with celibacy, elevating the separate cloistering of men and women in monasteries and convents as the highest form of spiritual expression, and demanding the practice from all male clergy.

Medieval theologians from the twelfth century onwards had access to the Church "Fathers" and to classical writers, especially Aristotle, who claimed that females were incomplete, naturally "deformed", monstrous males. Thomas Aquinas admitted that women had souls and could be saved, but he argued that women needed men's help in everything because they were physically and mentally weak. Beginning in the twelfth century, the devotional cult to Mary, the virgin mother of Jesus, spread throughout Europe. Though Mary emerged as a motherly spiritual intercessor, able to calm God's wrath, her virginity created a countermodel of pure goodness to Eve's association with sexual evil. For women there was no spiritual or sexual middle ground.[6]

In late medieval Europe, women could pursue three religious paths: as nuns, wives, or lay "sisters" living collectively. Nuns swore formal religious vows and followed regulations that defined their celibate lives, separated from the world within an enclosed convent. Often founded by queens or noble women for their own daughters or widowhood, many convents had become houses where membership was restricted to elite women or where the entry fee, literally a dowry for these "brides of Christ", was so high as to prohibit poorer women from joining, though they often served as lay sisters, doing the menial work.

Boniface VIII had decreed in 1298 that all religious women were to be cloistered, cut off from contact with the social world, though this was sporadically enforced. Many urban convents had visiting rooms where the nuns regularly met family members and sometimes suitors, and rumours of sexual impropriety and occasional court cases stained the reputation of all such communities. No reader found it unusual that an abbess and nun would be among Chaucer's pilgrims. Early medieval abbesses had been politically significant figures, but cloistering and the demand that convents submit to the higher authority of a male abbot or bishop limited the political voice of nuns. Late medieval convents instead became intellectual centres for private devotion and mystical religiosity. The Observant reform movements of the fifteenth century resulted in closer episcopal supervision of convents and renewed efforts to enforce cloistering. The zeal for stricter observance among the nuns themselves strengthened devotion, collective spirituality, and the authority of the abbess within the convent.[7]

In the wake of the Black Death, many widowed or unmarried European women took to living collectively in devotional communities that did not require a spiritual dowry as an entry fee. These communities of "Beguines" often supported themselves by weaving or sewing and provided social services by caring for the sick. Anger or envy from male artisans who felt these women "poached" on their markets, and concerns among the male ecclesiastical authorities that Beguines lived in the world without male supervision, resulted in charges of heresy or in calls that they submit to formal vows and cloistering. The Devotio Moderna in the Netherlands also fostered communities of lay women, known as the Sisters of the Common Life, who faced similar male resistance. Throughout the Middle Ages especially in England, individual women, known as anchoresses, walled themselves into tiny cells attached to churches or cathedrals, where they could meditate in seclusion. These holy hermits attracted devotees, and Julian of Norwich's recorded meditations reflected a deep feminine spirituality woven into God, "for in our Mother Christ we profit and increase".[8] Many women also attached themselves less formally to mendicant orders, such as the Franciscans and Dominicans. As tertiaries, or member of a "third" form of these orders, lay women could pursue a more intense devotional life in the world. These groups were not formally recognized by the Church, but they did have male guardians. Many Beguine houses when pressured to reform sought third-order status.[9]

The bulk of women lived as wives and mothers, and the Church's emphasis on virginity left them spiritually alienated. Mary, as a virgin mother, was an awkward role model, so devotion sprang up around Mary's mother Anne, who had a normal marriage and pregnancies. Here the popular thirst for spiritual models that spoke to women's lives led to a "vulgarization" of faith as non-scriptural legends sprang up around Mary's mother and her grandmother, Emerentia. In all, active lay female piety faced many obstacles on the eve of the Reformation, yet women endowed religious centres, became pilgrims, and flocked to penitential preachers. The feminization of spirituality reflected the hunger for faith "from below". Male Protestant and Catholic reformers would respond to women's needs and voices with ambivalence.

The Protestant reformers sought to transform religion but did little to transform women's place within faith. Protestant writers denounced clerical celibacy and advocated marriage as the norm, especially for women, who they felt could not resist sexual temptation. For Luther and others, monogamous marriage fostered the procreation of children, helped avoid sin, and encouraged mutual help and companionship between husband and wife. Protestant writers thus advocated a much more positive and affectionate model of conjugal relations. Nevertheless, all of the reformers, except for radical Anabaptists, felt that wives should remain submissive even to their unbelieving husbands. Even Anabaptists insisted that believing women who "divorced" recalcitrant husbands should immediately remarry within the congregation. Many priests willingly embraced the reform movement and married their longtime concubines, yet there remained residual hostility or ambivalence to pastor's wives deep into the sixteenth century.[10] In England, Elizabeth refused to acknowledge episcopal wives.[11]

The Protestant Reformation at first appeared to expand the religious opportunities for women under the banner of the priesthood of all believers, which could imply spiritual equality. Embedded in the concept, however, was a tension between the glorification of the "common man" as the true Christian, and the vilification of "common women" because of the association of female sexuality with male property rights.[12] Despite the Pauline call for female silence, many women engaged in the evangelical debate through preaching or, as in the case of Argula von Grumbach and Katharina Zell, pamphlet writing. Anne Askew was an outspoken early reformer in England who was executed for her beliefs, and numerous Anabaptist women gave witness to their faith through martyrdom. For male Protestants the visibility of women as reformers was embarrassing and suggested potential disorder, and as official Protestant churches sprang up in the Empire and elsewhere in Europe, female advocates were enjoined to silence. Their writings were soon limited to hymns and small works for private devotion. In England male reformers discouraged women, except for those of the upper classes, even from reading the Bible aloud to others, as this put them in the role of teachers. In Amsterdam, Calvinist women who assisted widows and others were called deaconesses, but held no formal place in the consistory. Marguérite of Navarre, Elizabeth of Braunschweig–Calenburg, and Mary and Elizabeth Tudor used their political influence to guide the pace and direction of reform, but as churches became established the visibility of women in religious roles diminished. Elizabeth as "Supreme Governor" of England couched her authority in male metaphors and in her personal virginity.[13]

The Protestant rejection of celibacy had the greatest impact on women, for Protestant officials attempted to close all convents and less formal religious communities. The drive liberated some women, whose families had forcibly cloistered them, but for most the closing of their convents spelled religious and personal disaster. In the relatively tolerant Netherlands dispossessed nuns, known as holy maidens (*geestelijke maagden*), resettled in small groups, which survived, attracting new members down into the eighteenth century. In many Imperial cities, the convents proved to be the Reformation's stiffest opponents, as many of the nuns came from the city's leading families and called on their support. Some convents were denied novices and allowed to die out; others survived for centuries after territories became officially Protestant. The abbess of Quedlinburg, who was an Imperial prince, signed the Augsburg Confession and secularized the male houses in her domains while preserving the convent. Quedlinburg and other Lutheran convents accepted novices from elite families into the nineteenth century.[14] On the whole then, Protestantism recognized marriage as the spiritual vocation for a woman, but political circumstances resulted in grudging accept-ance of other forms of female religious life.

As we have seen in earlier chapters, the Catholic reforms spelled out at Trent preserved much of late medieval religiosity and did little to alter the ecclesiastical order. For women, Tridentine Catholicism's most pro-found impact was its efforts, carried over from the fifteenth-century Observant movement and the assault on the Beguines, to enforce clois-tering. Initially sixteenth-century Catholic renewal produced spiritual movements among lay women as it had among men. The Company of St Ursula, founded by Angela Merici (1470/4–1540) in Italy, served victims of a new disease, syphilis, who were often prostitutes. From this base the company combated poverty and ignorance, the sources of prostitution, through charitable work and education. Their teaching activity and unwillingness to cloister, however, raised concerns over their public ministry.[15] Isabel Roser, an associate of Ignatius Loyola during his early days at Barcelona, failed to receive papal sanction for a female branch of the Jesuits, who would engage in active ministry. Despite Loyola's opposition the group continued its informal growth, attracting novices, educating young girls, and nursing the sick. The Council of Trent reaffirmed the late medieval papal call for enclosure of all female religious communities, but as with other conciliar decrees, enforcement depended on the cooperation of local lay authorities and was thus sporadic. Into the seventeenth century, many Ursuline communities effectively resisted cloistering through the patronage of elite families whose daughters they educated. By 1700, Catholic insistence on cloistering had relaxed in some parts of Europe, and communities of women active in Christian social services, such as the French Daughters of Charity, fed the poor and nursed the ill, while other female orders, founded to teach young girls or the poor, used the virgin mother Mary, a virgin active in the world, as their spiritual model.

In Protestant England, Catholic women risked their lives as missionaries and recusants. Mary Ward received provisional approval from Pope Paul V in 1616 to send English Catholic girls, whom she had educated in the Spanish Netherlands, home as missionaries. Later her efforts to establish houses for lay women to engage in active ministry on the continent led to her temporary imprisonment by the Inquisition in Munich and the condemnation of her "Jesuitesses".[16] Meanwhile, among wealthy English recusants, worship had necessarily become domestic and managed by women, who harboured priests and sustained the network through private correspondence. Under English law a wife controlled no property and the ecclesiastical fines for her recusancy were uncollectable. Authorities were also reluctant to imprison these well-to-do women and disrupt their families.[17]

Reformed Catholicism recognized the sacramental nature of marriage, but continued to value virginity above marriage, honouring men and women who embraced celibacy. Among the human family surrounding Jesus, Joseph replaced Anne as the critical third party in religious plays and iconography. He offered a spiritual model for husbands and fathers, while Mary again became the complex inspiration for women. Everywhere in Catholic Europe women continued to pursue an active apostolate outside the convent, but such roles, even where tolerated, were limited to domestic and nurturing functions such as nursing or the religious education of girls.

Female Catholic saints of the renewal and Counter-reform were neither missionaries nor lay teachers but rather cloistered reformers and contemplatives such as Teresa of Ávila (1515–82). She spent much of her life composing a spiritual autobiography, inspired by St Augustine's *Confessions*, which would become a template for hundreds of self-reflective spiritual diaries for men and women in the seventeenth century. She revitalized her Carmelite order in what was essentially an Observant movement, which reformed existing houses and spawned dozens of new foundations. Although presented officially as a cloistered nun, Teresa travelled throughout Spain to establish new houses and reached thousands through her published *Life* (1570) and her mystical writings. Her biography could be read by Church authorities as submissive acceptance of enclosure, and by women as an inspiration for an active spiritual life.

In the seventeenth and eighteenth centuries the Arminian, Pietistic, and Jansenist reforms, with their emphasis on personal conversion and direct contact with God, provided new opportunities for women to achieve spiritual equality without a male intermediary. Many of these movements had women among their founders and a disproportionate number of women among their members. Much of the criticism levelled against these movements by officials in the established churches highlighted the threat to godly order implicit in outspoken female spirituality. The increasing publication of spiritual diaries in the seventeenth century gave women a vehicle to transform private faith into public religious discourse. The emphasis on the power of prayer also armed women with a new tool of faith, to which they had equal access with men. Puritanism had brought prayer to the fore; and under the freedom of the press during the English Civil War, women such as Elizabeth Poole and Lady Eleanor Douglas spoke out from religious conviction in the political arena. Once again churchmen enforced silence when the Restoration re-established the royal Church and religious order.[18]

In the late seventeenth century, the Quakers emerged as dissenters against this order, and women played a prominent and visible role among the leaders. George Fox, the movement's founder, supported female preaching at Quaker meetings and their leadership roles in organizing charitable work for the sick, poor, and children. Like the earlier Anabaptists, Quaker women were whipped and imprisoned for their obstinacy. Margaret Fell Fox, who married John Fox after years of religious activism, published *Women's Speaking Justified* (1669), which cited numerous biblical examples of women bearing public witness to their faith. Anglican officials were troubled by spiritually empowered women and the threat they posed to male-dominated social and political order, but the Quakers were not gender revolutionaries.

On the continent women were less public and vocal in their call for spiritual equality. Emphasizing direct inspiration from the spirit of God, women among the Jansenists and Pietists downplayed the male-dominated established religious order as a vehicle for faith. Their approach was "quietist", calling for a simple surrender to God's will and encouraging public inactivity, since contemplation of God was enough. As empowering as this was for Madame Guyon, one of quietism's chief advocates, Catholic officials found her views heretical and imprisoned her on five occasions. Seventeenth-century French Jansenism became closely associated with the nuns at Port-Royal, who advocated prayer meetings, women reading and commenting on the Scriptures, and a moderated quietism.[19] Jesuit opposition eventually drew papal censure of the movement, but Jansenist cells survived at several convents under noble protection. In Germany the Pietist Anna Hoyer published a sharp religious satire entitled *Spiritual Conversation between a Mother and Child about True Christianity* (1651), against the rigidity of Lutheran Orthodox clericalism. She encouraged mothers to instil true religious knowledge in their children at home and spare them the false indoctrination of clerical catechizing.

In all, women actively advocated religious renewal and ecclesiastical reform throughout the Reformation era. In convents and conventicles, where they could freely express their vision of faith, vital forms of Christian piety emerged, while male officials sought to restrict female devotion, confining it to the cloister and godly household. Nevertheless, women constantly struggled for permission to engage in spiritual ministry within the world. Finally, in the eighteenth century, male authorities began to relax their restrictions. As with other efforts at confessionalization and social discipline, it was at a point when religious ideology was losing its appeal to the elite that it was permissible for women to express themselves in "irrational" piety. The church had become a woman's sanctuary, but the ministry remained entirely male.

Witchcraft and Witch-hunting

During the sixteenth and seventeenth centuries, between 100,000 and 200,000 people were officially tried and between 50,000 and 100,000 executed for witchcraft. Of these, over 80 percent were women. Witches appeared before Catholic inquisitors, Protestant consistories, and secular courts. The trials normally emerged out of complex disputes within local communities, in which the accusers assumed harmful magic had played a role. Once a case was brought to trial, prosecutors, guided by a belief that the accused witch belonged to a widespread and dangerous movement, hunted for accomplices. Witch-hunting in early modern Europe spanned a time from the fifteenth to the eighteenth centuries but peaked between 1560 and 1660, when confessional rivalries threatened religious order and confessionalized states were pressing to regulate the behaviour of immoral subjects.[20] Thus the bloodiest witch-hunts combined widespread popular views on the efficacy of magic and learned assumptions associating witchcraft with heresy, at a point when official anxiety about "disorder" was acute. Embedded in all three aspects were assumptions about women that made them vulnerable to accusation and punishment as witches.

Medieval Christian ritual was "miraculous", in which changes in physical reality often had spiritual forces behind them. At the centre of the sacramental Mass, bread became the body of Christ in substance, though it appeared to remain bread. In other religious settings parish priests blessed newly ploughed fields and animals with holy oil and water to ward off blight and illness. In the later Middle Ages Christian writers began to distinguish magical practices from religious rituals, accepting the efficacy of both but relegating magic to harmful or sinful behaviour.[21] In this new mind set, magic was not wrong because it failed to work; it was wrong because it worked effectively for the wrong reasons, because the practitioner collaborated with demons who aided the magician or witch in doing harm. For most Europeans, however, witchcraft was a normal part of everyday life, and witches helped people deal with concerns over health, love, and family honour. The village wise woman, who knew herbs and who was often called, along with the priest, to assist the ill or to deliver a baby, held positions of ritual power within the community. When things went wrong, no one questioned the spiritual power of priestcraft or witchcraft, though people did question whether the witch intended harm rather than healing.

Latin texts defined the rituals of harmful witchcraft as *maleficia*, "doing harm", which might involved a gesture, a recitation of a curse, or the placing of harm-bearing objects near a victim. Maleficent magic was a felony, and court proceedings normally required evidence of actions. The accused might have been seen putting a hex sign on a barn that later burned down, or tying knots in leather or rope to cause impotence in a robust man, or seducing a reluctant lover by seasoning food with menstrual blood. The cases required a belief in the power of magic but, more importantly, evidence of actions and consideration of intent. They might lead to individual prosecutions and even executions but not to mass arrests.

In the late fifteenth century, judicial officials began to equate witchcraft with heresy, and this connection radically changed the prosecutorial procedures and the effects of the trials. The new conceptual framework derived primarily from an inquisitors' manual, the *Malleus Malificarum* or *Hammer of Female Witches*, initially published in 1486 by two Dominican inquisitors, Heinrich Krämer and Jacob Springer. This "how to" guide for prosecuting witches was republished in numerous Latin editions and vernacular translations, providing the vocabulary for accusations and a sexually charged imagery of deviance that could be elicited by torture, a practice increasingly regularized by the revival of Roman law. Drawn from medieval struggles against "underground" heresies, the *Malleus* transformed witchcraft into a diabolical conspiracy to overthrow the established Church. The witch's sin and crime was her declared allegiance with the devil, offered up in a ritualized pact and reinforced by secret nocturnal gatherings called "sabbaths". The witch had access to magical powers that could ruin crops, kill babies, or seduce men, but in the gender-soaked imagery of diabolical witchcraft, the masculine devil used female witches for his own purposes.

At the centre of diabolical witchcraft was a pact with the devil charged with sexual fantasy. The devil supposedly appeared to men at night, in dreams or drunken stupours, as a beautiful woman, a *succubus*, to gather semen from their uncontrolled ejaculations. The devil then used the stored semen when assuming a male form, an *incubus*, to sexually seal the pact with the witch, after which the devil left a mark on her body, the "witch's tit", that her animal agents, black dogs and such, could suckle. Contemporary male writers believed that female sexual appetites grew as women aged, so that older single women and widows, who lacked male partners, would be particularly vulnerable to the devil's temptations. In the social nexus of witchcraft and witch-hunting, these were often women who served as the village healers, or due to local rules of inheritance, were significant female property-holders and targets for envy. In a Faustian male variant of this tale, learned male sorcerers sought magical powers by conjuring up dead souls, a practice known as necromancy, and might even bargain with the devil for those powers. In these accounts, composed by males, the sorcerers exercised a degree of control, whereas the female witch was entirely dependent on the devil's power.

If belief in the diabolical pact allowed prosecutors to try individual women without any evidence of *maleficia*, the concurrent belief in the witches' sabbath made possible extensive and deadly hunts. Belief in the sabbath fed on popular and elite anxieties, for the common folk feared that the witches gathered to ruin crops, while the elite prosecutors suspected sexual orgies and acts of religious desecration. The witches' sabbath was an inverted holy day, a gathering of witches who had flown on pitchforks or brooms at night to worship the devil. Some historians believe that this was the residue of ancient shamanistic practices, but it seems more likely that much of this imagery derived more from the prosecutors' imagining deviance.[22] Witches were said to dance naked around open fires, masking the social distinctions exhibited by clothing. They sometimes said Christian prayers backwards, burned babies to use the ashes for evil acts, or engaged in perverse group sex. In the court-room, belief in the sabbath implied accomplices; and when diabolical witches were questioned under torture, officials most often sought the identities of the sabbath's participants. That information could touch off "panics" of fifteen or twenty trials. In the tiny Catholic ecclesiastical state of Ellwangen in south-western Germany, a series of panics between 1611 and 1618 resulted in at least 400 executions, including local priests and eventually the judge and his wife.[23]

Trials often began with a dispute among neighbours that escalated into an accusation of witchcraft. The accused was questioned about the incident of *maleficium*, but soon the case shifted to concerns about the diabolical forces at work. The accused, nearly always a woman, was strip-searched for her "witch's tit" and badgered or tortured to determine the details of her pact and her conspirators at the sabbath. The prosecutors were seeking devil worshippers, and if that search was aggressive, a conspiracy was not hard to find. Judges may have framed the model of diabolical witchcraft in many cases, but in other instances the visions and spiritual experiences of the accused baffled the officials and demon-strated complex underlying beliefs. In the better known cases, of witch-hunters exposing the divergent religious world views of a Bavarian village shaman, Chonrad Stoeckhlin, or the Italian *benandanti*, the practitioners were men.[24] Overall, the mix of crimes involving harmful magic and fear of a diabolical conspiracy generated murderous rounds of witch-hunting, which peaked during the age of religious wars.

Though Lutherans, Calvinists, and Catholics, all punished witches, there are significant differences even within regions regarding the structure and patterns of trials. For example, diabolism normally did not inform witchcraft trials among the English, Dutch, and Scandinavian Protest-ants, so witch-hunts were rare and execution rates were normally under

25 percent.[25] Sweden's largest hunt, however, occurred in the late 1670s after mass prosecutions had died out elsewhere. It began when a young boy accused other youths and a seventy-year-old woman of stealing innocent children for the devil, and led to over 200 executions.[26] The English witch-hunter Matthew Hopkins triggered mini-panics during the height of the English Civil War, when fear of social and religious disorder gave added urgency to combating witches. The normal pattern in England involved isolated cases.

There was also little consistency within confessions. In Calvinist regions, the consistory at Geneva normally understood witchcraft as the product of ignorance or residual Catholic beliefs, and executed only one in five witches. In the nearby Calvinist courts in the mountainous Pays du Vaud, a region traditionally associated with the medieval Waldensian heresy, over 90 percent of the accused faced death. In the ecclesiastical principalities of Catholic Germany, individual bishops could be aggressive witch-hunters, while there is no evidence that the Roman Inquisition ever executed a witch. The only significant witch-hunt on the Catholic Iberian peninsula took place in the Basque regions between 1609 and 1614. As with the pastors at Geneva, the Inquisitors treated witchcraft as peasant superstition not heresy, and favoured education rather than corporal punishment. The third factor that may have contributed to the variations of timing and intensity in witch-hunting was the relationship between the state and popular culture. When officials were anxious about heresy, particularly in regions such as south-western Germany where confessional districts often overlapped, persecution could be harsh. In Eastern Europe witch-hunting only began in earnest in the late seventeenth and early eighteenth centuries as political authorities gained the wherewithal to intervene in local affairs.

Tied to the rise and decline of witch-hunting was a rise and decline of Christian obsession with the devil. Since the outset of Luther's reform programme, all religious parties dichotomized confessional struggles as battles between good and evil. Catholic views on the palpable nature of spirituality, Jesus made flesh by word and gesture at every Mass, made it easy to imagine the palpable nature of evil. In confessional diatribes Protestant writers referred to the pope as Antichrist, while Catholics identified Luther and Calvin as agents of the devil. Theologians, prosecutors, and judges at the witch trials believed that the magic-laced religiosity of the people grew out of explicit or implicit negotiations with the devil. Only after 1650 did the rhetoric of evil began to focus more on personal acts of human and social weakness. By the end of the seventeenth century, there was growing scepticism about hell and eternal torment among elite "enlightened" thinkers.

Nevertheless, the religious psychology of evil continued to play a role in moral policing. The gendered assumption that associated women with evil endured, and informs the modern imagery of witches in children's stories and television. In a recent essay, Lyndal Roper has examined the association of witchcraft with children in confessionally-mixed eighteenth-century Augsburg.[27] Here again, *maleficia*, often directed against the parental bed, pacts with the devil, and sabbath gatherings charged with sexual imagery, emerge from testimony provided by the children, whom parents had identified as "incorrigible". The child-witches, some as young as seven, were beaten, partially starved, and imprisoned for years. Roper argues that the assault on witches reflected a deep anxiety among common folk to defend the means for nurturing – be that the mother and child connection, the availability of food, or the sexual potency of the father to reproduce – from unseen forces. In each instance children were actual or potential victims of harmful magic. As belief in witchcraft waned, the threat to nurturing came from the wickedness of the child itself as new concerns regarding child sexuality and masturbation shifted the source of evil from older women to incorrigible children. Throughout, accusations of witchcraft remained wound up in sexual anxieties and the association of evil with sexuality.

Did women have a Reformation? The answer is Yes, but by rereading the Reformation for the perspective of women and questions of gender, we discover a very different account. Late medieval piety was profoundly influenced by women and their spiritual concerns. The attack of the power of good works, and an emphasis on the word, in many ways restored male dominance in an age when so few women could read. Women responded to, participated in, and when possible influenced the energies of spiritual renewal and ecclesiastical reform in all the religious movements, but their voices were most prominent on the radical fringes of Anabaptism and dissent. A second thrust of the reform called for "godly households" and social discipline, which reinforced the power of male patriarchs in the home and of male control in church and in politics.[28] The most significant battleground of this transformation of patriarchy was the witch-hunts, but the parish confessional, consistorial courts, and catechetical instruction instilled distinctly gendered models of proper Christian behaviour for men and women, which reinforced male power. Thus the long European Reformation provided the religious thread to the broader social and political transformation that bound women more tightly to men's authority in early modern Europe.

CONCLUSIONS

On 11 March 1715, a party of Catholic and Lutheran officials surveyed the sanctuary of the thirteenth-century Franciscan church in the Alsatian city of Colmar. The church had sheltered Protestant services for more than a century. Louis XIV, who had outlawed French Calvinism, could not expel his Alsatian Lutheran subjects, who were protected by Imperial law, so he had ordered that the sanctuary be walled off from the nave and re-consecrated for Catholic services. The decision generated a protracted legal struggle in which Colmar's Catholics and Protestants constructed distinct and false confessional histories for the city in an effort to justify their rights to the contested sanctuary. Colmar's Lutherans "forgot" that their community had initially aligned with Swiss reformers and not Luther, while the Catholics "remembered" the popularly supported civic reformation as the act of two self-indulgent civic officials. In the end the royal judges ruled that the wall would stay.[1]

The contested sacred space was first consecrated in the thirteenth century. It had fallen into disuse prior to the city's reformation in 1575 and was claimed and remodelled by the city's Protestant community. Given doubts over the legal authority of civic leaders to reform Colmar's churches, under the rubrics of the religious peace of Augsburg and the powerful allies that local Catholic clergy could call on, the municipal regime recognized the rights of all citizens to choose their place of worship, and the city became a bi-confessional town with a Catholic and a Reformed parish. Colmar's reformation religiously divided families, guilds, and neighbourhoods, but bi-confessional choice became a civic norm, for open religious conflict might draw in outside interference and threaten civic autonomy. The Reformed Protestant community that had worshipped in the church was eventually expelled by Habsburg Imperial forces in 1628 during the Thirty Years War, and Jesuit missionaries took over the church under the guidelines of the Edict of Restitution. Four years later, Swedish soldiers restored Protestant worship to the church, cutting off the noses and ears of the Jesuit priests and driving them from

217

the city. Over the next few decades, Orthodox Lutheran ministers rooted out all vestiges of Colmar's "crypto-Calvinist" past, while in an effort to preserve civic peace, Catholic and Lutheran leaders encouraged tolerance between the confessional communities. When Louis XIV conquered the city in 1673, he could not banish the Lutherans, who were protected by legal rights grounded in the Peace of Westphalia, but he sought every means to restrict Lutheran influence in civic politics and culture. Confiscating the sanctuary was the final act in this second counter-reformation offensive. Down to the end of the twentieth century, the wall in the Lutheran church symbolized the confessional divisions among Colmarians, who continued to live next to one another but not together.[2]

Colmar's story is in many ways a microcosm of the themes addressed in this book. Unlike most texts on Reformation history, I have traced the roots of the Reformation deep into the Middle Ages and followed its ramifications into the eighteenth. Though I have presented an outline of the key events, from the Avignese papacy to the expulsion of Protestants from the archdiocese of Salzburg, the chronological span of the analysis highlights continuities more than dramatic historical change. Since its appearance and initial growth in the Roman Empire, Christianity has been a dynamic and multi-headed movement. The message of Jesus's teachings, his call to faith, and his sacrificial death and resurrection promise eternal "life" to those who believe. The love that God offers "his chosen people", the community of faith, as witnessed in this story, has touched millions, yet determining the proper way to express faith has divided Christians since the age of Paul. Moreover, the chameleon mutability of Christianity, which adjusted and continues to adjust to new and differing social and cultural contexts by syncretizing rituals, sacred calendars, spiritual metaphors, and holy sites, was a key factor in allowing this Jewish reform movement to become a world church. Yet as Christianity has grown and spread across the globe, self-proclaimed leaders from antiquity to the present have sought to define true doctrine, codify rituals, and police the Church of heretical believers. To secure their faith, all Christians need to claim a direct legacy from Jesus and his immediate followers, but in constructing these genealogies of apostolic origins, all parties must "forget" and "remember" aspects of the historical primitive Church in order to find the mirror image for their own community of faith.

Calls for spiritual renewal and structural reform of the late medieval Roman Catholic Church triggered the break-up of what had been an unwieldy ecclesiastical structure and the formation of numerous churches distinct from one another, each modelled in the minds of its founders after the true apostolic church. Faith had long been an expression of community solidarity, and the presence of communities of believers who practised their faith differently was, at first, unimaginable. Political and religious authorities attempted to force the righteousness of their image of true Christianity on those harbouring dissenting views, through persecution and warfare, but in the end all had to settle for their right to disagree about faith. Authorities also sought to instil a deeper religiosity among the less committed, but learned to accept that the "ignorance" or indifference of the masses confirmed the personal worth of the new internalized faith for the elite. In this increasingly modern religious environment, there was even room for unbelief. This grudging tolerance from religious and political authorities was the Reformation's greatest impact on European culture, and it was not fully realized until the eighteenth century.

The ecclesiastical infrastructure of the late medieval Church derived from a ninth-century Carolingian base that was centralized by the eleventh-century Gregorian reforms. Under the system the pope, as "head" of the Church, claimed spiritual authority over all Christendom. Given the degree to which ecclesiastical institutions and personnel were integrated into lay governance and social hierarchies, papal claims generated political tensions. Christendom comprised thousands of parishes collected into hundreds of dioceses, so that every place and everyone had an ecclesiastical identity as a member of some religious corporation. Yet this coherent administrative landscape was racked with inconsistencies and anomalies. Monastic communities, nunneries, and mendicant preaching orders operated independently of the diocesan system. Thousands of "parish" churches could only claim partial parochial rights, while systems of lay patronage resulted in bishops having little or no authority over their diocesan clergy. The foundation of late medieval Christian spirituality also had earlier roots. In 1215 the Fourth Lateran Council had declared the centrality of the sacraments, administered by a consecrated male clergy, to personal salvation. Lay folk, however, continually reworked religious expression to meet their own needs, discovering new saints and pilgrimage sites or accumulating blessed objects to protect their household from the evil eye. This late medieval "vulgarization" of faith was symptomatic of sincere popular religiosity and reflects the success in inculcating the religious values spelled out at the Fourth Lateran Council.

The demographic shock of the Black Death exposed disparities of wealth among the clergy at a time when the papacy was unwilling to reform itself or the Church, culminating in the disastrous schism when two, then three, popes demanded obedience. At the same time, lay rulers were beginning the long struggle to centralize territorial political power, and privileged ecclesiastical institutions whose officials owed some allegiance to Rome formed the most visible obstacles in that quest. The lengthy papal schism gave European rulers tremendous leverage over their territorial churches, and a series of concordats drawn up in the century after the Council of Constance confirmed the new balance of power between Church and state, as Christendom devolved into regional Catholic churches. Even the heretical Hussites successfully defended their breakaway church, with the assistance of the Bohemian nobility. Given linguistic barriers and the absence of printing, however, Hussite religiosity remained local and Czech.

Luther's initial call for reform of the Church resonated throughout the Holy Roman Empire, whose political leaders had not previously secured concordats. The support of princes and magistrates would quickly transform the Martinists into Protestants. Yet what made Luther's evangelical movement so central to the history of the Reformation was his programme for spiritual renewal. Justification by faith alone, achieved through the Word of God rather than participation in collective rituals, was a dramatically different approach to being Christian. Furthermore, the challenge to clerical spiritual power embedded in Luther's call for a priesthood of all believers gave lay officials the authority to reform their regional churches and empowered the common folk to personalize their faith. The religious enthusiasm spawned by the possible meanings of Luther's message produced an evangelical movement among men and women from all walks of life, who, confident in their faith, refashioned themselves and attempted to reform society under godly law. The visibility of women and common folk within the evangelical movement hinted at the depth of faith unleashed by Luther's pamphlets and the revolutionary potential of Christian renewal. With Luther's approval political authorities soon crushed advocates of the "social Gospel" and silenced women. Though lay authorities now controlled the pace and direction of further reformation, Luther's emphasis on the Word as the source of faith meant that it would be impossible for Catholic authorities to restore religious unity without force, and that the unfolding Protestant movement itself would be as diverse as scriptural interpretations warranted.

By the 1560s versions of Lutheranism had become officially sanctioned in many Imperial states, in Scandinavia, and among German-speaking communities in Eastern Europe. A second "Reformed" Protestant movement associated with the writings of Jean Calvin had also sprung up, with or without official support, in Switzerland, France, the Low Countries, parts of the Empire, Scotland, England, and Eastern Europe. In England the Elizabethan Church did not recognize the authority of the pope, but it had yet to take on a unique confessional stamp. In addition there were scattered communities of Anabaptists, limited to regions like Moravia where local lords could promise tolerance. Catholicism itself had undergone renewal in the form of new religious orders and devotional practices and had developed an ecclesiastical reform programme at the Council of Trent, which placed more responsibility and authority in the hands of the bishops. Europe's leading confessions had separated from one another into distinct camps, but even within the confessions proponents remained divided on numerous issues.

Within each movement a cadre of leaders emerged who sought to unify their church under a strict set of doctrinal guidelines and to purge their communities of religious opponents and the unrighteous. Within confessionally mixed regions such as France, the Netherlands, and eventually the Holy Roman Empire, civil unrest soon triggered violence and religious warfare, punctuated by atrocities that solidified the barriers between confessions permanently. In England differences over faith within the official Church precipitated civil war and the public execution of the king. Warfare had become ideological. Even in regions spared wholesale bloodshed, the persecution of religious minorities, moral deviants, and witches increased as sin became criminalized. Having cleansed their communities of Christians from other confessions, self-righteous Calvinist elders, Jansenist nobles or Jesuit confessors, and Lutheran Orthodox ministers then turned on dissenters within their own Church. In the end, these efforts to force faith failed, and with a few notable exceptions official violence ended by the 1660s.

Though efforts to construct a "godly" society "from above" had borne little fruit, religious commitment and religiosity bloomed in the century after the Peace of Westphalia. New and revitalized forms of Catholic devotion spread throughout the countryside as communities appropriated official forms of religious expression for their own needs. Lutheran Pietism again exposed the potential for faith when direct contact with the Word made all believers "priests". Milder forms of Arminian Calvinism flowered into numerous churches, whose congregations experienced

a great awakening. In an increasing environment of tolerance, Mennon-
ite Anabaptists could practise their faith unharmed, while dissenters
developed new forms of religious expression that would inspire much of
nineteenth-century Protestantism. All of these religious developments
were fruits from the late harvest of the Reformation. They had finally
grown because European states had accumulated enough power to be
able to reduce their ideological reliance on an official religion. At the
same time the urban elites were drawn to a new faith in reason and a new
passion for materialism that relegated traditional religion to superstition,
best suited to keep the poor in line. The long European Reformation had
ended, and a new era had begun. The dynamic ideologies of Europe's
future, democracy, nationalism, socialism, capitalism, and racism, would
be secular ideologies grounded in worldly interests.

NOTES

Introduction

1. AAEB, A 19b, Mappe 7, p. 902.
2. Lewis W. Spitz, *The Protestant Reformation, 1517–1559* (New York, 1985). Three recent texts have carried their account into the seventeenth century. See Euan Cameron, *The European Reformation* (Oxford, 1991); Carter Lindberg, *The European Reformations* (Oxford, 1996); and James D. Tracy, *Europe's Reformations, 1450–1650* (Oxford, 1999).
3. Wolfgang Reinhard, "Gegenreformation als Modernisierung? Prolegomena zu einer Theorie des konfessionellen Zeitalters", *ARG*, 68 (1977), pp. 226–52; and Jean Delumeau, *Sin and Fear: The Emergence of Western Guilt Culture, Thirteenth–Eighteenth Centuries* (New York, 1990).
4. A. G. Dickens and John Tonkin, with Kenneth Powell, *The Reformation in Historical Thought* (Cambridge, MA, 1985).
5. Michael Stanford, *A Companion to the Study of History* (Oxford, 1994), pp. 1–7.
6. James Fentress and Chris Wickham, *Social Memory* (Oxford, 1992).
7. Joyce Appleby, Lynn Hunt, and Margaret Jacob, *Telling the Truth about History* (London, 1994); and Peter Novick, *That Noble Dream: The "Objectivity Question" and the American Historical Profession* (Cambridge, 1988), esp. pp. 1–46.
8. Keith Jenkins, *Re-thinking History* (London, 1991); cf. Richard J. Evans, *In Defense of History*, rev. edn (London, 1999).
9. Dickens and Tonkin, *The Reformation*, pp. 7–38.
10. Ibid., pp. 93–118; and Lindberg, *The European Reformations*, pp. 8–22, here at p. 10.
11. Dickens and Tonkin, *The Reformation*, pp. 119–49.
12. Ibid., pp. 119–75 and 264–77; cf. Thomas Nipperday, "The Reformation and the Modern World", in E. I. Kouri and Tom Scott (eds), *Politics and Society in Reformation Europe: Essays for Sir Geoffrey Elton on his Sixty-Fifth Birthday* (London, 1987), pp. 535–52.
13. Steven Ozment, (ed.), *Reformation Europe: A Guide to Research* (St Louis, 1982); John W. O'Malley, SJ (ed.), *Catholicism in Early Modern History: A Guide to Research* (St Louis, 1991); and William S. Maltby (ed.), *Reformation Europe: A Guide to Research*, vol. II (St Louis, 1992).
14. This historical genealogy, from religious communities to national communities, is most clearly drawn in Benedict Anderson, *Imagined Communities:*

223

Reflections on the Origins and Spread of Nationalism, rev. edn (London, 1991), esp. pp. 37–47.

15. Heiko A. Oberman, "The Impact of the Reformation: Problems and Perspectives", in Kouri and Scott (eds), *Politics and Society*, pp. 3–31.

16. See *OER* and *HEH*.

17. E. P. Sanders, *The Historical Figure of Jesus* (New York, 1993); cf. Alan F. Segal, *Rebecca's Children: Judaism and Christianity in the Roman World* (Cambridge, MA, 1986).

18. Wayne A. Meeks, *The First Urban Christians: The Social World of the Apostle Paul* (New Haven, 1983); see also Arland A. Hultgren, *The Rise of Normative Christianity* (Minneapolis, 1994).

19. Richard A. Horsley and John S. Hanson, *Bandits, Prophets, and Messiahs: Popular Movements in the Time of Jesus* (Minneapolis, 1985); John E. Stambaugh and David L. Balch, *The New Testament in its Social Environment* (Philadelphia, 1986).

20. Linwood Urban, *A Short History of Christian Thought*, rev. edn (Oxford, 1995), pp. 255–76.

21. Robert Lane Fox, *Pagans and Christians* (New York, 1987).

22. Joseph H. Lynch, *The Medieval Church: A Brief History* (London, 1992), pp. 8–10; see also Brent D. Shaw, "The Passion of Perpetua", *P&P*, 139 (May 1993), pp. 3–45.

23. The root of the word *clergy* suggests an individual chosen by lot as occurred when the apostles chose Matthias to replace Judas. See Acts 2: 21–6.

24. Fox, *Pagans and Christians*, pp. 493–545.

25. Urban, *A Short History*, pp. 45–65, 73–98, and 316–26.

26. Lynch, *The Medieval Church*, pp. 10–17.

27. H. A. Drake, "Lambs into Lions: Explaining Early Christian Intolerance", *P&P*, 153 (November 1996), pp. 3–36.

28. Fox, *Pagans and Christians*, pp. 601–24.

29. Lynch, *The Medieval Church*, pp. 26–8.

30. Samuel N. C. Lieu, *Manichaeism in the Later Roman Empire and Medieval China: A Historical Survey* (Manchester, 1985), pp. 117–53.

31. Peter Brown, *Augustine of Hippo: A Biography*, new edn (Berkeley, CA, 2000).

32. James C. Russell, *The Germanization of Early Medieval Christianity: A Sociohistorical Approach to Religious Transformation* (Oxford, 1994), pp. 145–54 and 211f.; see also John van Engen, "The Christian Middle Ages as an Historiographical Problem", *AHR*, 91 (1986), pp. 519–52.

33. Joan M. Hussey, *The Orthodox Church in the Byzantine Empire* (Oxford, 1986).

34. Thomas F. X. Noble, *The Republic of St Peter: The Birth of the Papal State, 680–825* (Philadelphia, 1984), pp. 1–56.

35. Hugh Kennedy, *The Prophet and the Age of the Caliphates: The Islamic Near East from the Sixth to the Eleventh Century* (London, 1986).

36. P. M. Holt, *The Age of the Crusades: The Near East from the Eleventh Century to 1517* (London, 1986), pp. 9–30.

37. Norman Housley, *The Later Crusades from Lyons to Alcazar, 1274–1580* (Oxford, 1992).

38. Adriaan H. Bredero, *Christendom and Christianity in the Middle Ages: The Relations between Religion, Church and Society* (Grand Rapids, 1994), pp. 16–18.

39. Ian Wood, *The Merovingian Kingdoms, 450–751* (London, 1994), pp. 273–93.
40. Rosamond McKitterick, *The Frankish Kingdoms under the Carolingians, 751–97* (London, 1983), pp. 46–50.
41. Lynch, *The Medieval Church*, pp. 54–96; and McKitterick, *The Frankish Kingdoms*, pp. 140–68.
42. On new views of feudalism, see Susan Reynolds, *Fiefs and Vassals: The Medieval Evidence Reinterpreted* (Oxford, 1994), pp. 1–16.
43. Colin Morris, *The Papal Monarchy: The Western Church from 1050 to 1250* (Oxford, 1989), pp. 11–33.
44. Ibid., pp. 57–78.
45. Ibid., pp. 109–73; and I. S. Robinson, *The Papacy, 1073–1198: Continuity and Innovation* (Cambridge, 1990), pp. 398–441.
46. Robinson, *The Papacy*, pp. 121–208.

Chapter 1: The Late Medieval Crisis, 1348–1517

1. Rosemary Horrox (trans.), *The Black Death* (Manchester, 1994), here at pp. 155–7.
2. Robert S. Gottfried, *The Black Death: Natural and Human Disaster in Medieval Europe* (New York, 1983), pp. 1–15.
3. From the introduction of *The Decameron*, quoted in Horrox, *The Black Death*, pp. 26–34, here at p. 27.
4. Samuel K. Cohn, *The Cult of Remembrance and the Black Death: Six Cities in Central Italy* (Baltimore and London, 1992), esp. pp. 25–8.
5. Wilhelm Abel, *Agricultural Fluctuations in Europe: From the Thirteenth to the Twentieth Centuries* (New York, 1980), pp. 21–3 and 40–2.
6. Georges Duby, *The Early Growth of the European Economy: Warriors and Peasants from the Seventh to the Twelfth Century* (Ithaca, NY, 1974), pp. 157–80.
7. Susan Reynolds, *Fiefs and Vassals The Medieval Evidence Reinterpreted* (Oxford, 1994), pp. 17–47; see also Susan Reynolds, *Kingdoms and Communities in Western Europe: 900–1200* (Oxford, 1984), pp. 104–54; and cf. Léopold Genicot, *Rural Communities in the Medieval West* (Baltimore and London, 1990), pp. 62–89.
8. Guy Bois, *The Crisis of Feudalism: Economy and Society in Eastern Normandy, c.1300–1550* (Cambridge, 1984), pp. 391–408.
9. Paul M. Hohenberg and Lynn Hollen Lees, *The Making of Urban Europe, 1000–1950* (Cambridge, MA, 1985), pp. 22–46; and David Nicholas, *The Growth of the Medieval City: From Late Antiquity to the Early Fourteenth Century* (London, 1997).
10. Rolf Kiessling, *Die Stadt und ihr Land: Umland, Bürgerbesitz und Wirtschafts-gefüge in Ostswaben vom 14. bis ins 16. Jahrhundert* (Cologne and Vienna, 1989); and Giovanna Benadusi, *A Provincial Elite in Early Modern Tuscany: Family and Power in the Creation of the State* (Baltimore and London, 1996).
11. Nicholas, *The Growth of the Medieval City*, pp. 169–83.
12. Abel, *Agricultural Fluctuations*, pp. 35–42.
13. Werner Rösener, *Peasants in the Middle Ages* (Urbana, IL, 1992), pp. 267–9.

14. Rösener estimates that overall, settlements dropped from 170,000 to 130,000. See Rösener, *Peasants*, p. 255.
15. Bois, *The Crisis of Feudalism*, esp. pp. 316–46.
16. Tom Scott, *Freiburg and the Breisgau: Town–Country Relations in the Age of Reformation and Peasants' War* (Oxford, 1986); see also S. R. Epstein (ed.), *Town and Country in Europe, 1300–1800* (Cambridge, 2001).
17. Hélène Millet and Peter Moraw, "Clerics in the State", in Wolfgang Reinhard (ed.), *Power Elites and State Building* (Oxford, 1996), pp. 173–88.
18. Quoted from Brian Tierney, in R. N. Swanson, *Religion and Devotion in Europe, c.1215–c.1515* (Cambridge, 1995), p. 6.
19. Edward Muir, *Ritual in Early Modern Europe* (Cambridge, 1997), pp. 19–55.
20. Genicot, *Rural Communities*, p. 95.
21. Colin Morris, *The Papal Monarchy: The Western Church from 1050 to 1250* (Oxford, 1989), p. 220.
22. Denys Hay, *The Church in Italy in the Fifteenth Century* (Cambridge, 1977), p. 10.
23. Merry E. Wiesner, *Women and Gender in Early Modern Europe*, 2nd edn (Cambridge, 2000), pp. 215–18.
24. From Innocent III (*1198–1216) to Boniface VIII (*1298–1303), eighteen men served as popes: 13 Italians; 3 Frenchmen, 1 Portuguese, and 1 Savoyard.
25. I. S. Robinson, *The Papacy, 1073–1198: Continuity and Innovation* (Cambridge, 1990), pp. 293–524; and Morris, *Papal Monarchy*, pp. 550–79.
26. Francis Oakley, *The Western Church in the Later Middle Ages* (Ithaca, NY, 1979).
27. Yves Renouard, *The Avignon Papacy, 1305–1403* (Hamden, CT, 1970).
28. Peter Moraw, "Die ältere Universität Erfurt in Rahmen der deutschen und europäischen Hochschulgeschichte", in Ulmann Weiß (ed.), *Erfurt: Geschichte und Gegenwart* (Weimar, 1995), pp. 200–2.
29. Renouard, *The Avignon Papacy*, pp. 74–8.
30. John A. F. Thomson, *Popes and Princes, 1417–1517: Politics and Polity in the Late Medieval Church* (London, 1980), pp. 3–28.
31. Joseph H. Lynch, *The Medieval Church: A Brief History* (London, 1992), p. 332; see also Philip H. Stump, *The Reforms of the Council of Constance, 1414–1418* (Leiden, 1984), pp. xii–xiv.
32. He became papal legate to the Marche of Ancona in central Italy.
33. Stump, *Reforms of the Council of Constance*, passim.
34. Thomson, *Popes and Princes*, pp. 62–3.
35. Paolo Prodi, *The Papal Prince, One Body and Two Souls: The Papal Monarchy in Early Modern Europe* (Cambridge, 1987), pp. 79–101.
36. Peter A. Dykema and Heiko A. Oberman (eds), *Anticlericalism in Late Medieval and Early Modern Europe* (Leiden, 1993).
37. Swanson, *Religion and Devotion*, pp. 235–56.

Chapter 2: Resistance, Renewal, and Reform, 1414–1521

1. R. I. Moore, *The Origins of European Dissent* (London, 1985).
2. Arno Borst, *Medieval Worlds: Barbarians, Heretics, and Artists in the Middle Ages* (Chicago, IL, 1992), pp. 99–100.

3. Malcolm Lambert, *Medieval Heresy: Popular Movements from the Gregorian Reform to the Reformation*, 2nd edn (Oxford, 1992), pp. 47–9.

4. Euan Cameron, *The Reformation of the Heretics: The Waldenses of the Alps, 1480–1580* (Oxford, 1984).

5. Lambert, *Medieval Heresy*, pp. 62–77, 96–7, and 189–214.

6. Ibid., pp. 105–46; cf. Malcolm Barber, *The Cathars: Dualist Heretics in Languedoc in the High Middle Ages* (London, 2000).

7. Emmanuel Le Roy Ladurie, *Montaillou: The Promised Land of Error* (New York, 1979).

8. Lambert, *Medieval Heresy*, pp. 201–2.

9. Bernard M. G. Reardon, *Religious Thought in the Reformation* (London, 1981), pp. 4–7.

10. Margaret Aston, *Lollards and Reformers: Images and Literacy in Late Medieval Religion* (London, 1984).

11. Robert E. Learner, *The Heresy of the Free Spirit in the Later Middle Ages* (Berkeley, 1972).

12. Robert E. Learner, "Medieval Prophecy and Religious Dissent", *P&P*, 72 (1976), pp. 3–24.

13. Howard Kaminsky, *A History of the Hussite Revolution* (Berkeley, CA, 1967), pp. 23–55; cf. Lambert, *Medieval Heresy*, pp. 294–6.

14. Thomas A. Fudge, "'Neither mine nor thine': Communist Experiments in Hussite Bohemia", *Canadian Journal of History*, 33 (April 1998), pp. 26–47.

15. John Van Engen, "The Church in the Fifteenth Century", *HEH*, vol. II, pp. 305–30.

16. R. W. Scribner, "Cosmic Order and Daily Life", in Kaspar von Greyerz (ed.), *Religion and Society in Early Modern Europe* (London, 1984), p. 17.

17. John Bossy, *Christianity in the West, 1400–1700* (Oxford, 1985), pp. 3–6.

18. Caroline Walker Bynum, *Holy Feast and Holy Fast: The Religious Significance of Food to Medieval Women* (Berkeley, CA, 1987).

19. Miri Rubin, *Corpus Christi: The Eucharist in Late Medieval Culture* (Cambridge, 1991).

20. Edward Muir, *Ritual in Early Modern Europe* (Cambridge, 1997), pp. 31–44.

21. Ibid., pp. 44–52.

22. R. N. Swanson, *Religion and Devotion in Europe, c.1215–c.1515* (Cambridge, 1995), pp. 93–101; see also Muir, *Ritual in Early Modern Europe*, pp. 55–80.

23. Swanson, *Religion and Devotion*, pp. 311–42; see also Andrew D. Brown, *Popular Piety in Late Medieval England: The Diocese of Salisbury, 1250–1550* (Oxford, 1995).

24. Van Engen, "The Church in the Fifteenth Century", pp. 319–22.

25. R. R. Post, *The Modern Devotion: Confrontation with Reformation and Humanism* (Leiden, 1968).

26. John Stephens, *The Italian Renaissance: The Origins of Intellectual and Artistic Change before the Reformation* (London, 1990).

27. Charles G. Nauert, Jr, *Humanism and the Culture of Renaissance Europe* (Cambridge, 1995), pp. 2–4.

28. Euan Cameron, *The European Reformation* (Oxford, 1991), pp. 177–89.

29. John A. F. Thomson, *Popes and Princes, 1417–1517: Politics and Polity in the Late Medieval Church* (London, 1992), pp. 145–215.

30. Andrew Vincent, *Theories of the State* (Oxford, 1987), pp. 51–65.
31. Thomson, *Popes and Princes*, pp. 145–6; cf. Susan Doran and Christopher Durston, *Princes, Pastors, and People: The Church and Religion in England, 1529–1689* (London, 1991), pp. 54–5.
32. Charles of Ghent held many crowns. As ruler of the Spanish kingdoms, he was Charles I, and as Holy Roman Emperor he was Charles V. Given the European scale of this narrative, I will consistently employ his Imperial designation.
33. For a well argued counter-point, see Heiko A. Oberman, *The Reformation: Roots and Ramifications* (Grand Rapids, MI, 1994).
34. R. W. Scribner, *For the Sake of Simple Folk: Popular Propaganda for the German Reformation*, rev. edn (Oxford, 1994), pp. 1–14.

Chapter 3: Evangelical Movements and Confessions, 1521–59

1. Carter Lindberg, *The European Reformations* (Oxford, 1996), pp. 91–110.
2. Susan C. Karant-Nunn, *Zwickau in Transition, 1500–1547: The Reformation as an Agent of Change* (Columbus, OH, 1987), pp. 106–9.
3. R. W. Scribner, *The German Reformation* (Atlantic Highlands, NJ, 1986), p. 23.
4. Tom Scott, *Freiburg and the Breisgau: Town–Country Relations in the Age of Reformation and Peasants' War* (Oxford, 1986), pp. 165–89.
5. Thomas A. Brady, Jr, *Turning Swiss: Cities and Empire, 1450–1550* (Cambridge, 1985).
6. Heiko Oberman, "The Gospel of Social Unrest", in Bob Scribner and Gerhard Benecke (eds), *The German Peasant War of 1525 – New Viewpoints* (London, 1979), pp. 39–51; cf. Peter Blickle, *From Communal Reformation to the Revolution of the Common Man* (Leiden, 1998).
7. Due to partible inheritance, there were two Saxonies at this time. Luther's protector, Frederick, held the duchy's electoral rights. His brother George would remain Catholic.
8. George H. Williams, *The Radical Reformation*, 3rd edn (Kirksville, MO, 1992).
9. James E. Stayer, "The Radical Reformation", in *HEH*, vol. II, pp. 249–82; and James E. Stayer, *The German Peasants' War and the Anabaptist Community of Goods* (Montreal, 1991).
10. R. Po-chia Hsia, *Society and Religion in Münster, 1535–1618* (New Haven, CT, 1984).
11. Lyndal Roper, "'The Common Man', 'the Common Good', 'Common Women': Gender and the Meaning of the German Reformation", *Social History*, 12 (1987), pp. 1–21.
12. Lyndal Roper, *The Holy Household: Women and Morals in Reformation Augsburg* (Oxford, 1989).
13. Lorna Jane Abray, *The People's Reformation: Magistrates, Clergy, and Commons in Strasbourg, 1500–1598* (Ithaca, NY, 1985).
14. Randolph C. Head, *Early Modern Democracy in the Grisons: Social Order and Political Language in a Swiss Mountain Canton, 1470–1620* (Cambridge, 1995).

15. W. P. Stephens, *Zwingli: An Introduction to his Thought* (Oxford, 1992).
16. Lee Palmer Wandel, *Voracious Idols and Violent Hands: Iconoclasm in Reformation Zurich, Strasbourg, and Basel* (Cambridge, 1995).
17. Thomas A. Brady, Jr, *Protestant Politics: Jacob Sturm and the German Reformation* (Atlantic Highlands, NJ, 1995).
18. Gerald Strauss, *Luther's House of Learning* (Baltimore, MD, 1978); see also Geoffrey Parker, "Success and Failure during the First Century of the Reformation", *P&P*, 136 (August 1992), pp. 43–82.
19. Ole Peter Grell, "Scandinavia", in *RNC*, pp. 111–30; cf. Ole Peter Grell (ed.), *The Scandinavian Reformation: From Evangelical Movement to Institutionalization of Reform* (Cambridge, 1995), esp. pp. 12–69.
20. Janusz Tazbir, "Poland", in *RNC*, pp. 168–80.
21. Katalin Peter, "Hungary", in ibid., pp. 155–67.
22. Richard A. Muller, *The Unaccommodated Calvin: Studies in the Foundation of a Theological Tradition* (Oxford, 2000), pp. 3–17.
23. Susan Doran and Christopher Durston, *Princes, Pastors and People: The Church and Religion in England, 1529–1689* (London, 1991), pp. 1–12.
24. R. Po-Chia Hsia, *The World of Catholic Renewal, 1540–1770* (Cambridge, 1998), pp. 1–9; cf. Robert Bireley, *The Refashioning of Catholicism, 1450–1700* (Washington, 1999).
25. Larissa Taylor, *Soldiers of Christ: Preaching in Late Medieval and Reformation France* (New York, 1992).
26. Euan Cameron, "Italy", in *ERE*, pp. 188–215.
27. Paolo Prodi, *The Papal Prince, One Body and Two Souls: The Papal Monarchy in Early Modern Europe* (Cambridge, 1987), pp. 79–101.

Chapter 4: Reformation and Religious War, 1550–1650

1. Jan de Vries, "Population", in *HEH*, pp. 1–50, here at p. 13.
2. Wally Seccombe, *A Millennium of Family Change: Feudalism to Capitalism in Northwestern Europe* (London, 1992), pp. 184–200.
3. Alison Rowlands, "The Conditions of Life for the Masses", in *EME*, p. 34.
4. Pavla Miller, *Transformations of Patriarchy in the West, 1500–1900* (Bloomington, IN, 1998), pp. 27–40.
5. David Warren Sabean, *Power in the Blood: Popular Culture and Village Discourse in Early Modern Germany* (Cambridge, 1984), pp. 113–43.
6. Robert S. Duplessis, *Transitions to Capitalism in Early Modern Europe* (Cambridge, 1997), pp. 76–82.
7. Rowlands, "The Conditions of Life", p. 46.
8. John H. Munro, "Patterns of Trade, Money, and Credit", in *HEH*, vol. I, pp. 147–95, here at pp. 172–5.
9. Sabean, *Power in the Blood*, pp. 1–36.
10. Rowlands, "The Conditions of Life", pp. 53f.
11. S. R. Epstein, "Introduction: Town and Country in Europe, 1300–1800", in S. R. Epstein (ed.), *Town and Country in Europe, 1300–1800* (Cambridge, 2001), pp. 1–29.

12. Christopher R. Friedrichs, *Urban Politics in Early Modern Europe* (London, 2000), pp. 65–71.

13. Robert Jütte, *Poverty and Deviance in Early Modern Europe* (Cambridge, 1994), pp. 100–42.

14. R. Po-Chia Hsia, *The World of Catholic Renewal, 1540–1770* (Cambridge, 1998), pp. 11–25.

15. Joseph Bergin, "The Counter-Reformation Church and its Bishops", *P&P*, 165 (November 1999), pp. 30–73.

16. Hsia, *The World of Catholic Renewal*, pp. 116–21.

17. William Monter, *Frontiers of Heresy: The Spanish Inquisition from the Basque Lands to Sicily* (Cambridge, 1990).

18. Carlo Ginzburg, *The Night Battles: Witchcraft and Agrarian Cults in the Sixteenth and Seventeenth Centuries* (Baltimore, MD, 1983).

19. Philip Benedict, "Settlements: France", *HEH*, vol. II, p. 425.

20. Mack P. Holt, *The French Wars of Religion, 1562–1629* (Cambridge, 1995), pp. 30–3.

21. Natalie Zemon Davis, "The Sacred and the Body Social in Sixteenth-Century Lyon", *P&P*, 90 (1981), pp. 40–70.

22. Barbara Diefendorf, *Beneath the Cross: Catholics and Huguenots in Sixteenth-Century Paris* (Oxford, 1991); and Holt, *French Wars of Religion*, pp. 76–97.

23. Menna Prestwich, "Calvinism in France, 1559–1629", in Menna Prestwich (ed.), *International Calvinism, 1541–1715* (Oxford, 1985), pp. 71–107.

24. On the Elizabethan church, see Susan Doran and Christopher Durston, *Princes, Pastors, and People: The Church and Religion in England, 1529–1689* (London, 1991); cf. Christopher Marsh, *Popular Religion in Sixteenth-Century England: Holding their Peace* (London, 1998), esp. pp. 197–219.

25. Ronald Hutton, "The English Reformation and the Evidence of Folklore", *P&P*, 148 (August 1995), pp. 89–116.

26. Jonathan I. Israel, *The Dutch Republic: Its Rise, Greatness, and Fall, 1477–1806* (Oxford, 1995), pp. 9–40.

27. Guido Marnef, *Antwerp in the Age of Reformation: Underground Protestantism in a Commercial Metropolis, 1550–1577* (Baltimore, MD, 1996), pp. 61–87.

28. Wiebe Bergsma, "The Low Countries", in *RNC*, p. 74.

29. Paul Warmbrunn, *Zwei Confessionen in Einer Stadt* (Wiesbaden, 1983).

30. Lorna Jane Abray, *The People's Reformation: Magistrates, Clergy, and Commons in Strasbourg, 1500–1598* (Ithaca, NY, 1985).

31. Heinz Schilling, *Religion, Political Culture and the Emergence of Early Modern Society: Essays in German and Dutch History* (Leiden, 1992), pp. 247–301.

32. Thorkild Lyby and Ole Peter Grell, "The Consolidation of Lutheranism in Denmark and Norway", in Ole Peter Grell (ed.), *The Scandinavian Reformation: From Evangelical Movement to Institutionalization of Reform* (Cambridge, 1995), pp. 114–43.

33. Ingun Montgomery, "The Institutionalisation of Lutheranism in Sweden and Finland", in ibid., pp. 144–78.

34. Janusz Tazbir, "Poland", in *RNC*, p. 168.

35. Katalin Peter, "Hungary", in ibid., pp. 155–67.

36. István György Tóth, *Literacy and Written Culture in Early Modern Central Europe* (Budapest, [1996] 2000).

37. R. J. W. Evans, *The Making of the Habsburg Monarchy, 1550–1700* (Oxford, 1979), pp. 41–79.

Chapter 5: Settlements, 1600–1750

 1. Carter Lindberg, *The European Reformations* (Oxford, 1996), p. 10.
 2. Robert Darnton, *The Great Massacre and Other Episodes in French Cultural History* (New York, 1984), pp. 31f.
 3. James C. Riley, "The Widening Market in Consumer Goods", in *EME*, pp. 233–62, here at p. 243.
 4. Ronald Hutton, "The English Reformation and the Evidence of Folklore", *P&P*, 148 (August 1995), pp. 89–116; cf. David Warren Sabean, *Power in the Blood: Popular Culture and Village Discourse in Early Modern Germany* (Cambridge, 1984), pp. 174–98.
 5. H. M. Scott, "Europe Turns East: Political Developments", in *EME*, pp. 298–344.
 6. Jeremy Black, *A Military Revolution? Military Change and European Society, 1550–1800* (Atlantic Highlands, NJ, 1991).
 7. Samuel Clark, *State and Status: The Rise of the State and Aristocratic Power in Western Europe* (Montreal and Kingston, 1995), pp. 29–125.
 8. Sharon Kettering, *Patrons, Brokers, and Clients in Seventeenth-Century France* (Oxford, 1986).
 9. Allyson M. Poska, *Regulating the People: The Catholic Reformation in Seventeenth-Century Spain* (Leiden, 1998).
10. Mack Walker, *The Salzburg Transaction: Expulsion and Redemption in Eighteenth-Century Germany* (Ithaca, NY, 1992).
11. Kaspar von Greyerz, *Religion und Kultur: Europe, 1500–1800* (Göttingen, 2000), pp. 152–4.
12. Paoli Prodi, *The Papal Prince, One Body and Two Souls: The Papal Monarchy in Early Modern Europe* (Cambridge, 1987), pp. 1–36.
13. R. Po-Chia Hsia, *The World of Catholic Renewal, 1540–1770* (Cambridge, 1998), pp. 92–105.
14. Joseph Bergin, "The Counter-Reformation Church and its Bishops", *P&P*, 165 (November 1999), pp. 30–73.
15. John McManners, *Church and Society in Eighteenth-Century France* (Oxford, 1998), vol. I, pp. 321–58.
16. Marc Forster, *The Counter-Reformation in the Villages: Religion and Reform in the Bishopric of Speyer, 1560–1720* (Ithaca, NY, 1992); and Keith P. Luria, *Territories of Grace: Cultural Change in the Seventeenth-Century Diocese of Grenoble* (Berkeley, CA, 1991).
17. Hsia, *The World of Catholic Renewal*, pp. 26–41.
18. Forster, *The Counter-Reformation in the Villages*, pp. 215–25; cf. Louis Châtellier, *The Religion of the Poor: Rural Missions in Europe and the Formation of Modern Catholicism, c.1500–1800* (Cambridge, 1997), pp. 19–30.
19. Patricia Ranft, *Women and the Religious Life in Premodern Europe* (New York, 1996), pp. 122–4.

20. Robert W. Scribner, "Incombustible Luther", *P&P*, 110 (1986), pp. 38–68.
21. John Stroup, *The Struggle for Identity in the Clerical Estate: Northwest German Protestant Opposition to Absolutist Policy in the Eighteenth Century* (Leiden, 1984), p. 19.
22. R. Po-Chia Hsia, *Social Discipline in the Reformation: Central Europe, 1550–1750* (London, 1989), pp. 19–22.
23. C. Scott Dixon, *The Reformation and Rural Society: The Parishes of Brandenburg-Ansbach-Kulmbach, 1528–1603* (Cambridge, 1996), pp. 128–42.
24. Thorkild Lyby and Ole Peter Grell, "The Consolidation of Lutheranism in Denmark and Norway", in Ole Peter Grell (ed.), *The Scandinavian Reformation: From Evangetical Movement to Institutionalization of Reform* (Cambridge, 1995), p. 137.
25. Sabean, *Power in the Blood*, pp. 138–43.
26. Stroup, *The Struggle for Identity*, pp. 30–2.
27. Nicholas Hope, *German and Scandinavian Protestantism, 1700–1918* (Oxford, 1995), pp. 78–80 and 154–8.
28. Mary Fulbrook, *Piety and Politics: Religion and the Rise of Absolutism in England, Württemberg, and Prussia* (Cambridge, 1983).
29. Menna Prestwich, "Introduction", in Menna Prestwich (ed.), *International Calvinism, 1541–1715* (Oxford, 1985), p. 5.
30. Élizabeth Labrousse, "Calvinism in France, 1598–1685", in ibid., pp. 285f.
31. Gregory Hanlon, *Confession and Community in Seventeenth-Century France: Catholic and Protestant Coexistence in Aquitaine* (Philadelphia, 1993), pp. 119–51.
32. Élizabeth Labrousse, *"Une foi, une loi, un roi?" La Révocation de l'édit de Nantes* (Paris, 1985), pp. 196–224.
33. Prestwich, "Introduction", in *International Calvinism*, p. 10.
34. Ronald Hutton, *The Rise and Fall of Merry England: The Ritual Year, 1400–1700* (Oxford, 1994).
35. J. C. D. Clark, *English Society, 1688–1832* (Cambridge, 1985), pp. 136–7.
36. Jean Delumeau, *Catholicism between Luther and Voltaire* (Philadelphia, 1977); cf. John Bossy, *Christianity in the West, 1400–1700* (New York, 1985).
37. Robert W. Scribner, "Elements of Popular Belief", in *HEH*, vol. I, pp. 231–62.
38. Marc Forster, *Catholic Revival in the Age of the Baroque: Religious Identity in Southwestern Germany, 1550–1750* (Cambridge, 2001), pp. 13–17, here at p. 13; see also Joel F. Harrington and Helmut Walser Smith, "Confessionalization, Community, and State Building in Germany, 1555–1870", *JMH*, 69 (1997), pp. 77–101.
39. Hans-Christoph Rublack (ed.), *Die lutherische Konfessionalisierung in Deutschland* (Gütersloh, 1992); cf. Dixon, *The Reformation and Rural Society*.
40. Wolfgang Reinhard and Heinz Schilling (eds), *Die katholische Konfessionalisierung* (Gütersloh, 1995).
41. Heiko A. Oberman, "Europa Afflicta: The Reformation of the Refugees", *ARG*, 83 (1992), pp. 91–111; and Heinz Schilling, *Konfessionskonflikt und Staatsbildung: Eine Fallstudie über das Verhältnis von religiösem und sozialem Wandel in der Frühneuzeit am Beispiel der Grafschaft Lippe* (Gütersloh, 1981).
42. Wolfgang Reinhard, "Reformation, Counter-Reformation, and the Early Modern State: A Reassessment", *Catholic Historical Review*, 75 (1989), pp. 383–404; and Heinz Schilling, "Confessional Europe", in *HEH*, vol. II, pp. 641–81.

43. Forster, *The Counter-Reformation in the Villages*, pp. 244–7.
44. Forster, *Catholic Revival*, pp. 83–103 and 131–47.
45. Châtellier, *The Religion of the Poor*, pp. 91–183, here at p. 92.
46. Hope, *German and Scandinavian Protestantism*, pp. 165–7.
47. Peter Zschunke, *Konfession und Alltag in Oppenheim: Beiträge zur Geschichte von Bevölkerung und Gesellschaft einer gemischtkonfessionellen Kleinstadt in der frühen Neuzeit* (Wiesbaden, 1984); and Étienne François, *Protestants et catholiques en Allemagne: identités et pluralisme: Augsburg, 1648–1806* (Paris, 1993).
48. István György Tóth, *Literacy and Written Culture in Early Modern Central Europe* (Budapest, [1996] 2000), pp. 76–7.
49. Jens Chr. V. Johansen, "Faith, Superstition and Witchcraft in Reformation Scandinavia", in Grell (ed.), *The Scandinavian Reformation*, 190–3.
50. David Gentilcore, *From Bishop to Witch: The System of the Sacred in Early Modern Terra d'Otronto* (Manchester, 1992), p. 4.
51. Luria, *Territories of Grace*.
52. James R. Jacob, *The Scientific Revolution: Aspirations and Achievement, 1500–1700* (Atlantic Highlands, NJ, 1998); see also Robin Briggs, "Embattled Faiths: Religion and Natural Philosophy", in *EME*, pp. 177ff.
53. Thomas S. Kuhn, *The Structure of Scientific Revolutions*, 3rd edn (Chicago, 1998).
54. Jacob, *The Scientific Revolution*, pp. 77–87.
55. Dorinda Outram, *The Enlightenment* (Cambridge, 1995), pp. 1–13, here at p. 2.
56. Jürgen Habermas, *The Structural Transformation of the Public Sphere: An Inquiry into a Category of Bourgeois Society* (Cambridge, MA, 1989), pp. 1–88.
57. Robert Darnton, *The Literary Underground of the Old Regime* (Cambridge, MA, 1982).
58. Norman Hampson, "The Enlightenment", in *EME*, pp. 265–97.
59. Outram, *The Enlightenment*, pp. 31–46.

Chapter 6: Rereading the Reformation through Gender Analysis

1. Merry E. Wiesner, "Studies of Women, Family, and Gender", in William S. Maltby (ed.), *Reformation Europe: A Guide to Research, II* (St Louis, 1992), pp. 159–87; see also Merry E. Wiesner, *Women and Gender in Early Modern Europe*, rev. edn (Cambridge, 2000), pp. 213–63, esp. pp. 254–63.
2. Joan Kelly, *Women, History, and Theory* (Chicago, 1984), pp. 19–50.
3. Joan Wallach Scott, "Gender a Useful Category of Historical Analysis", in Joan Wallach Scott (ed.), *Feminism and History* (Oxford, 1996), pp. 152–80, here at p. 167.
4. Merry Wiesner, *Christianity and Sexuality in the Early Modern World* (London, 2000), pp. 23–5.
5. Peter Brown, *The Body and Society: Men, Women, and Sexual Renunciation in Early Christianity* (New York, 1988).
6. Marina Warner, *Alone of All Her Sex: The Myth and Cult of the Virgin Mary* (London, 1976).
7. Wiesner, *Women and Gender*, pp. 215–20.

8. Patricia Ranft, *Women and Spiritual Equality in Christian Tradition* (New York, 1998), pp. 179–89, here at p. 188.

9. Patricia Ranft, *Women and the Religious Life in Pre-Modern Europe* (New York, 1996), pp. 80–5.

10. C. Scott Dixon, *The Reformation and Rural Society: The Parishes of Brandenburg-Ansbach-Kulmbach, 1528–1603* (Cambridge, 1996), pp. 82–3.

11. Wiesner, *Christianity and Sexuality*, p. 73.

12. Lyndal Roper, "'The Common Man', 'the Common Good', 'Common Women': Gender and the Meaning of the German Reformation", *Social History*, 12 (1987), pp. 1–21.

13. Wiesner, *Women and Gender*, pp. 220–5.

14. Ibid., p. 228.

15. Ranft, *Women and the Religious Life*, pp. 101–6.

16. Ibid., pp. 124–8.

17. Patricia Crawford, *Women and Religion in England, 1500–1720* (London, 1993), p. 78.

18. Wiesner, *Women and Gender*, pp. 243–5.

19. Alexander Sedgwick, *Jansenism in Seventeenth-Century France* (Charlottesville, VA, 1977).

20. Brian P. Levack, *The Witch-Hunt in Early Modern Europe*, rev. edn (London, 1996).

21. Stuart Clark, *Thinking with Demons: The Idea of Witchcraft in Early Modern Europe* (Oxford, 1997).

22. On the difficulty of defining witchcraft, see Wolfgang Behringer, *Witchcraft Persecutions in Bavaria: Popular Magic, Religious Zealotry and Reason of State in Early Modern Europe* (Cambridge, 1997), pp. 14–15.

23. H. C. Eric Midelfort, *Witch-Hunting in Southwestern Germany, 1562–1684* (Stanford, CT, 1984) pp. 212–14.

24. Wolfgang Behringer, *Shaman of Oberstdorf: Chonrad Stoeckhlin and the Phantoms of the Night* (Charlottesville, VA, 1998); cf. Carls Ginzburg, *The Night Battles: Witchcraft and Agrarian Cults in the Sixteenth and Seventeenth Centuries* (Baltimore, MD, 1983).

25. Levack, *The Witch-Hunt*, pp. 170–211.

26. Jens Chr. V. Johansen, "Faith, Superstition, and Witchcraft in Reformation Scandinavia", in Ole Peter Grell (ed.), *The Scandinavian Reformation: From Evangelical Movement to Institutionalization of Reform* (Cambridge, 1995), pp. 179–211.

27. Lyndal Roper, "'Evil Imaginings and Fantasies': Child-Witches and the End of the Witch Craze", *P&P*, 167 (May 2000), pp. 107–39.

28. Pavla Miller, *Transformations of Patriarchy in the West, 1500–1900* (Bloomington, IN, 1998), pp. 1–40.

Conclusions

1. Archives municipales de Colmar, GG 172.

2. Peter G. Wallace, *Communities and Conflict in Early Modern Colmar, 1575–1730* (Atlantic Highlands, NJ, 1995).

SELECT BIBLIOGRAPHY

General Works on Church History and the European Reformations

Brady, Thomas A., Jr, Heiko A. Oberman, and James D. Tracy (eds), *Handbook of European History, 1400–1600: Later Middle Ages, Renaissance and Reformation* (Leiden, 1994), 2 vols.

Cameron, Euan, *The European Reformation* (Oxford, 1991).

—— (ed.), *Early Modern Europe: An Oxford History* (Oxford, 1999).

Dickens, A. G. and John Tonkin, with Kenneth Powell, *The Reformation in Historical Thought* (Cambridge, MA, 1985).

Dykema, Peter A. and Heiko A. Oberman (eds), *Anticlericalism in Late Medieval and Early Modern Europe* (Leiden, 1993).

Friesen, Abraham, *Reformation and Utopia: The Marxist Interpretations of the Reformation and its Antecedents* (Wiesbaden, 1974).

Greengrass, Mark, *The Longman Companion to the European Reformation c.1500–1618* (London, 1998).

Grell, Ole Peter and Bob Scribner (eds), *Tolerance and Intolerance in the European Reformation* (Cambridge, 1996).

Greyerz, Kaspar von (ed.), *Religion and Society in Early Modern Europe, 1500–1800* (London, 1984).

——, *Religion und Kultur: Europa, 1500–1800* (Göttingen, 2000).

Hillerbarnd, Hans (ed.), *The Oxford Encyclopedia of the Reformation* (New York, 1996), 4 vols.

Lindberg, Carter, *The European Reformations* (Oxford, 1996).

Maltby, William S. (ed.), *Reformation Europe: A Guide to Research, II* (St Louis, 1992).

Monter, William, *Ritual, Myth, and Magic in Early Modern Europe* (Athens, OH, 1983).

Oberman, Heiko A., *The Dawn of the Reformation: Essays in Late Medieval and Early Reformation Thought* (Grand Rapids, MI, 1992).

——, *The Reformation: Roots and Ramifications* (Grand Rapids, MI, 1994).

Ozment, Steven (ed.), *Reformation Europe: A Guide to Research* (St Louis, 1982).

Pettegree, Andrew (ed.), *The Early Reformation in Europe* (Cambridge, 1992).

Reardon, Bernard M. G., *Religious Thought in the Reformation* (London, 1981).

Scribner, Bob, Roy Porter, and Mikuláš Teich (eds), *The Reformation in National Context* (Cambridge, 1994).

Tracy, James D., *Europe's Reformations, 1450–1650* (Oxford, 1999).

The Late Medieval Crisis and the Church

Aston, Margaret, "Corpus Christi and Corpus Regni: Heresy and the Peasants' Revolt", *P&P*, 143 (May 1994), pp. 3–47.

Black, Anthony, *Council and Commune: The Conciliar Movement and the Fifteenth-Century Heritage* (London, 1979).

Bredero, Adriaan H., *Christendom and Christianity in the Middle Ages: The Relations between Religion, Church and Society* (Grand Rapids, MI, 1994).

Brown, Andrew D., *Popular Piety in Late Medieval England: The Diocese of Salisbury, 1250–1550* (Oxford, 1995).

Cameron, Euan, *The Reformation of the Heretics: The Waldenses of the Alps, 1480–1580* (Oxford, 1984).

Cohn, Samuel K., *The Cult of Remembrance and the Black Death: Six Cities in Central Italy* (Baltimore, MD, 1992).

Dohar, William J., *The Black Death and Pastoral Leadership: The Diocese of Hereford in the Fourteenth Century* (Philadelphia, 1995).

French, Katherine L., *The People of the Parish: Community Life in a Late Medieval Diocese* (Philadelphia, 2001).

Hay, Denys, *The Church in Italy in the Fifteenth Century* (Cambridge, 1977).

Housley, Norman, *The Later Crusades from Lyons to Alcazar, 1274–1580* (Oxford, 1992).

Kaminsky, Howard, *A History of the Hussite Revolution* (Berkeley, CA, 1967).

Lambert, Malcolm, *Medieval Heresy: Popular Movements from the Gregorian Reform to the Reformation*, 2nd edn (Oxford, 1992).

Lerner, Robert E., *The Heresy of the Free Spirit in the Later Middle Ages* (Berkeley, CA, 1972).

Le Roy Ladurie, Emmanuel, *Montaillou: The Promised Land of Error* (New York, 1979).

Lynch, Joseph H., *The Medieval Church: A Brief History* (London, 1992).

Moore, R. I., *The Origins of European Dissent* (London, [1977] 1985).

Mormando, Franco, *The Preacher's Demons: Bernardino of Siena and the Social Underworld of Early Renaissance Italy* (Chicago, 1999).

Oakley, Francis, *The Western Church in the Later Middle Ages* (Ithaca, NY, 1979).

Post, R. R., *The Modern Devotion: Confrontation with Reformation and Humanism* (Leiden, 1968).

Renouard, Yves, *The Avignon Papacy, 1305–1403* (Hamden, CT, 1970).

Rubin, Miri, *Corpus Christi: The Eucharist in Late Medieval Culture* (Cambridge, 1991).

Stump, Philip H., *The Reforms of the Council of Constance (1414–1418)* (Leiden, 1984).

Swanson, R. N., *Religion and Devotion in Europe, c.1215 – c.1515* (Cambridge, 1995).

Thomson, John A. F., *Popes and Princes, 1417–1517: Politics and Polity in the Late Medieval Church* (London, 1980).

——, *The Western Church in the Middle Ages* (New York, 1998).

Van Engen, John, "The Christian Middle Ages as an Historiographical Problem", *AHR*, 91 (1986), pp. 519–52.

Wunderli, Richard, *Peasant Fires: The Drummer of Niklashausen* (Bloomington, IN, 1992).

The Renaissance and Humanism

Goodman, Anthony and Angus MacKay, *The Impact of Humanism on Western Europe* (London, 1990).

Martines, Lauro, *Power and Imagination: City States in Renaissance Italy* (Baltimore, MD, 1988).

Nauert, Charles G., Jr, *Humanism and the Culture of Renaissance Europe* (Cambridge, 1995).

Rummel, Erika, *Erasmus and His Catholic Critics* (Nieuwkoop, 1989).

——, *The Humanist–Scholastic Debate in the Renaissance and Reformation* (Cambridge, MA, 1995).

Stadtwald, Kurt W., *Roman Popes and German Patriots: Anti-Papalism in the Politics of the German Humanist Movement* (Geneva, 1995).

Stephens, John, *The Italian Renaissance: The Origins of Intellectual and Artistic Change before the Reformation* (London, 1990).

Tracy, James, *Erasmus of the Low Countries* (Berkeley, CA, 1996).

The German Reformation

Abray, Lorna Jane, *The People's Reformation: Magistrates, Clergy, and Commons in Strasbourg, 1500–1598* (Ithaca, NY, 1985).

Blickle, Peter, *The Communal Reformation: The Quest for Salvation in Sixteenth-Century Germany* (Atlantic Highlands, NJ, 1992).

Brady, Thomas A., Jr, *Protestant Politics: Jacob Sturm (1489–1553) and the German Reformation* (Atlantic Highlands, NJ, 1995).

——, *Ruling Class, Regime, and Reformation at Strasbourg, 1520–1555* (Leiden, 1978).

——, *Turning Swiss: Cities and Empire, 1450–1550* (Cambridge, 1985).

Brecht, Martin, *Martin Luther* (Philadelphia, 1985–93), 3 vols.

Chrisman, Miriam Usher, *Conflicting Visions of Reform: German Lay Propaganda Pamphlets, 1519–1530* (Atlantic Highlands, NJ, 1996).

——, *Lay Culture, Learned Culture in Strasbourg* (New Haven, CT, 1982).

Edwards, Mark U., *Printing, Propaganda, and Martin Luther* (Berkeley, CA, 1994).

Estes, James M., *Christian Magistrate and State Church: The Reforming Career of Johannes Brenz* (Toronto, 1982).

Hendrix, Scott, *Luther and the Papacy* (Philadelphia, 1981).

Karant-Nunn, Susan, "Luther's Pastors: The Reformation in the Ernestine Countryside", *Transactions of the American Philosophical Society*, 68/69 (Philadelphia, 1979).

——, *Zwickau in Transition, 1500–1547* (Columbus, OH, 1987).

Marius, Richard, *Martin Luther: The Christian between God and Death* (Cambridge, MA, 1999).

Oberman, Heiko A., *Luther: Man between God and the Devil* (New Haven, CT, 1989).

Russell, Paul, *Lay Theology in the Reformation: Popular Pamphleteers in Southwest Germany, 1521–1525* (Cambridge, 1986).

Scribner, R. W., *The German Reformation* (Atlantic Highlands, NJ, 1986).

Steinmetz, David, *Luther in Context* (Bloomington, IN, 1986).

The Swiss Reformation

Biel, Pamela, *Doorkeepers at the House of Righteousness: Heinrich Bullinger and the Zurich Clergy* (Bern, 1991).

Guggisberg, Hans, *Basel in the Sixteenth Century* (St Louis, 1982).

Locher, Gottfridt W., *Zwingli's Thought: New Perspectives* (Leiden, 1981).

Potter, G. R., *Zwingli* (Cambridge, 1976).

Stephens, W. P., *The Theology of Huldrych Zwingli* (Oxford, 1986).

——, *Zwingli: An Introduction to his Thought* (Oxford, 1992).

Wandel, Lee Palmer, *Voracious Idols and Violent Hands: Iconoclasm in Reformation Zurich, Strasbourg, and Basel* (Cambridge, 1995).

The Radical Reformation, the Peasants' War and Anabaptism

Bender, Harold, "The Anabaptist Vision", *Church History*, 13 (1944), pp. 3–24.

Blickle, Peter, *From Communal Reformation to the Revolution of the Common Man* (Leiden, 1998).

——, *The Revolution of 1525: The German Peasants' War from a New Perspective* (Baltimore, MD, 1981).

Clasen, Claus-Peter, *Anabaptism: A Social History, 1525–1618* (Ithaca, NY, 1972).

Conrad, Franziska, *Reformation in der baüerliche Gesellschaft* (Wiesbaden, 1984).

Goertz, Hans-Jürgen, *The Anabaptists* (New York, 1996).

Hillerbrand, Hans (ed.), *Radical Tendencies in the Reformation: Divergent Perspectives* (Kirksville, MO, 1988).

Packull, Werner O., *Hutterite Beginnings: Communitarian Experiments during the Reformation* (Baltimore, MD, 1995).

Scott, Tom, *Freiburg and the Breisgau: Town–Country Relations in the Age of Reformation and Peasants' War* (Oxford, 1986).

Scribner, Bob, "Practical Utopias: Pre-modern Communism and the Reformation", *Comparative Studies in Society and History*, 36 (1994), pp. 743–74.

—— and Gerhard Benecke (eds), *The German Peasant War of 1525: New Viewpoints* (London, 1979).

Stayer, James M., *Anabaptists and the Sword* (Lawrence, KS, 1972).

——, *The German Peasants' War and the Anabaptist Community of Goods* (Montreal, 1991).

The English Reformation under the Tudors

Brigdon, Susan, *London and the Reformation* (Oxford, 1989).

Collinson, Patrick, *The Elizabethan Puritan Movement* (Oxford, [1967] 1990).

Dickens, A. G., *The English Reformation*, 2nd edn (University Park, PA, 1989).

Doran, Susan and Christopher Durston, *Princes, Pastors and People: The Church and Religion in England, 1529–1689* (London, 1991).

Duffy, Eamon, *Stripping the Altars: Traditional Religion in England, ca.1400–ca.1580* (New Haven, CT, 1992).

Haigh, Christopher, *English Reformations: Religion, Politics, and Society under the Tudors* (New York, 1993).

Jones, Norman, *The Birth of the Elizabethan Age: England in the 1560s* (Oxford, 1993).

Marsh, Christopher, *Popular Religion in Sixteenth-Century England: Holding their Peace* (London, 1998).

Marshall, Peter (ed.), *The Impact of the English Reformation, 1500–1640* (London, 1997).

Mcigs, Samantha A., *The Reformation in Ireland* (New York, 1997).

Whiting, Robert, *The Blind Devotion of the People: Popular Religion and the English Reformation* (Cambridge, 1989).

——, *Local Responses to the English Reformation* (London, 1998).

The Second Reformation: Calvin, Geneva, France, and beyond

Benedict, Philip, *The Faith and Fortune of France's Huguenots, 1600–85* (Aldershot, 2001).

Bouwsma, William, *Jean Calvin: A Sixteenth-Century Portrait* (New York, 1988).

Cottret, Bernard, *Calvin: A Biography* (Grand Rapids, MI, 2000).

Crew, Phyllis Mack, *Calvinist Preaching and Iconoclasm in the Netherlands, 1544–1569* (Cambridge, 1978).

Davis, Natalie, *Society and Culture in Early Modern France* (Stanford, CT, 1975).

Duke, Alastair C., *Reformation and Revolt in the Low Countries* (London, 1990).

Duplessis, Robert, *Lille in the Dutch Revolt* (Cambridge, 1991).

Greengrass, Mark, *The French Reformation* (Oxford, 1987).

Höpfl, Harro, *The Christian Polity of John Calvin* (Cambridge, 1985).

Kaplan, Benjamin, *Calvinists and Libertines: Confessions and Community in Utrecht, 1578–1620* (Oxford, 1995).

Lottin, Alain, *Lille, Citadelle de la Contre-Réforme (1598–1668)?* (Dunkirk, 1984).

Marnef, Guido, *Antwerp in the Age of Reformation: Underground Protestantism in a Commercial Metropolis, 1550–1577* (Baltimore, MD, 1996).

Marshall, Sherrin, *The Dutch Gentry, 1500–1650: Faith, Family, and Fortune* (Westport, CT, 1987).

McGrath, Alastair, *A Life of John Calvin* (Oxford, 1990).

Muller, Richard A., *The Unaccommodated Calvin: Studies in the Foundation of a Theological Tradition* (Oxford, 2000).

Nischan, Bodo, *Princes, People, and Confession: The Second Reformation in Brandenburg* (Philadelphia, 1994).

Parker, Charles H., *The Reformation of the Community: The Diaconate and Municipal Poor Relief in Holland, 1572–1617* (Cambridge, 1998).

Pettegree, Andrew, *Emden and the Dutch Revolt* (Oxford, 1992).

Press, Volker, *Calvinismus und Territorialstaat: Regierung und Zentralbehörden der Kurpfalz, 1559–1619* (Stuttgart, 1970).

Schilling, Heinz, *Civic Calvinism in Northwest Germany and the Netherlands* (Kirkesville, MO, 1992).

—— (ed.), *Die reformierte Konfessionalisierung in Deutschland – Das Problem der "Zweiten Reformation"* (Gütersloh, 1986).

Steinmetz, David C., *Calvin in Context* (Oxford, 1995).

Tracy, James D., *Holland under Habsburg Rule* (Berkeley, CA, 1990).

Northern and Eastern Europe

Evans, R. J. W., *The Making of the Habsburg Monarchy, 1550–1700* (Oxford, 1979).
Kirby, David, *Northern Europe in the Early Modern Period: The Baltic World, 1492–1772* (London, 1990).
Grell, Ole Peter (ed.), *The Scandinavian Reformation: From Evangelical Movement to Institutionalization of Reform* (Cambridge, 1995).

Age of the Religious Wars

Benedict, Philip, *Rouen during the Wars of Religion* (Cambridge, 1981).
Bireley, Robert, SJ, *Religion and Politics in the Age of the Counter Reformation: Emperor Ferdinand II, William Lamormiani SJ, and the Formation of Imperial Policy* (Chapel Hill, NJ, 1981).
Crouzet, Denis, *Les Guerriers de Dieu: La violence au temps du trouble de religion* (Seyssel, 1990), 2 vols.
Diefendorf, Barbara, *Beneath the Cross: Catholics and Huguenots in Sixteenth-Century France* (Oxford, 1991).
Holt, Mack, *The French Wars of Religion, 1562–1629* (Cambridge, 1995).
Robbins, Kevin, *City on the Ocean Sea: La Rochelle, 1530–1650* (Leiden, 1997).
Warmbrunn, Paul, *Zwei Confessionen in Einer Stadt* (Wiesbaden, 1983).

Confession and Church Building

Catholic Renewal

Bergin, Joseph, "The Counter-Reformation Church and Its Bishops", *P&P*, 165 (November 1999), pp. 30–73.
Bilinkoff, Jodi, *The Avila of St Teresa: Religious Reform in a Sixteenth-Century Spanish City* (Ithaca, NY, 1989).
Bireley, Robert, SJ, *The Refashioning of Catholicism, 1450–1700: A Reassessment of the Counter Reformation* (Washington, 1999).
Black, Christopher F., *Italian Confraternities in the Sixteenth Century* (Cambridge, 1989).
Bossy, John, "The Counter-Reformation and the People of Catholic Europe", *P&P*, 47 (1970), pp. 51–70.
Delumeau, Jean, *Catholicism between Luther and Voltaire* (Philadelphia, 1977).
Forster, Marc R., *The Counter-Reformation in the Villages: Religion and Reform in the Bishopric of Speyer, 1560–1720* (Ithaca, 1992).
——, *Catholic Revival in the Age of the Baroque: Religious Identity in Southwest Germany, 1550–1750* (Cambridge, 2001).
Hallman, Barbara McClung, *Italian Cardinals, Reform, and the Church as Property* (Berkeley, CA, 1985).
Hoffman, Philip, *Church and Community in the Diocese of Lyon, 1500–1789* (New Haven, CT, 1984).
Hsia, R. Po-chia, *Society and Religion in Münster, 1535–1618* (New Haven, CT, 1984).

——, *The World of Catholic Renewal, 1540–1770* (Cambridge, 1998).

Hudon, William V., "Religion and Society in Early Modern Italy – Old Questions, New Insights", *AHR*, 101 (1996), pp. 783–804.

Kamen, Henry, *Inquisition and Society in Spain in the Sixteenth and Seventeenth Centuries* (Bloomington, IN, 1985).

——, *The Phoenix and the Flame: Catalonia and the Counter Reformation* (New Haven, CT, 1993).

Luria, Keith P., *Territories of Grace: Cultural Change in the Seventeenth-Century Diocese of Grenoble* (Berkeley, CA, 1991).

Meyers, W. David, *Poor Sinning Folk: Confession and Conscience in Counter-Reformation Germany* (Ithaca, NY, 1996).

Mullett, Michael A., *The Catholic Reformation* (London, 1999).

Nalle, Sara T., *God in La Mancha: Religious Reform and the People of Cuenca, 1500–1650* (Baltimore, MD, 1992).

Olin, John, *The Catholic Reformation* (New York, 1993).

O'Malley, John W. SJ (ed.), *Catholicism in Early Modern History: A Guide to Research* (St Louis, 1991).

——, *The First Jesuits* (Cambridge, MA, 1993).

Phillips, Henry, *Church and Culture in Seventeenth-Century France* (Cambridge, 1997).

Prodi, Paolo, *The Papal Prince: Papal Monarchy in Early Modern Europe* (Cambridge, 1987).

Reinhard, Wolfgang and Heinz Schilling (eds), *Die Katholische Konfessionalisierung* (Münster, 1995).

Sedgwick, Alexander, *Jansenism in Seventeenth-Century France* (Charlottesville, VA, 1977).

Lutheranism

Gawthorp, Richard L., *Pietism and the Making of Eighteenth-Century Prussia* (Cambridge, 1993).

Hope, Nicholas, *German and Scandinavian Protestantism, 1700–1918* (Oxford, 1995).

Scribner, Bob, "Incombustible Luther: The Image of the Reformer in Early Modern Germany", *P&P*, 110 (February 1986), pp. 38–68.

Stoeffel, F. Ernest, *The Rise of Evangelical Pietism* (Leiden, 1965).

Stroup, John, *The Struggle for Identity in the Clerical Estate: Northwest German Protestant Opposition to Absolutist Policy in the Eighteenth Century* (Leiden, 1984).

Tolley, Bruce, *Pastors and Parishioners in Württemberg during the Late Reformation* (Stanford, CT, 1995).

Tracy, James D. (ed.), *Luther and the Modern State in Germany* (Kirksville, MO, 1986).

Calvinism

Bangs, Carl, *Arminius: A Study of the Dutch Reformation*, 2nd edn (Grands Rapids, MI, 1985).

Graham, W. Fred (ed.), *Later Calvinism: International Perspectives* (Kirksville, MO, 1994).

Mentzer, Raymond A., *Blood and Belief: Family Survival and Confessional Identity among the Provincial Huguenot Nobility* (West Lafayette, IN, 1994).
Pettegree, Andrew, Alastair Duke, and Gillian Lewis (eds), *Calvinism in Europe, 1540–1620* (Cambridge, 1995).
Prestwich, Menna, *International Calvinism, 1541–1715* (Oxford, 1985).

The Stuarts, Puritanism, Civil War and the Anglican Church

Barbour, Hugh, *The Quakers in Puritan England* (Richmond, 1985).
Carlton, Charles, *Archbishop William Laud* (London, 1987).
Champion, J. A. I., *The Pillars of Priestcraft Shaken: The Church of England and Its Enemies, 1660–1730* (Cambridge, 1992).
Cliffe, J. T., *Puritans in Conflict: The Puritan Gentry During and After the Civil Wars* (London, 1988).
Coward, Barry, *Oliver Cromwell* (London, 1991).
Gillespie, Raymond, *Devoted People: Belief and Religion in Early Modern Ireland* (Manchester, 1997).
Gregory, Jeremy, *Restoration, Reformation, and Reform, 1660–1828: Archbishops of Canterbury and their Diocese* (Oxford, 2000).
Hunt, Arnold, "The Lord's Supper in Early Modern England", *P&P*, 161 (November 1998), pp. 39–83.
Sachs, William L., *The Transformation of Anglicanism: From State Church to Global Communion* (Cambridge, 1993).
Spufford, Margaret (ed.), *The World of Rural Dissenters, 1520–1725* (Cambridge, 1995).
Todd, Margo (ed.), *Reformation to Revolution: Politics and Religion in Early Modern England* (London, 1995).
Tyacke, Nicholas (ed.), *England's Long Reformation, 1500–1800* (London, 1998).
——, *Anti-Calvinists: The Rise of English Arminianism, c.1590–1640* (Oxford, 1987).
Webster, Tom, *Godly Clergy in Early Stuart England* (Cambridge, 1997).
White, Peter, *Predestination, Policy, and Polemic: Conflict and Consensus in the English Church from the Reformation to the Civil War* (Cambridge, 1992).

Social Discipline and Popular Religious Culture

Beaver, Daniel C., *Parish Communities and Religious Conflict in the Vale of Gloucester, 1590–1690* (Cambridge, MA, 1998).
Bossy, John, *Christianity in the West, 1400–1700* (Oxford, 1985).
Bottigheimer, Ruth B., "Bible Reading, 'Bibles' and the Bible for Children in Early Modern Germany", *P&P*, 139 (May 1993), pp. 66–89.
Châtellier, Louis, *Europe of the Devout* (Cambridge, 1989).
——, *The Religion of the Poor: Rural Missions in Europe and the Formation of Modern Catholicism, c.1500–1800* (Cambridge, 1997).
Christian, William, *Local Religion in Sixteenth-Century Spain* (1982).
Delumeau, Jean, *Sin and Fear: The Emergence of Western Guilt Culture, Thirteenth–Eighteenth Centuries* (New York, 1990).

Dixon, C. Scott, *The Reformation and Rural Society: The Parishes of Brandenburg-Ansbach-Kulmbach, 1528–1603* (Cambridge, 1996).

Eire, Carlos M., *From Madrid to Purgatory: The Art and Craft of Dying in Sixteenth-Century Spain* (Cambridge, 1995).

Fehler, Timothy G., *Poor Relief and Protestantism: The Evolution of Social Welfare in Sixteenth-Century Emden* (Aldershot, 1999).

Gordon, Bruce, *Clerical Discipline and the Rural Reformation: The Synod of Zurich, 1532–1580* (New York, 1992).

Hsia, R. Po-Chia, *Social Discipline in the Reformation: Central Europe, 1550–1750* (London, 1989).

Hutton, Ronald, "The English Reformation and the Evidence of Folklore", *P&P*, 148 (August 1995), pp. 89–116.

Karant-Nunn, Susan C., *The Reformation of Ritual: An Interpretation of Early Modern Germany* (London, 1997).

McManners, John, *Church and Society in Eighteenth-Century France* (Oxford, 1998), 2 vols.

Monter, William, *Frontiers of Heresy: The Spanish Inquisition from the Basque Lands to Sicily* (Cambridge, 1990).

Muchembled, Robert, *Popular Culture and Elite Culture in France, 1400–1700* (Baton Rouge, LA, 1984).

Muir, Edward, *Ritual in Early Modern Europe* (Cambridge, 1997).

Parker, Geoffrey, "Success and Failure during the First Century of the Reformation", *P&P*, 136 (August 1992), pp. 43–82.

Pettegree, Andrew (ed.), *The Reformation of the Parishes: The Ministry and the Reformation in Town and Country* (Manchester, 1993).

Poska, Allyson M., *Regulating the People: The Catholic Reformation in Seventeenth-Century Spain* (Leiden, 1998).

Sabean, David, *Power in the Blood: Popular Culture and Village Discourse in Early Modern Germany* (Cambridge, 1984).

Schilling, Heinz, *Religion, Political Culture, and the Emergence of Early Modern Society* (Leiden, 1992).

Schmidt, Heinrich Richard, *Dorf und Religion: Reformierte Sittenzucht in Berner Landgemeinden der Frühen Neuzeit* (Stuttgart, 1995).

Scribner, R. W., *For the Sake of Simple Folk: Popular Propaganda for the German Reformation*, rev. edn (Oxford, 1994).

Strauss, Gerald, *Luther's House of Learning* (Baltimore, MD 1978).

——, "Success and Failure in the German Reformation", *P&P*, 65 (1975), pp. 30–63.

Tóth, István György, *Literacy and Written Culture in Early Modern Central Europe* (New York, 2000).

Witchcraft and Witch-hunting

Behringer, Wolfgang, *Witchcraft Persecutions in Bavaria: Popular Magic, Religious Zealotry, and Reason of State in Early Modern Europe* (Cambridge, 1997).

Genticore, David, *From Bishop to Witch: The System of the Sacred in Early Modern Terra d'Otranto* (Manchester, 1992).

Gregory, Annabel, "Witchcraft, Politics and 'Good Neighbourhood'", *P&P*, 133 (November 1991), pp. 31–66.

Levack, Brian P., *The Witch-Hunt in Early Modern Europe*, rev. edn (London, 1996).

Midelfort, H. C. Eric, *Witch-Hunting in Southwestern Germany, 1562–1684* (Stanford, CT, 1984).

Monter, E. William, *Witchcraft in France and Switzerland: The Borderlands of the Reformation* (Ithaca, NY, 1976).

Roper, Lyndal, "'Evil Imaginings and Fantasies': Child-Witches and the End of the Witch Craze", *P&P*, 167 (May 2000), pp. 107–39.

Sharpe, James, *The Bewitching of Anne Gunther: A Horrible and True Story of Deception, Witchcraft, Murder, and the King of England* (New York, 2000).

Thomas, Keith, *Religion and the Decline of Magic* (Oxford, 1971).

Gender Analyses

Bynum, Caroline Walker, *Holy Feast and Holy Fast: The Religious Significance of Food to Medieval Women* (Berkeley, CA, 1987).

Conn, Marie A., *Noble Daughters: Unheralded Women in Western Christianity, 13th to 18th Centuries* (Westport, CT, 2000).

Crawford, Patricia, *Women and Religion in England, 1500–1720* (London, 1993).

Diefendorf, Barbara B., "Give Us Back Our Children: Patriarchal Authority and Parental Consent to Religious Vocations in Early Counter-Reformation France", *JMH*, 68 (1996), pp. 265–307.

Farr, James R., "The Pure and Disciplined Body: Hierarchy, Morality and Symbolism in France during the Catholic Reformation", *The Journal of Interdisciplinary History*, 21 (1991), pp. 391–414.

Hendrix, Scott, "Masculinity and Patriarchy in Reformation Germany", *Journal of the History of Ideas*, 56 (1995), pp. 177–93.

Kelly, Joan, *Women, History, and Theory* (Chicago, 1984).

Marshall, Sherrin (ed.), *Women in Reformation and Counter-Reformation Europe: Private and Public Worlds* (Bloomington, IN, 1989).

Miller, Pavla, *Transformations of Patriarchy in the West, 1500–1900* (Bloomington, IN, 1998).

Peters, Christine, "Gender, Sacrament, and Ritual: The Making and Meaning of Marriage in Late Medieval and Early Modern England", *P&P*, 169 (November 2000), pp. 63–96.

Ranft, Patricia, *Women and Spiritual Equality in Christian Tradition* (New York, 1998).

Reuther, Rosemary Radford, *Women and Redemption: A Theological History* (Minneapolis, 1998).

Roper, Lyndal, "'The Common Man', 'the Common Good', 'Common Women': Gender and the Meaning of the German Reformation", *Social History*, 12 (1987), pp. 1–21.

——, *The Holy Household: Women and Morals in Reformation Augsburg* (Oxford, 1989).

——, *Oedipus and the Devil: Witchcraft, Sexuality, and Religion in Early Modern Europe* (London, 1994).

Safley, Thomas Max, *Let No Man Put Asunder: The Control of Marriage in the German Southwest: A Comparative Study, 1550–1600* (St Louis, 1984).

Wiesner, Merry E., *Women and Gender in Early Modern Europe*, rev. edn (Cambridge, 2000).

——, *Christianity and Sexuality in the Early Modern World: Regulating Desire, Reforming Practice* (London, 2000).

Wunder, Heidi, *He is the Sun, She is the Moon: Women in Early Modern Germany* (Cambridge, MA, 1998).

Inter-Confessional Relations in the Late Seventeenth and Eighteenth Centuries

Breuer, Dietrich (ed.), *Religion und Religiosität im Zeitalter des Barock* (Wiesbaden, 1995), 2 vols.

François, Étienne, *Protestants et catholiques en Allemagne: Identités et pluralisme Augsbourg, 1648–1806* (Paris, 1993).

Fulbrook, Mary, *Piety and Politics: Religion and the Rise of Absolutism in England, Württemberg, and Prussia* (Cambridge, 1983).

Hanlon, Gregory, *Confession and Community in Seventeenth-Century France: Catholic and Protestant Coexistence in Aquitaine* (Philadelphia, 1993).

Mentzer, Raymond A., Jr, "The Persistence of 'Superstition and Idolatry' among Rural French Calvinists", *Church History*, 65 (June 1996), pp. 220–33.

Luria, Keith P., "Separated by Death? Burials, Cemeteries, and Confessional Boundaries in Seventeenth-Century France", *French Historical Studies*, 24 (Spring 2001), pp. 185–222.

Sedgwick, Alexander, *The Travails of Conscience: The Arnauld Family and the Ancien Régime* (Cambridge, 1998).

Walker, Mack, *The Salzburg Transaction: Expulsion and Redemption in Eighteenth-Century Germany* (Ithaca, NY, 1992).

Wallace, Peter G., *Communities and Conflict in Early Modern Colmar, 1575–1730* (Atlantic Highlands, NJ, 1995).

Ward, W. R., *Christianity under the Ancien Régime, 1648–1789* (Cambridge, 1999).

Whaley, Joachim, *Religious Toleration and Social Change in Hamburg, 1529–1819* (Cambridge, 1985).

INDEX

Aachen (Holy Roman Empire), 146, 147
abbesses
  Benedictine, 37–8
  in *Canterbury Tales*, 205
  Quedlinburg, 207
absenteeism
  condemned at Trent, 126
  parish clergy and, 34
absolute monarchies *see* monarchy, absolute
Adam, sin of, 203
Advent, 65, 66
Africa
  Jesuit missions and, 178
  south, Huguenot refugees in, 186
Alba, duke of, Fernand Alvárez de Toledo
  (1508–82), 141–2
  Council of Troubles (Council of Blood)
    and, 141–2
Albert of Brandenburg, archbishop of Mainz
  and Magdeburg (1490–1545), 76
Albert of Hohenzollern, grand master of
  the Teutonic Knights, then margrave
  of Brandenburg and duke of Prussia
  (1490–1568), 97
Albigensians, 57; *see also* Cathari
  crusade against, 17, 57
Alcalá, university of, 69, 73, 112
Alès, Peace of (1629), 133
Alexander V, Pisan antipope (*1409–10), 45, 46
Alexander VI, pope (*1492–1503), 50, 51
Alfonso V, king of Aragon (*1416–58), 73
Alsace (Holy Roman Empire then France), 160
  German Peasants' war and, 87
Americas, the, 168
  Great Awakening in, 200
  Huguenot refugees, 186
  Jesuit missions and, 178
  John Wesley in, 190
  silver and, 121
Amsterdam (Dutch Republic), 157, 167, 168, 207
Anabaptists, 88–9, 159, 221
  baptism, views on, 88, 97
  in Bohemia, 88
  Dutch Republic and, 143
  excommunication (shunning), 88
  German Peasants' war and, 88

Mennonites, 89, 143, 222
  in Moravia, 88
  in Netherlands, 89, 140
  in Switzerland (Swiss Brethren), 88
  women and, 206, 209
  at Zurich, 95
Anagni (Italy), 41, 42
anchoresses, 205
Andersson, Lars (*c*.1470–1552), Reformation
  in Sweden and, 101–2
Andreae, Jacob (1529–90), 145
Anglican *see* England, Church of
Anhalt-Köthen (Holy Roman Empire), county
  of, 97
annates, 43, 49; *see also* Papacy
Anne, mother of Virgin Mary, cult of, 64,
  205–6, 208
Anne of Cleves, queen of England (*1540), 108
Annunciation, feast of, 66
Antichrist, 59–60, 89
  pope as, 58, 180, 214
anti-clericalism, 52, 67
anti-Trinitarianism, 152, 154
Antoine, duke of Lorraine (*1508–44),
  German Peasants' war, 87
Antoine de Bourbon, king of Navarre and
  duke of Béarn (1518–62), 131
Antwerp (Netherlands), 122, 140, 142
Anvers (Netherlands), 129
Apocalypse, 82; *see also* Antichrist
  Black Death and, 25
  Book of Daniel and, 60
  Book of Revelations and, 60
  early Church and, 9
  English Civil War and, 135
  Jews and, 60
  Millennium and, 59–60
  Münster and, 89
Apostolic Chamber *see* Papacy
Aquinas, Thomas (1225–74)
  human nature and, 125
  women and, 204
Aquitaine (France), duchy of, 40
Aragon (Spain), kingdom of
  Church in, 73
  claims in Italy, 42, 51, 73–4